PREDICTIVE METHODS FOR FOOTBALL AND BETTING MARKETS

Enrique Dóal Pérez Frías

© Enrique Dóal Pérez Frías

Second edition, 2022

Original title: *Métodos Predictivos para Fútbol y Mercados de Apuestas*

Cover design: Manuel Martín García

ISBN-13: 979-8364780379

ISBN-10: 8364780379

Without data you are just another person with an opinion.

William Edwards Deming

*I am a great believer in luck.
The harder I work, the more of it I seem to have.*

Coleman Cox

Can't see the forest for the trees

Popular saying

ACKOWLEDGEMENTS

I would like to express my deepest gratitude to the following individuals:

To my mother, for all the time you devoted to turn me into a good student, to show me how to deal with numbers and to teach me that "every day has its bright side". I owe you everything.

To my father, for teaching me to think like an economist, to manage money properly and for your dispassionate and rational vision of sports and markets.

To my wife, Karín, for your support, immense patience, love and understanding, without which this book would never have been possible.

To my daughter, Diana, for surprising me every day, for filling me with smiles and for those hugs at the height of the knees.

To my son, Adrián, for the enthusiasm you show every day when you see me walk through the front door.

To my brother, Oscar, for the valuable comments on the drafts and your always constructive and sincere criticism.

To my former boss, Jaime Muruais, for everything you taught me about modelling and programming in that office on Hermosilla Street.

To my friend, Alfredo Vasallo, for your dedication in the review, your enriching contributions, and your encouragement.

To Raju Thapa, for your help in proofreading the English version of this book.

And finally, thank you very much also to all the relatives, friends and colleagues who have supported me in this adventure.

Thank you very much from the bottom of my heart.

FOREWORD TO THE SECOND EDITION

Four years ago, the first edition of this book went on sale. The good reception it has had during this time has encouraged me to write a second version in Spanish and to publish it for the first time in English.

One third of the content of this second edition is new and covers aspects such as:

- The importance of the age of the footballers, the size of the squads and their market value.
- The differences in the style of play of the best and worst teams (level of possession, type of passes used, playing areas, etc.).
- The predictive capacity of new metrics such as expected goals and their potential use in sports betting.
- The relevance of the scoreboard at halftime and the probability of comebacks.
- Additional biases incurred by bettors and measurable factors that affect team motivation.

The remainder of the book is an updated and revised version of all the chapters from the first edition. The four additional years of information have allowed me to increase the robustness of the analyses and revalidate their conclusions.

Finally, I have incorporated several suggestions from readers from both sides of the Atlantic.

CONTENTS

INTRODUCTION

For several years I was a consultant, working on different projects for banks. Many of these projects were of a statistical nature and allowed me to become familiar with the analyses that these institutions carry out when deciding whether to grant a loan.

Within the financial industry these statistical models are usually called scorings or ratings. A scoring is nothing more than a regression in which, by means of a combination of explanatory variables (for example, age, income level, length of relationship, etc.), the probability of default of the loan is estimated.

The selection of the variables that enter a scoring is made, mainly, according to statistical criteria. A database made up of actual loans granted in previous years is used. This database contains both the client's information at the time of application, as well as information on whether that loan was paid back normally or if, on the contrary, it was unpaid.

Thanks to this historical information, it is possible to study which customer characteristics are most closely related to their payment behaviour. Once identified, these key variables will be used to automatically evaluate new loan applications.

The use of these statistical models has become very popular in the banking industry in recent years and, in many cases, although not always, has replaced the people dedicated to assessing the risk level of loans. Are these statistical models more predictive than a human being? The answer depends on the type of banking transaction and its complexity. When assigning a probability of default to, for example, a credit card, it is very likely that the statistical model will be, in general, more reliable than a person (above all, it will be more homogeneous when evaluating, faster and less expensive). For more complex deals, for which historical information is scarcer, the traditional risk analyst still has a lot to say, although the statistical model can serve as a support tool.

The vast majority of the scoring models used by banks are constructed in the form of a logistic regression. Most people have never heard of this term. Without going into mathematical details, it is sufficient to know that a logistic regression is a normal regression (such as linear regressions) commonly used to calculate the probability (between 0% and 100%) that a certain event will occur.

This can be whether a customer repays or not a loan or, why not, whether or not a team wins a football game.

Several years ago, I started building models to calculate the probabilities of home win, draw and away win in football matches. The idea was apparently simple: if I managed to build a good enough model, I could compare the odds provided by it with the odds offered by the bookmakers and, this way, bet money on those matches in which the offered odds were interesting enough.

All the content of this book is the result, direct or indirect, of that search for the perfect statistical model to predict soccer results. After all these years working on this topic, I have the feeling, not of having found the Holy Grail, but of having learned a lot, both about statistics and about football.

In the search for this model, I have compiled a database with the results of 262,598 soccer matches from 28 different leagues from 17 countries. With this database, I have tested, one by one, more than 2,000 different possible explanatory variables to predict football results and I have also been able to study which strategies would have made a profit by betting, since for the matches played from the year 2000, I have the full-time result odds offered by various bookmakers.

COUNTRY	LEAGUE	FROM	TO	MATCHES	ODDS
BELGIUM	PRO LEAGUE	1995	2020	6,954	5,405
BRAZIL	BRASILEIRÃO	2003	2020	7,084	7,053
CHINA	SUPER LEAGUE	2009	2020	2,802	2,797
ENGLAND	PREMIER LEAGUE	1974	2020	18,992	7,678
	CHAMPIONSHIP	1993	2020	15,036	11,169
	LEAGUE ONE	1993	2020	14,885	11,019
	LEAGUE TWO	1993	2020	14,752	11,064
	NATIONAL	2005	2020	8,132	8,096
FRANCE	LIGUE 1	1975	2020	16,722	7,445
	LIGUE 2	1996	2020	9,282	7,580
GERMANY	BUNDESLIGA	1993	2020	8,325	6,183
	BUNDESLIGA 2	1993	2020	8,395	6,180
GREECE	SUPER LEAGUE	1994	2020	6,757	4,691
ITALY	SERIE A	1993	2020	9,516	7,365
	SERIE B	1997	2020	10,086	8,786
JAPAN	J1 LEAGUE	1998	2020	6,611	6,408
MEXICO	PRIMERA	2005	2020	5,116	5,086
NETHERLANDS	EREDIVISIE	1993	2020	8,259	6,115

PERU	PRIMERA	2005	2020	5,014	4,910
PORTUGAL	PRIMEIRA LIGA	1994	2020	7,490	5,643
SCOTLAND	PREMIERSHIP	1994	2020	5,668	4,587
	CHAMPIONSHIP	1994	2020	4,656	3,566
	LEAGUE ONE	1997	2020	4,119	3,566
	LEAGUE TWO	1997	2020	4,117	3,561
SPAIN	PRIMERA	1970	2020	18,012	7,683
	SEGUNDA	1968	2020	21,701	9,348
TURKEY	SÜPER LIG	1994	2020	7,999	6,154
USA	MLS	1998	2020	6,116	6,043
TOTAL		**1968**	**2020**	**262,598**	**185,181**

When building a statistical model, you have to decide what information to use. Not all historical information is relevant. In the case of models for predicting soccer results, two questions arise almost immediately:

- Is it possible to build a single model with information from several different leagues (Spain, England, Germany, etc.) or is it better to build a different model for each of these competitions, given their possible different characteristics?
- Should the model be built with all the available historical information, or should it be built only with information from recent seasons, since only these seasons would reflect the characteristics of modern football?

To answer these two questions, we must explore the data. As a general rule, **if soccer was quite similar between countries and / or had changed little over the years, we should opt for a single model** using all available seasons and information from different leagues, as it would be more robust.

To start investigating, we have prepared the following table with the number of goals scored per game in the Spanish La Liga, in the English Premier League, in the German Bundesliga and in the Spanish Second Division from the 1975-76 season to the present.

AVERAGE GOALS PER GAME				
SEASONS	**LA LIGA**	**PREMIER LEAGUE**	**BUNDESLIGA**	**SECOND DIVISION**
1975 - 1984	2.6	2.6	3.4	2.4
1985 - 1994	2.4	2.6	2.9	2.3
1995 - 2004	2.7	2.6	2.9	2.3
2005 - 2014	2.7	2.7	2.9	2.5
2015 - 2020	2.7	2.8	3.0	2.2

In the case of La Liga and the Premier League it is observed that:

- The number of goals per game has remained stable since at least 1975, oscillating between 2.6 and 2.7 in most campaigns.
- The number of goals per game is very similar in both competitions.

The German Bundesliga seems to have other characteristics:

- The number of goals per game has changed over the last few decades. Until 1987, more than 3 goals were scored on average per game. Since 1988 the average number of goals per game has stayed between 2.9 and 3.0.
- Out of the 46 seasons analysed, in 44 of them the German Bundesliga has achieved a higher scoring average than the Spanish La Liga, the English Premier League and the Spanish Second Division.

Finally, the Spanish Second Division is, out of the four leagues analysed, clearly the competition with the fewest goals with an average of just 2.3 per game.

After this first study we could be inclined to develop a joint model for the La Liga and the Premier League, taking advantage of all the historical information from at least 1975 onward; but let's continue studying the available information. Another relevant analysis consists of studying how the percentage of matches that have ended in home win, draw and away win has evolved over time.

For the same four competitions and with information from 1975 onwards we obtain the following tables:

LA LIGA			
SEASONS	HOME WIN	DRAW	AWAY WIN
1975 – 1984	59.0%	25.2%	15.9%
1985 – 1994	51.4%	27.8%	20.8%
1995 - 2004	48.2%	26.9%	24.8%
2005 - 2014	47.8%	23.7%	28.4%
2015 - 2020	46.3%	25.5%	28.2%

PREMIER LEAGUE			
SEASONS	HOME WIN	DRAW	AWAY WIN
1975 - 1984	49.9%	27.0%	23.1%
1985 - 1994	46.1%	28.2%	25.7%
1995 - 2004	46.4%	27.1%	26.5%
2005 - 2014	46.9%	25.0%	28.1%
2015 - 2020	45.4%	23.7%	30.9%

BUNDESLIGA			
SEASONS	HOME WIN	DRAW	AWAY WIN
1975 - 1984	56.7%	24.2%	19.1%
1985 - 1994	49.4%	29.1%	21.5%
1995 - 2004	48.5%	25.8%	25.8%
2005 - 2014	45.1%	25.5%	29.4%
2015 - 2020	44.4%	24.4%	31.1%

SECOND DIVISION			
SEASONS	HOME WIN	DRAW	AWAY WIN
1975 - 1984	57.5%	27.9%	14.6%
1985 - 1994	49.2%	29.7%	21.0%
1995 - 2004	42.5%	31.2%	26.3%
2005 - 2014	45.9%	28.5%	25.6%
2015 - 2020	45.3%	30.9%	23.8%

It can be observed that in the 70s more than 50% of the matches ended in a local victory and only between 10% and 20% ended in an away victory.

17

Currently, less than 50% end in home victory and more than 25% end in away victory. The percentage of matches that end up tied has remained unchanged over time[1]. This trend towards fewer home victories and more away victories can be observed with greater or lesser intensity in the four competitions analysed[2].

It is striking that this change in home and away winning percentages has occurred even though the number of goals per game has remained unchanged (except in Germany). What has produced this change? Speculatively, several possible causes can be considered:

- Over the years, football has become more "civilized". Both the players of the visiting teams and the referees have gradually felt safer and less intimidated when playing or officiating on certain fields.
- The increase in the number of televised matches, recordings, etc., has decreased violence in soccer. No longer does the team that elbows the most wins, but the one with the best players.
- Inequality in football has been increasing. In the 70s a great team like Real Madrid, Barcelona or Bayern normally considered a draw away from home as a good result. Today, everything that is not a victory is considered by these teams as a failure[3].

Whatever the reason, the fact is that, if we were to construct a statistical model to assign probabilities to 1, X, 2 of each match with historical information since 1975, our model would tend to overestimate the probability of local victory and underestimate the probability of away victory for the matches that are played nowadays. The solution would be to build the model only with information from the most recent decades, making sure that the percentages of home wins,

---

[1] In the 1995-96 season, the system that awards 3 instead of 2 points to the winner of the match was introduced in Spain and Germany. Apparently, this regulatory change has failed to reduce the number of matches that end in a tie. In England 3 points are awarded to the winner of the match since the 1981-82 season.

[2] For simplicity we refer to each season by the year in which it began. The data used for these analyses covers all matches played until November 2020.

[3] Nowadays, in places like Nigeria more than 60% of the matches still end in a local victory. Allegations of corruption in the country's football league are not uncommon.

draws and away wins have remained stable throughout the time window and are similar to those of modern football[4].

The possible increase in the degree of inequality between the different teams that participate in the same competition is something that we can try to measure. The following table shows the percentage of points that the winner of each of these four leagues has obtained over time:

POINTS OBTAINED BY THE WINNER				
SEASONS	LA LIGA	PREMIER LEAGUE	BUNDESLIGA	SECOND DIVISION
1975 - 1984	71.3%	70.5%	71.6%	65.7%
1985 - 1994	75.4%	70.7%	71.5%	69.1%
1995 - 2004	69.0%	73.7%	70.3%	62.4%
2005 - 2014	79.7%	76.7%	76.1%	64.3%
2015 - 2020	79.1%	82.6%	81.2%	62.2%

If in the 70s a team could be a winner by getting 70% of all possible points, today it needs to get close to 80% to finish the championship in the first position. This phenomenon is observed in La Liga, the Premier League and in the Bundesliga. In the Second Division, inequality has not increased since both the best teams and the worst teams are "eliminated" from the competition from one edition to the next through promotions and relegations. In the first tier leagues the best teams do remain in the category, since there is no other national competition to which they can be promoted.

This book is divided into 4 sections:

- Section 1 focuses on **teams and the information that can be used to predict their future performance**: significant variables, relevant historical information, etc.
- Section 2 focuses on **betting markets, bookmakers and their odds**: types of bookmakers, margins charged, predictive capacity, evolution of odds, etc.
- Section 3 lists the **tips a bettor can follow**, summarizes the **inefficiencies that exist in betting markets** and the **strategies that can be employed to try to exploit them**.

---

[4] Alternatively, the model could be built using all available historical information and later be recalibrated. A recalibration is a statistical technique that transforms the outcome of the model into the current probabilities of home win, draw and away win.

- Finally, section 4 lists the advice that **may be useful for the players, coaching staff and the board of a football club** derived from the analyses carried out.

A series of annexes is included with detailed quantitative information on several of the aspects covered in this book.

Although each section can be read independently, it is recommended to follow the proposed order, since the aspects exposed in each of them help understand the content of the subsequent ones.

SECTION 1: PREDICTIVE METHODS FOR FOOTBALL

POINTS OR GOALS

Normally, in a season the team that achieves the greatest difference between goals scored and goals conceded gets the highest number of points. For example, the 2018-19 La Liga season was won by FC. Barcelona with 87 points, being the team with the best goal difference (90 goals scored versus 36 conceded).

However, sometimes there are teams that obtain a higher number of points than other participants in the competition, despite having a worse goal difference. For example, the following season, 2019-20, Real Madrid won the championship without achieving the best goal difference. Throughout the season, Real Madrid scored 70 goals and conceded 25 so their goal difference was +45. For their part, FC. Barcelona finished the season in second place with a goal difference of +48.

Let's imagine a madridista and a culé. The Real Madrid supporter thinks that his team will finish the 2020-21 season above Barcelona, as they got more points in the previous season. The Barça fan thinks differently. He believes that his team will probably end up in a better position, as the best goal difference from the previous season indicates that, in reality, his beloved Catalan team is better than the Madrid team.

Who of them is right? Of course, we don't know for sure what will happen in the next season. However, we know what has happened in the past. When a team got one season more points than another squad, but had worse goal difference than its opponent, which of them is more likely to finish higher the following season?

Fortunately, for this analysis we have a large historical sample. In total it is possible to find in the entire history of La Liga 974 pairs of teams that meet the following conditions:

- One of them finished the season ahead of the other in the standings but had a worse goal difference.
- Both teams played the following season in La Liga (neither of them was relegated).

In this sample, the same team can be part of one or more pairs. For example, let's imagine the following situation:

	POINTS	GOAL DIFFERENCE
TEAM A	52	4
TEAM B	50	-5
TEAM C	45	-1
TEAM D	43	2
TEAM E	38	-7

In this case, there would be three pairs for our analysis, since all three meet the condition that the team with the worse goal difference got more points than the other:

- Pair 1: Team B and Team C.
- Pair 2: Team B and Team D.
- Pair 3: Team C and Team D.

Out of the 974 pairs that have satisfied this condition throughout La Liga history, in 557 cases (57% of the total sample) the team with the best goal difference ended up the following season in a better place than the team that got the most points. In the remaining 417 cases (43% of the total sample), it was the team with the most points and the worst goal difference that ended up in a better place at the end of the following campaign.

This is a very revealing piece of information. **Goal difference is a better predictor of a team's future performance than points. The best team is not the one that gets the most points during a season, but the one with the best goal difference.**

Therefore, going back to the previous example, the Barça fan is right. Even if his team ranked lower than Real Madrid this year, it is likely that next season it will end up higher than its rivals. It is also likely that next season Barça will also beat Real Madrid on goal difference again, since, out of these 974 pairs, in 559 cases the team with the best goal difference also got the best goal difference the following season. In 401 cases it obtained a worse goal difference the following season than its rival and in the remaining 14 cases both teams obtained the same goal difference. This means that **goal difference is a better variable than**

points to predict both the points and the goal difference that a team will obtain in the future[5].

Looking at this analysis, one may wonder why the team with the most points is proclaimed the league champion instead of the team with the best goal difference. Although goals are a better indicator of a team's level, there are several factors that make points preferable when establishing the ranking:

- The point system gives equal importance to all matches. It is a system that rewards consistency.
- The point system limits the risk of fraud. For example, if the champion were decided on the basis of goal difference, a virtually relegated team could be bribed to be thrashed on the final matchday by a team with a chance of winning the league[6].

Based on our analysis, a league champion who did not get the best goal difference should be less likely to win the league again the following year than a champion that has also obtained the best goal difference.

The following table divides the 88 league winners in the history of La Liga into 4 groups:

1. League winners that got the best goal difference that season, and that managed to win again the season after.
2. League winners that got the best goal difference that season but failed to win again the season after.
3. League winners that did not get the best goal difference that season but managed to win again the season after.
4. League winners that did not get the best goal difference that season and failed to win again the season after.

---

[5] In practice, this means that if, just at the end of the season, F.C. Barcelona and Real Madrid played on a neutral field, such as in a hypothetical Cup final, we should consider F.C. Barcelona as favourites given their best goal difference.

[6] The opposite situation could also be possible, since the team about to be relegated could have incentives to buy the game, as it could save itself by scoring a scandalously high number of goals.

		TITLE RENEWED	
		YES	NO
CHAMPION WITH BEST GOAL DIFFERENCE	YES	25	37
	NO	9	17

Out of the 88 league winners only 34 managed to win again the following season. That is, the probability of renewing the title was (25 + 9) / (88) = 38.6%. If we focus only on the 62 league winners (25 + 37) that also got the best goal difference, 40.3% managed to renew their titles. Finally, of the 26 league winners that did not get the best goal difference only 34.6% ended up first the following season.

In any case, it is interesting to have a look at the most recent La Liga seasons to see in which cases the champion was not the team with the best goal difference.

SEASON	WINNER	BEST GOAL DIFFERENCE
2000-01	REAL MADRID	YES
2001-02	VALENCIA	NO
2002-03	REAL MADRID	YES
2003-04	VALENCIA	YES
2004-05	BARCELONA	YES
2005-06	BARCELONA	YES
2006-07	REAL MADRID	NO
2007-08	REAL MADRID	YES
2008-09	BARCELONA	YES
2009-10	BARCELONA	YES
2010-11	BARCELONA	YES
2011-12	REAL MADRID	YES
2012-13	BARCELONA	YES
2013-14	ATLÉTICO	NO
2014-15	BARCELONA	YES
2015-16	BARCELONA	YES
2016-17	REAL MADRID	NO
2017-18	BARCELONA	YES
2018-19	BARCELONA	YES
2019-20	REAL MADRID	NO

Since the 2000-01 season, only on 5 occasions the winner has not been the team with the greatest goal difference. Valencia, in the 2001-02 season,

Atlético, in 2013-14, and Real Madrid, in the 2006-07, 2016-17 and 2019-20 seasons, won the title without obtaining the best goal difference. **In those five seasons, the team with the best goal difference was FC. Barcelona.** If the champions were decided based on goal difference, Barcelona would have won 5 more leagues in the last 20 years[7].

This is not to say that a champion that has not got the best goal difference is an unworthy champion. Rather the complete opposite. A champion that has not got the best goal difference has been a team that, having faced stronger teams in the competition, has managed to win the key games, maintain concentration throughout the season and get better results from its qualities. A team that has won the goal difference, but has not won the league, is possibly a team that has failed to maintain motivation or intensity in games that, in principle, should have won.

It can also be speculated that the teams that did not win the league despite obtaining the best goal difference had a worse coach in those seasons and that the teams that won without the best goal difference had excellent coaches. The following table shows who were the coaches in those seasons:

SEASON	WINNING COACH	BETTER GOAL DIFFERENCE
2001-02	RAFAEL BENÍTEZ	CARLES REXACH
2006-07	FABIO CAPELLO	FRANK RIJKAARD
2013-14	"CHOLO" SIMEONE	"TATA" MARTINO
2016-17	ZINEDINE ZIDANE	LUIS ENRIQUE
2019-20	ZINEDINE ZIDANE	QUIQUE SATIÉN

Did Benítez, Capello, Simeone and Zidane achieve better results with worse squads than Rexach, Rijkaard, "Tata" Martino, Luis Enrique and Quique Setién in those five seasons? It is a hypothesis. It is not easy at all to isolate the performance of a coach from the performance of his footballers.

Finally, another possibility is that those five seasons the team that won the championship had the luck on its side. The luck that the team with the best goal difference lacked. In the long run, after a long series of matches, the better

---

[7] A well-known international case of a league winner that did not achieve the best goal difference was Leicester. They won the 2015-16 Premier League, but the team with the best goal difference was Tottenham. The following three seasons Tottenham ended up higher than Leicester.

team gets more points and wins more games than the worse team. But in the short term, the worst team can get more wins. Whereas 38 is usually a sufficient number of games for the best team to win, it may not be always the case. If the leagues were shorter there would be more "surprises" and if they were longer there would be fewer.

DEFENCE OR ATTACK

A recurring debate in team sports is about the importance of defence and attack. Clearly having both a good attack and a good defence is essential for any team that wants to win games. But is any of these two elements more important than the other?

Let's imagine two teams. The first one scores quite a few goals, but also concedes quite a few goals. Their matches, on many occasions, end with high scores. The second team scores far fewer goals, but also concedes very few goals. Their matches usually end up with low scores. What style of play allows you to obtain better results?

Taking all the historical information from 1995 onwards we have constructed the following table:

	NUMBER OF GOALS SCORED AND CONCEDED	OBSERVATIONS	NUMBER OF POINTS OBTAINED
DEFENSIVE TEAMS	3	572	7.55
	4	1,707	7.82
	5	3,469	7.89
	6	5,334	8.01
	7	6,066	8.11
	3-7	**17,148**	**7.99**
OFFENSIVE TEAMS	8	5,563	8.11
	9	4,131	8.18
	10	2,512	8.21
	11	1,335	8.31
	12	665	8.35
	8-12	**14,206**	**8.18**

The first column divides the teams by the number of total goals scored and conceded in their previous six games. **To make a fair comparison we have only selected teams that scored and conceded the same number of goals in the previous six games.** This way the upper rows of the table show the most defensive teams. These are teams that score and concede few goals. The bottom rows show the most offensive teams. They are teams that score and receive many goals.

The most defensive teams obtained fewer points in their previous 6 games than the most offensive teams. The teams that scored and conceded 7 goals or fewer obtained, on average, slightly less than 8 points out of a possible total of 18. Teams that scored and received 8 or more goals got, on average, more than 8 points in their last 6 matches.

Although the difference is very small, it is clear that in a world where victory is worth 3 points and a draw is worth only 1 point, it is worth being an offensive team. The teams that score and concede few goals see how a higher percentage of their matches end in a draw and that hurts them. To get 3 points a team must necessarily score.

We have added an additional column to the previous table with the percentage of victories obtained in their next game by the offensive and defensive teams. Offensive teams achieved a slightly higher winning percentage than defensive teams.

	NUMBER OF GOALS SCORED AND CONCEDED	PERCENTAGE OF WINS NEXT MATCH	POINTS NEXT MATCH
DEFENSIVE TEAMS	3	34.4%	1.32
	4	33.6%	1.29
	5	33.4%	1.30
	6	35.0%	1.33
	7	35.6%	1.35
	3-7	**34.7%**	**1,328**
OFFENSIVE TEAMS	8	35.3%	1.32
	9	36.2%	1.35
	10	36.6%	1.35
	11	35.1%	1.30
	12	37.6%	1.36
	8-12	**35.9%**	**1,332**

The difference between the winning percentage of offensive teams (35.9%) and that of defensive teams (34.7%) is very small. About every 100 matches an offensive team achieves an additional victory over a defensive team of the same level. A good team is one that manages to score more goals than it concedes. **In order to win matches and get points, it is not very relevant if you achieve that positive goal difference with low scoring or with high scoring games. Defence is practically as important as attack.**

Teams that have scored and conceded few goals in the recent past tend to score and concede few goals in subsequent matches. Likewise, teams that have scored and conceded many goals tend to score and receive, in their subsequent matches, more goals than most teams.

However, **this relationship is weaker than you might expect**. For example, highly defensive teams that have scored and conceded only 3, 4 or 5 goals in their last 6 games, that is, an average of less than 1 goal scored and conceded per game, score and concede more than 1 goal on average in their next match. Similarly, highly offensive teams that have scored and conceded 9 or more goals in their last 6 matches, an average of at least 1.5 goals conceded and scored per match, score and concede, on average, less than 1.5 goals in their next match. The following table summarizes these figures:

	NUMBER OF GOALS SCORED AND CONCEDED	NUMBER OF GOALS PER GAME	GOALS SCORED NEXT MATCH	GOALS CONCEDED NEXT MATCH
DEFENSIVE TEAMS	3	3/6 = 0.5	1.16	1.20
	4	4/6 = 0.67	1.17	1.26
	5	5/6 = 0.83	1.21	1.27
	6	6/6 = 1	1.24	1.27
	7	7/6 = 1.17	1.28	1.31
	3-7	**[0.5-1.17]**	**1.24**	**1.28**
OFFENSIVE TEAMS	8	8/6 = 1.33	1.27	1.35
	9	9/6 = 1.5	1.33	1.35
	10	10/6 = 1.67	1.37	1.42
	11	11/6 = 1.83	1.36	1.48
	12	12/6 = 2	1.44	1.55
	8-12	**[1.33-2]**	**1.32**	**1.38**

What happens when an offensive team faces a defensive team? Who usually wins? The one that plays more offensive football or the one that plays more defensive football?

Let's look at 5 hypothetical matches as an example:

	HOME TEAM		AWAY TEAM	
	GOALS SCORED LAST 6 GAMES	GOALS CONCEDED LAST 6 GAMES	GOALS SCORED LAST 6 GAMES	GOALS CONCEDED LAST 6 GAMES
MATCH 1	12	6	9	3
MATCH 2	4	3	7	6
MATCH 3	7	12	5	10
MATCH 4	3	5	5	7
MATCH 5	3	4	3	4

These 5 matches are between teams of a similar level, since, in all of them, both the home team and the away team got the same goal difference, either positive or negative, in their respective 6 previous matches.

In matches 1 and 3 the home team is more offensive than the away team, as it has scored more goals. In matches 2 and 4 the home team is more defensive than the away team, as it has conceded fewer goals. In game 5 no team is more offensive or defensive than the other[8].

If we search through all the available historical information for all the games with these characteristics, we obtain the following results:

HOME TEAM STYLE	AWAY TEAM STYLE	MATCHES	HOME WIN	DRAW	AWAY WIN
DEFENSIVE	OFFENSIVE	4,385	46.2%	26.9%	27.0%
NEUTRAL	NEUTRAL	1,459	44.3%	28.7%	27.0%
OFFENSIVE	DEFENSIVE	4,283	44.8%	28.2%	27.0%

When we focus on these games, any advantage that the offensive teams may have over the defensive ones seems to disappear completely. In a higher percentage of occasions, the defensive team wins.

---

[8] This means that, in this case, the concept of defensive and offensive team is relative depending on which of the two rivals is more or less offensive / defensive than the other.

And from a gambler's point of view? We compare below the number of victories of the defensive teams and of the offensive teams with the number of victories expected according to the odds offered by the bookmakers.

HOME TEAM STYLE	AWAY TEAM STYLE	LOCAL WINS / EXPECTED LOCAL WINS	AWAY WINS / EXPECTED AWAY WINS
DEFENSIVE	OFFENSIVE	103%	98%
NEUTRAL	NEUTRAL	98%	101%
OFFENSIVE	DEFENSIVE	98%	102%

In the available sample, the defensive teams obtained better than expected results when they faced teams of the same level, but with a more offensive profile[9]. It is not easy to determine the cause of this phenomenon. Perhaps it is because **a team that scores and concedes few goals is perceived by bettors as a worse team than one that scores and concedes many goals**. This perception could skew the odds to some extent, making them more interesting for those who decide to bet in favour of the defensive team. It may also be because, as we have seen, teams that have recently scored few goals tend to score more in their subsequent matches.

---

[9] A detailed explanation of how bookmaker odds are related to the probabilities of each outcome can be found in section 2 of this book.

TREND OR REVERSION TO THE MEAN

It is summer in Donostia-San Sebastián. Three friends, Real Sociedad fans, chat animatedly around glasses of chacolí while savouring some pinchos. It's been a few weeks since the season ended and there are still a few more before the new one begins. Real Sociedad finished the previous campaign in ninth place. It was not a spectacular season, but not a bad one either. In any case, it represented an improvement over the previous campaign in which Real Sociedad finished in twelfth place. The three friends comment on their team's prospects for the new season:

— "I believe that next season we will end up above the ninth position. The team improved last season and it is sure to continue on that upward path. Hopefully we will qualify for Europe".

— "I don't agree, Aitor. Most likely, we will end up in a position very similar to last year".

— "Well, I think we will end up below the ninth position because two seasons ago we finished in the twelfth position. The improvement that we saw last season was just a mirage".

Which one of the three friends is right? When a team improves one season with respect to the previous one, can you expect it to continue on that upward path, to stay at the same level, or to see its performance drop again? Let's see what has happened historically.

In total, since the Spanish league was created, on 451 occasions the same team has played three consecutive seasons in La Liga and has achieved a better position in the second season than in the first[10]. What happened in the third?

Only 111 times out of 451 (24.6%) the team did manage to improve the results of the second season in the third season. On 73 occasions, 16.2%, the team repeated in the third season the position achieved in the second. Finally, in 267

---

[10] In this case, when we talk about three consecutive seasons in La Liga, we are not necessarily referring to the first three campaigns after a promotion, but to any continuous period of three seasons in which the has played in La Liga. These three-year periods may be partially overlap. For example, if a team has played four seasons in La Liga, we would be looking at two periods of three years. Therefore, in this sample the same team appears once for every campaign in which it improved its position over the previous one.

cases, 59.2%, the team finished in the third season in a worse position than in the second.

PERFORMANCE IN THE THIRD SEASON AFTER IMPROVING IN THE SECOND SEASON		
BETTER THAN THE SECOND	111	24.6%
SAME AS IN THE SECOND	73	16.2%
WORSE THAN THE SECOND	267	59.2%
TOTAL	451	100%

Of the three friends, clearly the third of them is the one who is right: it is most likely that Real Sociedad will end up in a worse position than the ninth place obtained last season. It is even relatively likely that it will rank worse than the 12th place achieved two years ago, since 124 times out of 451 the position in the third season was even worse than the one achieved in the first.

PERFORMANCE IN THE THIRD SEASON AFTER IMPROVING IN THE SECOND SEASON		
WORSE THAN THE SECOND, BUT NOT WORSE THAN THE FIRST	143	31.7%
WORSE THAN THE FIRST	124	27.5%
TOTAL	267	59.2%

It is also worth analysing the opposite situation: what happens to the teams that end up one season in a worse place than the previous season? Do they continue to worsen, or do they tend to improve their performance the following season?

In this case, we have a historical sample of 490 teams that played one season in La Liga and in the next one got worse – without being relegated. What happened in the third season?

In 192 cases out of 490, 39.2%, the team ended up in the third season in a worse position than in the previous two seasons. In 42 cases (8.6%) the team repeated in the third season the same position as in the second season. Finally, in 256 cases (52.2%) the team achieved a better position in the third season than in the second. Out of these 256 cases, in 104 the position achieved was even better than that of the first campaign.

PERFORMANCE IN THE THIRD SEASON AFTER GETTING WORSE IN THE SECOND SEASON		
WORSE THAN THE SECOND	192	39.2%
SAME AS IN THE SECOND	42	8.6%
BETTER THAN THE SECOND, BUT NOT BETTER THAN THE FIRST	152	31.0%
BETTER THAN THE FIRST	104	21.2%
TOTAL	490	100%

When studying what happens after an improvement or after a decrease in the performance of a team, two things must be taken into account:

- Obviously, in the case of improving, if the team wins the league, it is not possible to keep improving the following season. That partly explains the higher percentage of "equals" after an improvement than after a deterioration.
- In several seasons the league has increased its number of participants. These expansions explain, in part, the historical probability of worsening between two seasons.

In any case, several interesting conclusions can be drawn from this analysis:

- Just because **a team has recently improved its performance does not mean that it will make further improvements. Rather the opposite**.
- Likewise, just because **a team has recently worsened its performance does not mean that it will continue to deteriorate. Rather the opposite**.
- Therefore, to adequately predict the future performance of a team it is not enough to consider only its latest season. Older behaviour contains valuable information that is useful in order to make more accurate predictions.

This last point is especially relevant. It is clear that the information from two seasons back, and not just the latest one, is valuable when forecasting the results of a team. And the results from three seasons ago? And the results from four seasons ago? Do they also help improve the forecasts? At what point is information so old that it no longer provides additional predictive capacity? We will try to answer this question later in this book.

AT THE EDGE OF THE ABYSS

In soccer, most of the time, the best team wins. It is the logical thing. It is the usual thing. However, we all know that this is not always the case. There are many other factors that influence the outcome of a match. In many cases we group these factors under the generic word luck: Shots on the woodwork, a red card for a foolish action, last minute penalties, untimely slips, etc.

Sometimes the deciding factor is neither which is the best team nor luck, but another very important factor: **motivation**.

In any human activity, motivation plays an essential role. Runners, for example, understand this perfectly well. It is not the same to run 10 kilometres training on your own as to run a 10-kilometre race competing. The difference in time can be enormous.

Coaches understand it too. A bad relationship with their players can lead to a situation where they want to "set him up" and underperform.

There are many factors that can affect a player's individual motivation. For example, playing against his former team after an unfriendly exit or playing in front of his national coach when he has to decide whether to include him in the next squad. These individual factors are likely to significantly affect that footballer's performance, but they may not be easily observable in the results of the team as a whole.

Fortunately, there are situations that do affect the motivation of an entire team. The home-field advantage is the clearest example. The same team tends, as a general rule, to win more games when playing at home than when playing away. Playing in your own stadium in front of your own fans affects the outcome of the game. It is something that we have internalized so much that it has even ceased to surprise us, although it is a fascinating phenomenon[11].

---

[11] The following video in English from German television explains the various psychological, hormonal and even evolutionary reasons behind the home-field advantage https://www.youtube.com/watch?v=YNBBuNAA9oU and why during the COVID-19 pandemic it weakened but did not fully disappear despite the absence of public in the stadiums.

When the final matchdays approach and a team is close to being relegated, all the players feel in their own flesh the importance of the upcoming games. This is also a situation that affects the motivation of the players.

What effect does this increase in motivation have? To what extent does a team improve its performance in critical situations? Is playing under pressure an advantage or could it turn out to be a disadvantage? Let's see what the numbers say.

To carry out this analysis, we have taken information from the Spanish La Liga from the 1995-96 season (in which victory began to be rewarded with 3 points instead of 2) until the 2019-20 season and we have calculated the percentage of matches won by teams that are ranked in the two spots immediately above the relegation line and in the two spots immediately below the relegation line. This corresponds, in most seasons, to positions 16, 17, 18 and 19, as, since 1999, relegation places have always corresponded to teams classified in positions 18, 19, 20.

Between matchday 1 and matchday 34, the teams classified in positions 16, 17, 18 and 19 won 31.7% of the matches they played. However, from matchday 35 to the end of the championship, the teams classified in these positions won 37.6% of their matches[12].

On the other hand, the teams classified in the middle of the table, in the "no man's land", without facing the risk of relegation and without the possibility of qualifying for the European competitions, experience a drop in performance in the final stretch of the championship. La Liga teams ranked between 5 and 8 places above the relegation line —that is, in positions 10, 11, 12 and 13 in a league with 20 teams— won 31.7% of the games played between matchday 1 and 34, but only 29.1% from matchday 35 onwards.

---

[12] We omit from this analysis the teams classified in 20th place, since their level of motivation may be very different in the final stretch of the season depending on whether they are already mathematically relegated or whether they still have a chance of maintaining the category.

The following table summarizes the commented data:

LA LIGA	MATCHES	VICTORIES	VICTORY PERCENTAGE
DAYS 1-34 POSITIONS 16, 17, 18, 19	3,401	1,078	31.7%
DAYS 35-38 POSITIONS 16, 17, 18, 19	431	162	37.6%
DAYS 1-34 POSITIONS 10, 11, 12, 13	3,402	1,080	31.7%
DAYS 35-38 POSITIONS 10, 11, 12, 13	430	125	29.1%

This phenomenon is not exclusive to the Spanish La Liga. It can also be observed in the Premier League. The following table has been constructed with information from this competition from the 1992-93 to the 2019-20 season:

ENGLISH PREMIER LEAGUE [13]	MATCHES	VICTORIES	VICTORY PERCENTAGE
DAYS 1-34 POSITIONS 16, 17, 18, 19	3,815	1,151	30.2%
DAYS 35-38 POSITIONS 16, 17, 18, 19	487	159	32.6%
DAYS 1-34 POSITIONS 10, 11, 12, 13	3,817	1,192	31.2%
DAYS 35-38 POSITIONS 10, 11, 12, 13	488	136	27.9%

Finally, we have the numbers for the Spanish Second Division since 1987[14]. 22 teams have taken part in this competition every season since 1997. Since then, the relegation line has always been between the 18th and 19th place, as the 4 worst-ranked teams are relegated at the end of each season.

SECOND SPANISH DIVISION	MATCHES	VICTORIES	VICTORY PERCENTAGE
DAYS 1-34 POSITIONS 17, 18, 19, 20	4,490	1,413	31.5%
DAYS 35-42 POSITIONS 17, 18, 19, 20	894	327	36.6%
DAYS 1-34 POSITIONS 11, 12, 13, 14	4,489	1,589	35.4%
DAYS 35-42 POSITIONS 11, 13, 13, 14	895	275	30.7%

Clearly **approaching the abyss provides a very significant extra motivation**. Likewise, reaching the final matchdays of the league in mid-table demotivates the squads. If, for example, on matchday 14 of the championship the team ranked 11th faces the team ranked 18th, the team ranked 11th will

---

[13] The Premier League was founded under its current format in 1992.
[14] We take the data from this season since in the previous one (1986-87) the promotion and relegation system was significantly different.

be, in general terms, the favourite. However, if this match is played on the last or second last matchday, the team in 18th place will be the favourite.

In statistical terms this means that the correlation between a team's past performance, whether measured by position, points or goals, and its future performance is not stable throughout the season. The correlations depend on what phase the championship is in.

For any modeler who wants to build regressions this presents a considerable challenge. If you build a single model for the whole season based on the position of the teams, your model will tend to underestimate the probability of victory of the teams in the dangerous positions in the final stretch of the season and it will tend to overestimate it for teams in the middle of the table on those same matchdays.

To solve this problem the modeler could try the following:

- Include some variable in the model that captures the relevance of the game for each team.
- Build, instead of a single model for the whole season, several models so that each one of them contains the correct correlations for each phase of the league.

Neither solution is easy. With the exception of the home team advantage, it is not easy to build a variable that adequately and systematically captures the level of motivation of each of the teams. Building several models is also complicated, since it requires correctly identifying when each one should start being applied and the previous one stop being used. Above all, it means using smaller samples to build each of them, which can lead them to being less reliable[15].

Probably the best option is to build a single model while being aware of its limitations. The user of the model should use it knowing that in situations where the motivation of one of the two teams is much higher or lower than usual, the model calculations will not be valid.

---

[15] Intuitively, any statistical analysis is more robust the more observations we have at our disposal in order to carry it out. If we use few observations, we run the risk that the results obtained will not be representative of reality but reflect only the specific characteristics of the sample we are analysing.

If the winning probabilities of the teams with decisive matches are higher than what their previous results seem to indicate, perhaps a good strategy for a bettor is precisely to bet in favour of these teams and against those that no longer risk anything. What results would a bettor have obtained if he had followed this strategy? To answer this question, we have collected the betting odds for these 3 competitions from the 2000-01 season onwards.

In the case of the Spanish La Liga, we would have made money if we had bet in favour of the teams "on the edge of the abyss" during the last matchdays.

LA LIGA	MATCHES	BETS WON	EXPECTED BETS WON	RATIO
MATCHDAYS 35-38 POSTS 16, 17, 18, 19	319	120	109.0	110%
MATCHDAYS 35-38 POSTS 10, 11, 12, 13	318	98	96.8	101%

A ratio greater than 100% means that teams in this situation won more matches than expected based on the implied probabilities in the betting odds. For the bettor to achieve a profit, this ratio must be greater than 100% and, additionally, be high enough to offset the bookmaker's margin.

In the case of the Premier League, we would also have been better off betting in favour of the teams in the lower zone of the table than in favour of the teams in the middle zone, although we would not have made any money.

ENGLISH PREMIER LEAGUE	MATCHES	BETS WON	EXPECTED BETS WON	RATIO
MATCHDAYS 35-38 POSTS 16, 17, 18, 19	315	97	94.7	102%
MATCHDAYS 35-38 POSTS 10, 11, 12, 13	315	92	94.7	97%

Finally, in the case of the Spanish Second Division, it is observed that it is also a better strategy to bet in favour of teams that risk being relegated than in favour of those in the quiet area of the table.

SECOND SPANISH DIVISION	MATCHES	BETS WON	EXPECTED BETS WON	RATIO
MATCHDAYS 35-42 POSTS 16, 17, 18, 19	636	242	208.5	116%
MATCHDAYS 35-42 POSTS 10, 11, 12, 13	638	187	197.2	95%

Although the available sample is small, it is observed that this strategy could provide some gains. In general, in these matches the initial odds published by some bookies pay generously for the victory of the hypermotivated team, since their statistical models probably have difficulty capturing this factor. As bettors place their bets, the odds move sharply, getting much closer to the real probabilities.

In any case, as always, it is vital to act prudently. Nothing guarantees that the motivated team will win and the one that does risk anything will lose.

The coach of the team that does not risk anything could, for example, consider fielding less habitual players who could be more motivated than their fellow starters. What works best for a team? Playing with your best eleven, even if they are not very motivated, or playing with substitutes who may be more motivated to show their skills?

There could even be a situation in which the team that does not risk anything is motivated by a third-party bonus. But that is a different story...

HOME OR AWAY

Matchday 11 is about to begin. On this day, Barcelona visits Seville and Real Madrid hosts Leganés. A group of friends looks at how the standings are at that moment:

RANK	EQUIPO	HOME			AWAY			POINTS
		WIN	DRAW	LOSS	WIN	DRAW	LOSS	
1	R. MADRID	3	2	0	4	1	0	24
2	BARCELONA	3	1	1	4	0	1	22
4	SEVILLE	5	0	0	1	3	1	21
17	LEGANÉS	0	1	4	3	0	2	10

"What a great game Seville-Barcelona!" says one of them. Seville are unbeatable in their home stadium. They have won all five games at the Pizjuán. Without a doubt, we should bet that they are going to defeat Barcelona.

"Seville are not that good," says another one of the friends. Look what has happened to them when they have played away from home. They have only won one match out of five.

"Yes, but in front of their crowd they are a totally different team. We have to look at what they have done in their previous home games, since today they are playing at home," the first friend argues again.

"Well, and what do you think of the match between Real Madrid and Leganés?" The third friend intervenes. "Very easy game for Real, or maybe not? Leganés are near the relegation zone, but they have obtained their three victories away from home".

This conversation reflects a relatively frequent debate when talking about football or team sports in general. When it comes to forecasting, is it better to take into account all the matches played by a team or is it better to focus only on the matches played at home or away depending on where its next match is going to be?

Our point of view will affect the odds we assign to Seville and Leganés of winning, as these teams have obtained very different results at home and away so far this season.

To try to answer this question we have initially constructed two variables:

- **Home Team Home Points**: points per game obtained this season in the matches played at home by the team that is going to play the next match at home. For example, in this case, for Seville the value of this variable would be 3, since they have got a total of 15 points in the 5 games they have played in their field. For Real Madrid it would be 2.2.

- **Away Team Away Points**: points per game obtained this season in the matches played away by the team that is going to play the next match away. For example, in this case, for Leganés the value of this variable would be 1.8, since they have got a total of 9 points in the 5 games they have played away. For Barcelona it would be 2.4.

To assess the different predictive capacity of these 2 variables, we have calculated them for the more than 185,000 matches included in the database described in the introduction.

With this sample we build a model that calculates the probability of local victory according to these two explanatory variables[16]. The following results are obtained:

ESTIMATED MODEL 1		
VARIABLE	COEFFICIENT	P-VALUE
HOME TEAM HOME POINTS	0.44	<0.01%
AWAY TEAM AWAY POINTS	-0.45	<0.01%

As it can be expected, the higher the percentage of points obtained by the home team in their home games, the greater the probability that they will win their next home game. This is indicated by the positive coefficient of 0.44. Likewise, the higher the percentage of points achieved by the visiting team in their away games, the lower the probability of a local victory (coefficient of -0.45)[17]. The p-values are less than 0.01% which indicates that both variables are highly significant[18].

---

[16] We use a logistic regression model for this.

[17] It is not easy to give an intuitive explanation for each coefficient. The logistic regression limits its output between 0% and 100%, so the coefficients 0.44 and -0.45 affect the local victory probabilities differently depending on the absolute values of the explanatory variables. Let's see this with an example:

Given that both explanatory variables take, by construction, the same range of values (between 0 and 3 points per game), that their coefficients take similar values (one with a positive sign and the other with a negative sign) and that their p-values are the same, it is possible to conclude that **the level of the home team and the visiting team have a similar influence on how the match will unfold**. Football is a two-team dance. What happens on the field depends on both of them.

Is this a good model? Could we make good predictions with it? The statistics of this model are the following:

GOODNESS OF MODEL 1	
CONCORDANCE	59.5%
ROC	60.1%

The concordance value indicates the percentage of matches in the construction sample for which the model makes a correct prediction. Correct predictions are of two types: when the model said that the probability of local victory was greater than 50% and the match effectively ended in a local victory and when the probability of a local victory was less than 50% and the match, indeed, did not end in a local victory. A perfect model would have a 100% concordance value and a model without any predictive ability would show a 50% concordance value (it would be like tossing a coin).

- The local team has obtained, on average, 1 point per game when playing at home and the visiting team has obtained on average 0.5 points per game when playing away. In this case the model indicates that the probability of a match between the two finishing in local victory is 45.8%.
- Instead, if the local team had obtained 2 points per game when playing on their turf the probability of a home victory would be 56.9%.
- Finally, if the local team had obtained on average 3 points per game when playing at home the probability of a local victory would be 67.3%.

Going from 1 point per game to 2 points per game, makes the probability of local victory go up by 11.1% (56.9% - 45.8%), while going from 2 points per game to 3 points per game makes the probability of local victory go up by just **10.4%** (67.3% - 56.9%).

In a traditional linear regression, the coefficient of each variable indicates exactly how much the dependent variable is going to move in response to a delta in the explanatory variable. In a logistic regression, this movement is not always the same, since it not only depends on the delta of the explanatory variable, but also on its starting and finishing values. It is this property what precisely makes the probability assigned by the logistic regression to always remain between 0% and 100%.

[18] It is common practice to consider relevant those variables with a p-value lower than 5%.

The ROC is an indicator of the model's ability to order the matches from lowest to highest probability of local victory. Its calculation is relatively complex[19]. For the time being, it is worth simply knowing that, as with concordance, a perfect model should have a ROC of 100% and a model with zero predictive capacity would have a ROC of 50%.

In fact, these statistics must be calculated not only with the sample of games used for the construction of the model, but also with a sample of different games. If the model achieves similar indicators with both samples, it is an excellent sign. If the indicators fall when calculated with a sample of different games, it means that the model is capturing patterns of the construction sample, but that cannot be extrapolated to other games. In practice this means that if we are building a statistical model with the aim of betting, we need its goodness of fit to be high, not only in the sample of historical information used to construct it, but also with the matches that are played in the future.

The model we have built has a concordance of 59.5% and a ROC of 60.1%. Are these values high or low? How high should they be to be able to make a profit gambling?

Luckily, the sample with which we have built this model also contains the odds offered by the bookmakers for the local victory. If we use these odds as an explanatory variable and build a model with it, we get the following:

ODDS MODEL		
VARIABLE	COEFFICIENT	P-VALUE
LOCAL ODDS	-0.67	<0.01%

Clearly the odds paid by the bookmakers are highly correlated with the results of the match. The negative coefficient indicates that the higher the odds offered by the bookmakers, the lower the probability of a local victory.

This model has the following goodness of fit:

ODDS MODEL - GOODNESS OF FIT	
CONCORDANCE	65.3%
ROC	66.0%

---

[19] Annex 1 contains a detailed explanation about it.

Both the concordance and the ROC of the odds model are significantly higher than our simple model based on the points per game of the home games for the home team and the points per game of the away games for the away team.

Our first model does not exceed in predictive power the odds offered by the bookmakers. Therefore, **it is insufficiently good to detect odds that offer value to the bettor**.

Of course, we are not going to give up on round one. We can try to add additional variables into our model to make it more predictive. **We already know the minimum predictive capacity we need for a model to be profitable.**

As a next step, we can see if the model improves by incorporating variables that capture the performance of the home team away from home and of the away team at home and, this way, answer the question with which we opened this chapter. For this purpose, we have created the following two additional variables:

- **Home Team Away Points**: points per game obtained this season in the matches played as a visitor by the team that is going to play at home. For example, in this case, for Seville the value of this variable would be 1.2, since they have got a total of 6 points in the 5 games they have played away from home. For Real Madrid it would be 2.6.

- **Away Team Home Points:** points per game obtained this season in the matches played at home by the team that is going to play as a visitor. For example, in this case, for Leganés the value of this variable would be 0.2, since they have got 1 point in the 5 games they have played away from home. For Barcelona it would be 2.

If we create a model with these two new variables, along with the previous two, we get the following:

MODEL 2		
VARIABLE	**COEFFICIENT**	**P-VALUE**
HOME TEAM HOME POINTS	0.37	<0.01%
HOME TEAM AWAY POINTS	0.33	<0.01%
AWAY TEAM AWAY POINTS	-0.38	<0.01%
AWAY TEAM HOME POINTS	-0.32	<0.01%

The two new variables also have a p-value lower than 0.01% and present coefficients with the expected sign. If the team that is going to play at home has got a lot of points away from home, it is likely that it will be a team that wins when it plays at home. If the visiting team usually wins when they play on their own turf, it is likely that they will also get points when they play away.

This new model has two explanatory variables related to the home team and two explanatory variables related to the visiting team. When introducing the two new variables we see how the coefficient of the two old variables decreases. This is because each of the new variables is partially correlated with one of the old variables, causing the old variables to lose some of their relevance. In other words, although a team may perform differently home and away, both aspects are undoubtedly related: a good team tends to win at home and away, and a bad team tends to lose at home and away.

The goodness of fit indicators of this model with 4 explanatory variables are the following:

MODEL 2 – GOODNESS OF FIT	
CONCORDANCE	61.7%
ROC	62.0%

By introducing the two new variables we obtain a more predictive model. The two new variables provide information that was not in the two initial variables. Their incorporation into the model allows for more accurate forecasts.

Despite having improved, we are still far from the predictive power of the odds model. We do not have a profitable model yet.

The coefficients of the four variables are very similar and so are their p-values, so it can be concluded that their relevance is the same. However, it can be observed that the coefficients of the new variables are slightly lower than those of the old variables: **the model gives a little more importance to the past behaviour at home of the teams that play at home than to their past behaviour as a visitor. Similarly, it gives a little more importance to the past behaviour as a visitor of the team that plays as a visitor than to its past behaviour at home.**

To get a clearer idea of this small difference in relevance, let's imagine the following three situations:

- **Situation 1**: both the home team and the away team have averaged 1.5 points per game so far in the league, both getting 50% of the points in their home games and 50% in their away games.
- **Situation 2**: both the home team and the visiting team have averaged 1.5 points per game so far in the league, both getting 66% of the points at stake in their respective home games and 33% as visitors.
- **Situation 3**: both the home team and the visiting team have averaged 1.5 points per game so far in the league, both getting 33% of the points at stake in their respective home games and 66% as visitors.

The following table summarizes the value of the four explanatory variables in these three situations:

	HOME TEAM HOME POINTS	HOME TEAM AWAY POINTS	AWAY TEAM HOME POINTS	AWAY TEAM AWAY POINTS
SITUATION 1	1.5	1.5	1.5	1.5
SITUATION 2	2	1	2	1
SITUATION 3	1	2	1	2

The probability of each match ending in a local victory according to the model is the following:

	LOCAL VICTORY PROBABILITY
SITUATION 1	45.8%
SITUATION 2	47.1%
SITUATION 3	44.4%

Situation 2 is the most favourable for the home team given their greater relative strength when playing on their field, but it is a small difference. **It is much more relevant how many points per game each team gets. Whether they get them at home or away is a secondary aspect when predicting what will happen in the next match**.

As a final test we have developed a model with only 2 explanatory variables. One of them indicates the number of points per game got by the home team (both in the games it played at home and away) and the other indicates the same, but for the visiting team:

- **Home Team Points:** points per game obtained this season, both in its home and away matches, by the team that is going to play at home. For example, in this case, for Seville the value of this variable would be 2.1, since they have got a total of 21 points in the 10 games they have played so far. For Real Madrid it would be 2.4. This variable is nothing more than the mean between the variables Home Team Home Points and Home Team Away Points.

- **Away Team Points:** points per game obtained this season, both in its matches played at home and away, by the team that is going to play as a visitor. For example, in this case, for Leganés the value of this variable would be 1, since they have got a total of 10 points in the 10 games they have played so far. For Barcelona it would be 2.2. This variable is nothing more than the average between the variables Away Team Away Points and Away Team Home Points.

With these two variables the model obtained is the following:

MODEL 3		
VARIABLE	**COEFFICIENT**	**P-VALUE**
HOME TEAM POINTS	0.70	<0.01%
AWAY TEAM POINTS	-0.69	<0.01%

It is a very similar model to the first one, only this time each of the explanatory variables is more powerful, as it is built with more information. Its indicators of goodness of fit are as follows:

MODEL 3 – GOODNESS OF FIT	
CONCONDANCE	61.6%
ROC	61.9%

Its goodness of fit is practically the same as the model with four explanatory variables. By having condensed all the information from each team in a single variable, we have basically not lost any predictive capacity.

Although this model loses the finesse of giving a slightly different importance to the past as a home or as a visitor, this loss is compensated by having 2 very robust variables, built with more games and, therefore, prone to fewer distortions due to outliers, correlation with other explanatory variables, etc. Applying the principle of parsimony, we would opt for this model among all those built in this chapter.

In any case, this model is not satisfactory. Its predictive capacity is still significantly below the odds of the bookmakers. This should come as no surprise, as this model only assigns probabilities based on the results of each team during the current season. This undoubtedly provides rather poor forecasts, especially during the first few matchdays. As we saw in previous chapters, at least the two previous seasons are also relevant.

Furthermore, the model uses only variables based on points and ignores any variables related to goals.

In the specific case of the matches between Real Madrid-Leganés and Sevilla-Barcelona, the three models built in this chapter would have assigned the following probabilities:

LOCAL VICTORY PROBABILITY	REAL MADRID - LEGANÉS	SEVILLE - BARCELONA
MODEL 1	44.6%	46.7%
MODEL 2	67.8%	44.7%
MODEL 3	70.0%	45.3%

Clearly, in both cases these models underestimate the real probabilities of victory for Real Madrid and Barcelona for the reasons stated above.

In the next chapters we will try to build a more predictive model by expanding the time window of the explanatory variables and incorporating information on the numbers of goals scored and conceded by each team.

THE IMPORTANCE OF THE PAST

The past performance of a team provides us with valuable information about its future performance. The question is: what part of the past is relevant and what part is already too far back to be useful? When modelling, what time window do the explanatory variables have to consider?

To answer this question, we have calculated, for every match of the Spanish La Liga of seasons 2000-01 to 2019-20, the difference between the goals scored and conceded by the team that is going to play at home and by the team that is going to play away in their previous matches. We have calculated this difference between goals scored and conceded considering different time windows[20]:

- The 6 previous games.
- The 19 previous games.
- The 38 previous games.
- The 76 previous games.
- All the matches already played by each team during the current season and the 2 previous seasons (between 76 and 113 games).
- All matches already played by each team in the current season and in the 3 previous seasons (between 114 and 151 games).
- All the matches already played by each team in the current season and in the 4 previous seasons (between 152 and 189).
- All the matches already played by each team in the current season and in the 5 previous seasons (between 190 and 227).

We have, therefore, constructed 8 variables in the same way with the only difference that each one takes more extensive information from the past to try to predict what will happen in the present.

---

[20] As we learned in previous chapters, these variables have been constructed with information on goals, not points, and giving equal importance to goals scored and conceded and to matches played at home and away from home. In the case of the teams that have been promoted or relegated during the seasons analysed, the variables are constructed only with the matches played in La Liga.

Which of them is the most predictive? These are the results:

6 PREVIOUS GAMES	
CONCORDANCE	61.0%
ROC	62.8%

19 PREVIOUS GAMES	
CONCORDANCE	66.1%
ROC	66.8%

38 PREVIOUS GAMES	
CONCORDANCE	66.7%
ROC	67.1%

76 PREVIOUS GAMES	
CONCORDANCE	67.2%
ROC	67.5%

Clearly 6 games are too few to properly assess the level of a team. Out of the first 4 variables analysed, the most powerful is the one that considers the previous 76 games. This result is consistent with what we saw in the chapter "Trend or reversion to the mean": the future performance of a team depends not only on the last season. Older results also provide valuable information.

The 4 variables that consider an even longer window obtained the following results:

CURRENT SEASON AND 2 PREVIOUS	
CONCORDANCE	67.5%
ROC	67.7%

CURRENT SEASON AND 3 PREVIOUS	
CONCORDANCE	67.3%
ROC	67.6%

CURRENT SEASON AND 4 PREVIOUS	
CONCORDANCE	67.1%
ROC	67.3%

CURRENT SEASON AND 5 PREVIOUS	
CONCORDANCE	67.0%
ROC	67.2%

The best of the 8 variables is the one that considers the current season and the 2 previous ones. The variables that consider older information have less predictive capacity. We can, therefore, conclude that in order to correctly assess the level of a team, **it is necessary to consider all the games it has played in the current season and in the 2 previous seasons**.

It is striking how the variable that considers the 5 previous seasons has a predictive power only slightly lower than that of the variable that considers the 2 most recent seasons. Intuitively, we might think that a variable that uses such old historical information should be much worse than the variable that focuses on more recent historical information. In fact, in so many years normally a large part of the squad, let alone the coach, will have changed. Why is this variable not much worse then?

Probably the reason is that, although the players and coaches change, the general level of the team does tend to be stable over time. The good team will sign new players who will probably also be good, and the bad team will possibly sign new bad players. Does anyone expect that Real Madrid and Barcelona will not continue to dominate the Spanish league in 5, 10 or 15 years?

It should be noted here that these 8 variables all give equal importance to all the games that fall within their time windows. We are not saying that what happened 2 seasons ago is as relevant as what happened last season. What we are saying is that **what happened 2 seasons ago enriches the information of what happened last season**.

If we divide the winning variable into 3 parts (current season, previous season and 2 seasons ago) we can see which part of the time window is more important and which is less:

VARIABLE	RELATIVE WEIGHT
CURRENT SEASON	41%
PREVIOUS SEASON	32%
2 SEASONS AGO	27%

When building a model with these 3 variables, the results of the current season are the most important with 41% of the weight, the previous season has an importance of 32% and what happened 2 seasons ago has an importance of 27%[21].

These percentages have been calculated with information from the Spanish La Liga. For other leagues, these percentages may be, to some extent, different depending on, for example, different practices when signing players and / or coaches, the typical duration of contracts, etc.

Of course, the importance of the current season will depend on the matchday we are in, being lower in the first ones and higher as the end of the competition approaches. The above percentages can be considered representative when the current season is in its middle phase.

To show the effect of the passage of time more intuitively on the predictive capacity of the variables, we have constructed the following table with all the available historical information:

BEST TEAM CURRENT SEASON	BEST TEAM PREVIOUS SEASON	BEST TEAM 2 SEASONS AGO	MATCHES	LOCAL WINS
LOCAL	LOCAL	LOCAL	17,215	63.1%
LOCAL	LOCAL	VISITOR	5,961	53.9%
LOCAL	VISITOR	LOCAL	4,813	50.4%
VISITOR	LOCAL	LOCAL	6,685	46.5%
LOCAL	VISITOR	VISITOR	6,177	45.2%
VISITOR	LOCAL	VISITOR	5,116	41.6%
VISITOR	VISITOR	LOCAL	6,198	38.2%
VISITOR	VISITOR	VISITOR	17,871	31.0%
TOTAL			70,036	46.3%

When the home team is being a better team this season —that is to say, it has a better goal difference— than the visiting team and it was also a better team in the 2 previous seasons, matches end in a local victory in 63.1% of cases. This probability is reduced if the away team is being better this season or if the visiting team was better than the home team in any of the 2 previous seasons.

---

[21] Readers with a statistical background may be interested to know that in this case the relative weight has been calculated as the Wald Chi-Square of each variable divided by the sum of the Wald Chi-Square of the 3 explanatory variables.

For example, if the away team was better than the home team 2 seasons ago [22], the local win percentage drops to 53.9%. On the other hand, if the visiting team is being better this season, the percentage falls to 46.5%. That is, it doesn't just matter how many of the past seasons one team has been better than the other, but obviously also which team is currently being better.

Therefore, by dividing the historical information into several variables, we can improve the predictive power of the model. When we use a variable for the current season, another one for the previous one and third one for 2 seasons ago, the indicators of goodness of fit reach the following values:

CURRENT SEASON AND 2 PREVIOUS SEASONS (USING 3 SPECIFIC VARIABLES)	
CONCORDANCE	67.7%
ROC	67.8%

These indicators of goodness of fit are somewhat better than when we use a single variable [23]. The improvement is, in any case, small since the three variables are partially correlated with each other.

What lessons can a bettor draw from this chapter? Is it a good strategy to build a model that uses information from the last 3 years and bet with it? Is it better to bet on matches between teams that have been in the same league for several seasons or is it better to bet on matches played by a newly promoted team?

Clearly, historical information allows for more reliable predictions in games between veteran teams than between newly promoted teams. Unfortunately, this does not mean that it is easier to beat the odds that the bookmakers offer in matches between veteran teams, since they also have more information to correctly estimate the probability of each result.

---

[22] In this chapter when we say that one team was better than the other, we mean that it got better goal differences than its rival in the past. We are not referring to the previous head-to-head matches between the two teams. The specific relevance of the previous head-to-head matches between the two teams is discussed later in this book.

[23] As we mentioned earlier, when modelling one must always be cautious when achieving greater predictive power by increasing the number of explanatory variables, since the greater number of degrees of freedom of the regression can lead to "overfitting". To minimize this risk, the predictive capacity of the model must be measured with a different sample than the one used for its construction.

To see how the availability of historical information affects the reliability of the odds, we have studied their predictive capacity in 3 types of matches:

1. Matches played between 2 teams that have been just promoted to the same league.
2. Matches played between 2 teams that played last season in the same league (and are still in it).
3. Matches played between 2 teams that played the 2 previous seasons in the same league (and continue to do so).

The results are the following:

ODDS MODEL 1	
CONCORDANCE	62.2%
ROC	63.1%

ODDS MODEL 2	
CONCORDANCE	64.4%
ROC	65.3%

ODDS MODEL 3	
CONCORDANCE	66.0%
ROC	66.7%

As it can be seen, the odds are also more predictive the longer the 2 teams have been in the same league. **The availability of historical information is a weapon available both to the bettor and to the bookie.**

Does this mean that there is no hope? Can't you use statistics to find value in odds? Let's go back to the table we saw earlier that divided the games according to the relative performance of each team in the last 3 seasons. What profit or loss would have made a bettor who had risked money in each type of match[24]?

---

[24] Returns have been calculated assuming that all bets would have been of the same amount. A percentage of 100% means that the bettor would have made neither a profit nor a loss. Therefore, percentages lower than 100% indicate losses for the bettor.

BEST TEAM CURRENT SEASON	BEST TEAM PREVIOUS SEASON	BEST TEAM 2 SEASONS AGO	HOME VICTORY RETURN	AWAY VICTORY RETURN
LOCAL	LOCAL	LOCAL	99.2%	88.7%
LOCAL	LOCAL	VISITOR	98.6%	93.1%
LOCAL	VISITOR	LOCAL	96.8%	91.3%
VISITOR	LOCAL	LOCAL	98.9%	89.9%
LOCAL	VISITOR	VISITOR	95.0%	96.1%
VISITOR	LOCAL	VISITOR	98.0%	92.0%
VISITOR	VISITOR	LOCAL	95.4%	94.3%
VISITOR	VISITOR	VISITOR	97.5%	95.9%
TOTAL			**97.9%**	**93.4%**

Although none of these strategies would have provided a positive return, there are significant differences between them. If we simplify the previous table to analyse what would have happened if we had systematically bet on the teams that are doing better in the current season than in the previous one, we obtain the following figures:

BEST TEAM CURRENT SEASON	BEST TEAM PREVIOUS SEASON	HOME VICTORY RETURN	AWAY VICTORY RETURN
LOCAL	VISITOR	95.8%	94.2%
VISITOR	LOCAL	98.5%	90.9%
TOTAL		**97.9%**	**93.4%**

These results indicate that, although the recent past is more predictive than the more remote past, **it is better to bet in favour of teams that are doing worse than the previous season. Equally, it is better to bet against teams that have recently performed better than in the previous season**. Why?

The market overestimates the importance of the latest results. When a team is on a winning streak or on a losing streak, many bettors get carried away. They begin to bet massively in favour of the team that is "on fire" and run away from the team that is apparently crumbling. This creates a bias in the odds that makes it more interesting to bet on the team that is going through a bad time.

Let's imagine, for example, a team in the middle of the table like Athletic or Celta. If one of these teams wins 3 or 4 matches in a row, they start to attract a lot of interest. The odds that are offered for their next victories decrease. But do those 3 or 4 wins in a row really mean that, all of a sudden, these teams are much better than before? Probably not. That little winning streak may be due, at least in part, simply to luck. These teams will most likely return to their usual level sooner or later[25]. **It is not advisable to bet in favour of the fashionable team**.

The table above also provides another interesting insight. Generally speaking, **it is better to bet in favour of home teams than in favour of visiting teams**. Someone who had always bet in favour of the local team would have recovered 97.9% of their investment. Someone who had always bet in favour of the visiting team would have recovered only 93.4%.

These tables hide another very relevant insight. In the top four rows the home team has been better than the visiting team in at least 2 of the last 3 seasons. On the other hand, in the bottom four rows it is the visiting team who has been better than the home team in at least 2 of the previous seasons. Well, **if you like to bet in favour of the home team, it is better to do it when it is a better team than the visiting team** (top four rows) than when it is not (bottom four rows). Likewise, **if you like to bet in favour of the visiting team, it is better to do it when it is a better team than the home team**. These are the returns for each of these options:

BEST TEAM CURRENT SEASON	BEST TEAM PREVIOUS SEASON	BEST TEAM 2 SEASONS AGO	HOME VICTORY RETURN	AWAY VICTORY RETURN
LOCAL	LOCAL	LOCAL		
LOCAL	LOCAL	VISITOR	98.8%	90.3%
LOCAL	VISITOR	LOCAL		
VISITOR	LOCAL	LOCAL		
LOCAL	VISITOR	VISITOR		
VISITOR	LOCAL	VISITOR	96.6%	95.2%
VISITOR	VISITOR	LOCAL		
VISITOR	VISITOR	VISITOR		
TOTAL			97.9%	93.4%

[25] Other authors also defend this idea, such as Kevin Pullein in his book *The Definitive Guide to Betting on Football* or Chris Anderson and David Sally in *The Numbers Game*.

In conclusion, according to the data in the table, the worst strategy is to bet in favour of:

- A visiting team
- that is on a winning streak
- which plays against a local team that is better
- that is on a losing streak.

On the contrary, the best strategy is to bet in favour of:

- A local team
- that is on a losing streak
- which plays against a visiting team that is worse
- that is on winning streak.

These results are due, to a large extent, to how the bookmakers set their odds and the behaviour of the bettors themselves. These aspects are covered in more detail in the second and third part of this book.

Given the statistical approach of this book, we are focusing on the games between teams that have been in the same league for some time. It is in these cases when there is historical information that can be used to construct explanatory variables.

This is not to say that matches between newly promoted or relegated teams cannot be of interest to a bettor. As we have seen, in these types of matches it is much more difficult for the bookies to estimate the correct odds. So presumably someone with a good knowledge of the squads, the strategy, the motivation of the players, the referee, etc., can make good predictions.

This type of qualitative information is, however, much more difficult to obtain, store in a database and analyse in a systematic way. In addition, a high number of matches is required to be able to assess with certainty whether a possible inefficiency or market bias is indeed such. For this reason, here we focus on quantifiable factors that apply to a large number of matches. We leave aside other factors that, although may be relevant, are qualitative or apply only to a small number of games.

The criteria used in this chapter to classify football matches and possible bets are relevant because their level of profitability is different. However, none of them provides a positive return. This should not come as a surprise, as it is not easy to beat the market. Whoever says that making money gambling is easy simply lies or does not know what is talking about.

In the following chapters we will continue to analyse other relevant factors that must be considered when predicting team performance and placing bets.

BEYOND GOALS

We have seen that the difference between goals scored and goals conceded is a more reliable indicator than points when it comes to predicting the future performance of a team.

Are there other variables even better than goals to predict the behaviour of a team? Yes, there are, and in this chapter we are going to talk about them.

If you have **historical information on the shots that each team makes and that each team receives, you can make more reliable forecasts.** Historical information on the number of shots taken by each team is not as easy to get as the information on goals. In any case, we are fortunate to have this type of data for a sample of 75,164 games from the following leagues and seasons[26]:

COUNTRY	COMPETITION	FROM	UNTIL	MATCHES
BELGIUM	PRO LEAGUE	2017	2020	803
ENGLAND	PREMIER LEAGUE	2000	2020	7,608
	CHAMPIONSHIP	2000	2020	11,046
	LEAGUE ONE	2000	2020	10,878
	LEAGUE TWO	2000	2020	10,950
FRANCE	LIGUE 1	2005	2020	5,484
	LIGUE 2	2017	2020	1,115
GERMANY	BUNDESLIGA	2006	2020	4,316
	BUNDESLIGA 2	2017	2020	962
GREECE	SUPER LEAGUE	2017	2020	754
ITALY	SERIE A	2005	2020	5,716
	SERIE B	2017	2020	1,215
NETHERLANDS	EREDIVISIE	2017	2020	902
PORTUGAL	PRIMEIRA LIGA	2017	2020	966
SPAIN	PRIMERA	2005	2020	3,924
	SEGUNDA	2017	2020	1,462
TURKEY	SÜPER LIG	2017	2020	978

---

[26] Part of the historical information used for this chapter and others in this book is freely available at http://www.football-data.co.uk/downloadm.php thanks to Joseph Buchdahl. The information can be downloaded in Excel format.

SCOTLAND	PREMIERSHIP	2000	2020	4,567
	CHAMPIONSHIP	2017	2020	505
	LEAGUE ONE	2017	2020	507
	LEAGUE TWO	2017	2020	506
TOTAL		**2000**	**2020**	**75,164**

For each of these matches we have constructed the following variables:

- **PointDif6**: difference between the points added by the home team and the visiting team in the previous 6 games.
- **GoalDif6**: difference between the goals scored and conceded by the home team and the visiting team in the previous 6 matches.
- **ShotDif6:** difference between the shots made and received by the home team and the visiting team in the previous 6 games.
- **ShotOnTargetDif6**: difference between the shots on goal made and received by the home team and the visiting team in the previous 6 games.

All these variables are divided by 6 to facilitate their comparison with other variables constructed with a larger number of matches that we will use later. This way, all the variables can be read as average values per game[27].

The two variables on shots present a relevant difference between them. ShotDif6 considers all the shots made and received by each of the contestants regardless of whether these shots were on target or not. The variable ShotOnTargetDif6 only considers the shots made and received by each team that were directed to the goal.

When talking about the 6 previous games we refer to the 6 previous matchdays played by each team.

---

[27] Obviously this change in the scale of the variables does not affect their predictive capacity.

Let's see an example with some numbers:

TEAM A PREVIOUS 6 GAMES		TEAM B PREVIOUS 6 GAMES		CALCULATED VARIABLES
TOTAL SHOTS MADE	TOTAL SHOTS RECEIVED	TOTAL SHOTS MADE	TOTAL SHOTS RECEIVED	SHOTDIF6
34	30	20	25	$((34 - 30) - (20 - 25)) / 6$ $= 9 / 6 = 1.5$
SHOTS ON TARGET MADE	SHOTS ON TARGET RECEIVED	SHOTS ON TARGET MADE	SHOTS ON TARGET RECEIVED	SHOTONTARGETDIF6
17	16	18	19	$((17 - 16) - (18 - 19)) / 6$ $= 2 / 6 = 0.33$
GOALS SCORED	GOALS CONCEDED	GOALS SCORED	GOALS CONCEDED	GOALDIF6
6	6	8	7	$((6 - 6) - (8 - 7))$ $= -1 / 6 = -0.17$
POINTS		POINTS		POINTDIF6
6		9		$(6 - 9)$ $= -3 / 6 = -0.5$

Team A, during their previous 6 matches, made 34 shots. 17 were on target and 6 were converted into goals. During those same matches they received 30 shots, 16 of them on target, and conceded 6 goals. In total they got 6 points. They scored and conceded the same number of goals.

Team B, meanwhile, in their previous 6 games got in total 9 points and scored 1 more goal than they conceded. Variables based on goal difference and point difference would say that team B is better than team A. However, the shooting statistics tell a different story. Despite having obtained better results in recent games, team B tends to receive more shots than they make while team A shoots more than they are shot. What variables are right?

By having calculated the variables on points, goals, and shots for the same sample of matches, we can compare their different predictive power. In a similar way as in the previous chapter, we build regression models with each variable. We start with the variable based on points. When using PointDif6 we obtain:

ESTIMATED MODEL		
VARIABLE	COEFFICIENT	P-VALUE
POINTDIF6	0.42	<0.01%

The indicators of goodness of fit for this model are the following:

GOODNESS OF FIT POINTDIF6	
CONCORDANCE	56.9%
ROC	59.6%

We now try with the goal-based variable (GoalDif6). As we already knew, this variable is more predictive than the one based on points:

ESTIMATED MODEL		
VARIABLE	COEFFICIENT	P-VALUE
GOALDIF6	0.36	<0.01%

The indicators of goodness of fit of this model are the following:

GOODNESS OF FIT GOALDIF6	
CONCORDANCE	58.8%
ROC	60.9%

The goals variable is associated with a lower coefficient in its regression than the points variable. This is solely due to the fact that the values taken by each variable move in different ranges (in a maximum of 6 games one team can get up to 18 more points than another, but the difference between the goals scored and conceded by one team and another can move in wider ranges). We know that the goals variable is more predictive than the points variable due to the higher concordance and ROC values obtained by the model.

Graphically this univariate model, based on goal difference, can be represented by a histogram.

The vertical bell-shaped bars represent the number of matches in the sample for which the variable DifGoal6 takes each of the values indicated on the horizontal axis. It should be read using the left axis. For instance:

- In 4,481 matches in the sample, the two teams facing each other had obtained the same goal difference in their respective 6 previous matches.
- In 966 matches in the sample, the home team had a goal average per game 2 goals worse than that of the visiting team.

The continuous line ascending from left to right represents the percentage of games that the home team won for each value of DifGoal6. When this variable takes the value 0, the home team wins 44.1% of the time. When this variable takes the value -2.0, the home team wins 28.4% of the time. When this variable takes the value +2.0, the home team wins 66.3% of the time. The coefficient of the variable DifGoal6 that we have obtained when building the model (0.36) represents in a synthetic way the slope of the continuous line.

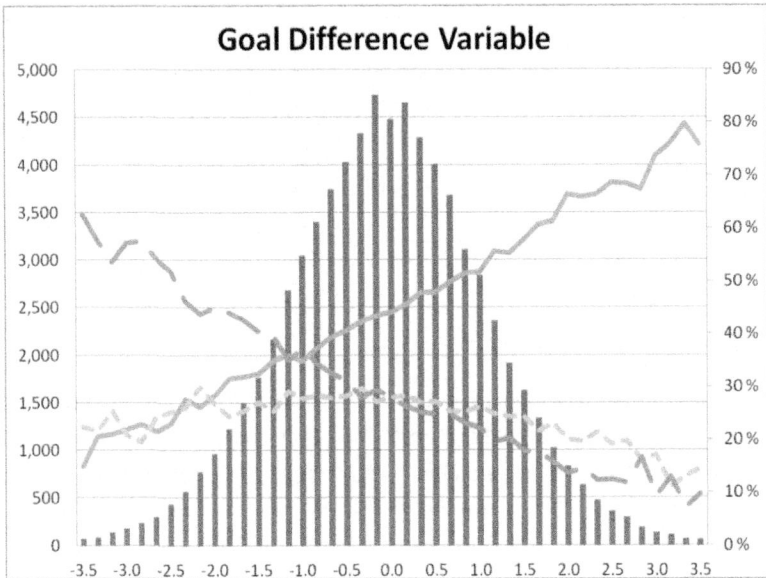

Goal Difference Variable

In the same way, the dashed lines represent the probability of away victory and draw. The almost flat shape of the shorter dashed line that represents the probability of a tie is striking. Indeed, the probability of a tie is only weakly related to the level of the two teams. It ranges from a maximum of 30%, if the two teams have a similar level, and a minimum of 10% if one of the teams is significantly better than the other.

The symmetric shape of the DifGoal6 variable is due to how it has been constructed. It is the difference between goals scored and goals conceded. We can be sure that in any given league and / or match the total number of goals scored is always equal to the number of goals conceded! This explains why the mean of this variable is 0. If there are teams that score more goals than they concede, there must be teams that concede more goals than they score.

Now let's try with the shot variables. This is the model that is obtained with the difference in shots made and received by the two teams (ShotDif6):

ESTIMATED MODEL		
VARIABLE	COEFFICIENT	P-VALUE
SHOTDIF6	0.083	<0.01%

The goodness of fit indicators of the model are the following:

GOODNESS OF FIT SHOTDIF6	
CONCORDANCE	61.2%
ROC	61.6%

The difference between the number of shots a team takes and receives gives more information about its future performance than the difference between the number of goals it scores and concedes.

This conclusion may seem counterintuitive at first glance, but it is correct. We all have seen football matches in which a team has attacked numerous times, has shot more than a dozen times, and yet has failed to score. Suddenly the opponent has made a counterattack and has managed to score having shot only once. Which team wins the match? Obviously, the team that has managed to score. But which team would we expect to win if these two teams played each other again in the future? The one that shot twelve times.

During short periods of time, the team that shoots the most may be unlucky and score few or no goals, but, in the medium run, it is very likely that those shots will end up paying off.

The reverse is also true. A team that has shot only once can win a match. You can even win a game without shooting if the other team scores an own goal! But **being lucky one day doesn't increase your chances of winning your next match**.

Be aware, a team that does not shoot much is not necessarily a bad team. A team that does not shoot much can be good if it can make its opponents shoot even less. **The best team is not the one that shoots the most, but the one that maximizes the difference between shots taken and shots received.**

The shots variable that we have used so far considers all shots. What happens if we use the variable that only considers the number of shots on target? This is the model that you get:

MODEL ESTIMATED SHOTONTARGETDIF6		
VARIABLE	COEFFICIENT	P-VALUE
SHOTONTARGETDIF6	0.16	<0.01%

GOODNESS OF FIT SHOTONTARGETDIF6	
CONCORDANCE	60.7%
ROC	61.6%

The goodness of fit indicators of the model that only considers shots on target are not higher than those of the model that considers all shots.

This, however, is due to the fact that in the model we are only taking into account the 6 previous matches played by each team. When we build the variable with information from a higher number of matches, the shots on target variable becomes more predictive than the variable of total shots. For example, when the models are built with the previous 12 games, the indicators are the following:

GOODNESS OF FIT SHOTDIF12	
CONCORDANCE	62.7%
ROC	62.9%

GOODNESS OF FIT SHOTONTARGETDIF12	
CONCORDANCE	62.9%
ROC	63.2%

Both models have improved by using the previous 12 games instead of the previous 6. The model that exclusively considers shots on target has improved to a greater extent. Intuitively this makes sense: since shots on target are less frequent than shots in general, it takes a greater number of matches to be able to correctly assess a team using this information.

We can further improve the predictive capacity of the model by using variables for points, goals, and shots at the same time. For example, if we simultaneously use the 4 variables calculated with the previous 12 matches, we obtain:

ESTIMATED MODEL		
VARIABLE	**COEFFICIENT**	**P-VALUE**
POINTDIF12	0.071	0.11%
GOALDIF12	0.274	<0.01%
SHOTDIF12	0.062	<0.01%
SHOTONTARGETDIF12	0.024	0.18%

GOODNESS OF FIT JOINT MODEL	
CONCORDANCE	64.3%
ROC	64.5%

The goodness of fit of the model has increased by using several explanatory variables at the same time. The rise is not spectacular, because, although each variable focuses on one aspect of the game, they are obviously correlated. We can analyse in more detail to what extent these variables are related by building a correlation matrix.

	VICLOCAL	**SHOT DIF6**	**SHOT ON TARGET DIF6**	**GOAL DIF6**	**POINT DIF6**
VICLOCAL	1	0.21	0.21	0.20	0.17
SHOTDIF6	0.21	1	0.82	0.49	0.40
SHOTONTARGETDIF6	0.21	0.82	1	0.64	0.55
GOALDIF6	0.20	0.49	0.64	1	0.87
POINTDIF6	0.17	0.40	0.55	0.87	1

	VICLOCAL	**SHOT DIF12**	**SHOT ON TARGET DIF12**	**GOAL DIF12**	**POINT DIF12**
VICLOCAL	1	0.23	0.23	0.23	0.20
SHOTDIF12	0.23	1	0.87	0.60	0.50
SHOTONTARGETDIF12	0.23	0.87	1	0.72	0.61
GOALDIF12	0.23	0.60	0.72	1	0.87
POINTDIF12	0.20	0.50	0.61	0.87	1

The first column and the first row show the correlation between each variable and the result of the next game. The other rows and columns show the correlation between each pair of explanatory variables.

The linear correlation coefficients that we have calculated can take values between -1 and +1. In this case they all take positive values, since, obviously, in general terms, the more a team shoots, the more shots it will make on target, the more goals it will score and the more points it will get. The fact that the correlation coefficients are lower than 1 means that the relationship between the variables is not perfect. The information from one of them enriches what the others tell us.

As you might expect, the number of shots and the number of shots on target are closely related. Goal difference is also closely related to point difference.

The most interesting fact is that the correlations are higher in the second table than in the first one. As we mentioned, during short periods of time a team can score while shooting infrequently or get many points while scoring few goals, but, in the medium term, these situations are not sustainable. Based on all the available data, on average, it takes 8.7 shots to score a goal. Of all the shots that the teams take, 42.1% go on target. Therefore, 3.7 shots on target are needed to score 1 goal[28].

Once we have reached this point, it is natural to wonder how the shooting information can be used to try to make money by betting.

There are two possible strategies. The first one is to use the most predictive model that we have built in order to compare the probabilities that it provides with the odds offered for a given match. Unfortunately, the models built in this chapter do not exceed the predictive capacity of the bookies, so using them would not be profitable.

The second strategy is to **bet in favour of teams that have been "unlucky" recently, that is to say, in favour of teams that have played well (according to the number of shots), but that have got few points in their latest games.**

---

[28] Annex 2 contains detailed information on the evolution of the number of shots, goals, fouls, corners, yellow cards and red cards over time for various European leagues.

Let's see it graphically:

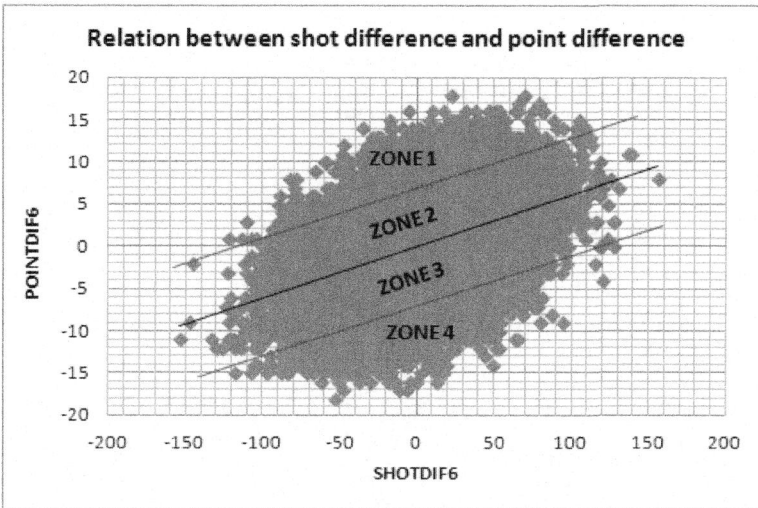

Relation between shot difference and point difference

Each dot represents the difference in shots and points obtained in the previous 6 games by the two teams that are going to play a match. The line with a positive slope in the middle of the scatter plot represents the relationship between these two variables. The line is ascending since the team that has got the larger shot difference is likely to have got more points in the previous games. Using Excel, this relationship between shots and goals can be easily calculated. In the analysed sample, the teams got 0.065 points more than their rivals for each additional shot they made or for each fewer shot they received compared to their rivals. 0.065 is precisely the slope of the line.

In the games located in the lower area of the graph (zone 4) we should bet in favour of the local team. In these cases, this team has obtained in its recent matches fewer points than it would have "deserved" according to its level of play. It has had relatively worse luck than the visiting team.

In the games located in the upper area of the graph (zone 1) we should bet in favour of the visiting team. In these cases, this team has obtained in recent matches fewer points than it would have "deserved" according to its level of play. It has had relatively worse luck than the local team.

In games located near the middle line (zone 2 and zone 3) we should simply not bet. In these cases, both teams have got a reasonable number of points, considering their level of play, so, in principle, there should be no bias in the odds.

Using this strategy, we would have obtained the following results betting in favour of the local team:

ZONE	MATCHES	OVERROUND	EXPECTED LOCAL VICTORIES	LOCAL VICTORIES	RATIO	RETURN
1	18,710	3.4%	9,648	9,533	98.8%	-4.9%
2	18,756	3.5%	8,642	8,707	100.7%	-3.1%
3	18,935	3.4%	7,995	8,104	101.4%	-2.3%
4	18,763	3.4%	6,930	7,296	105.3%	2.0%

If we had bet in favour of the visiting team, these would have been the results by zone:

ZONE	MATCHES	OVERROUND	EXPECTED VISTOR VICTORIES	VISITOR VICTORIES	RATIO	RETURN
1	18,710	3.4%	4,273	4,489	105.0%	-0.4%
2	18,756	3.5%	5,079	5,157	101.5%	-3.2%
3	18,935	3.4%	5,773	5,731	99.3%	-5.5%
4	18,763	3.4%	6,704	6,541	97.6%	-5.9%

As it can be seen, zone 1 is the best one to bet in favour of the visiting team and zone 4 is the best one to bet in favour of the home team. Zone 4 lets you make a small profit when betting in favour of the local team. In order to make a profit by betting in favour of the visitor, it would be necessary to subdivide zone 1 and bet only in its upper half.

This strategy is interesting because **the odds and behaviour of most bettors are based excessively on the results obtained by the teams and tend to give less importance than they should to their level of play in the previous games**.

This creates an opportunity that can be exploited by the bettor who decides to risk his money in favour of teams that have recently obtained relatively poor results but are playing relatively well.

If you want to use this tactic, take the difference of shots of both teams in the previous 6 games and multiply it by 0.065. If during those 6 matches a team has got 4 or more additional "unwarranted" points than its rival then bet against it, especially if it has to play away.

EXPECTED GOALS

In recent years the world of football has begun to talk about a metric called expected goals. This metric is an evolution of the traditional variables on goals and shots.

This metric tries to measure the quality of the shots by assigning to each of them a probability of ending up in a goal based on the distance from where it was executed, its angle, the part of the body with which it was taken, etc. The objective is to have a more reliable indicator of the level of play of each footballer and each team, regardless of the role that "luck" may have played in the outcome of each scoring opportunity.

This variable exists in both offensive and defensive versions. This way it is possible to know how many goals each team "should have" scored and conceded.

The expected goals are calculated by analysing historical databases, seeing what percentage of shots with the same characteristics ended up as a goal. Its value, therefore, depends on the data provider and on the modelling techniques used. A company can assign a probability of 10% to a given shot and another company a probability of 20% to the very same shot. Even a company can refine and review its expected goal calculations over time.

It is, without a doubt, a metric with great educational value. As a footballer it is clearly interesting to know what kind of shots are the most effective or the most dangerous. But, one may wonder, to what extent is it a good predictor? Are expected goals better than the variables we have considered so far?

To answer these questions, we have collected the expected goals data from the Understat.com website on the big five European leagues from the 2014-15 season onwards[29].

---

[29] Other data providers that calculate expected goals are Opta, Wyscout, and Instat.

When we put this new variable against the traditional variable of goal difference, we observe the following:

- **If you have a large set of matches** to evaluate teams, such as a full season, **the expected goals variable is not more powerful than the traditional goal difference variable**. For example, if you want to forecast how each team in a league will do next season, you can look at any of the two variables from the previous season. Both are equally predictive[30].

- **If there is a small sample of matches** to evaluate the teams, **then the expected goals variable is more powerful**. For example, if the seventh matchday of a league is going to be played and we want to assign probabilities based on what each team has done in the previous six games, then we will achieve better results using this new metric[31].

Therefore, something similar to what we observed when comparing the shooting variables with the goal variables occurs. When just a few games have been played by each team, the expected goals predict better, but, after a substantial number of games, they do not beat the actual goal difference.

Some analysts have drawn attention to the fact that, for example, Messi consistently manages to score more goals than he "should" based on his expected goals statistic[32]. This simply means that the probability of scoring goals not only depends on the distance, angle, or part of the body with which you shoot, but also depends on other intrinsic characteristics of the player that are not captured by this variable.

Can the expected goals information be used for betting? Let's imagine a possible strategy that consists of comparing the actual number of goals each team has scored and conceded in their previous 6 games with the expected goals in those same 6 games. If two teams are going to face each other and the

---

[30] When predicting the results of the next season, both variables achieved an R^2 of 59%. The R^2 is the statistic used to measure the fit of linear regressions. It takes values between 0% and 100%. 0% means that the model does not explain any of the variability of the dependent variable and 100% means that it explains all of it.

[31] When it comes to predicting the outcome of the next match based on the 6 previous games of each team, the goal difference variable reaches a ROC of 65% whereas expected goals reach 67%.

[32] See, for example, the following article: https://www.footballcritic.com/features/lionel-messi-is-he-as-good-as-ever-or-are-his-numbers-fallingc/831

actual number of goals in their previous games is lower than the expected amount, we bet over[33].

	BET OVER YIELD	BET UNDER YIELD	MATCHES
ACTUAL GOALS <EXPECTED GOALS	1.7%	-4.3%	1,654
ACUTAL GOALS> EXPECTED GOALS	-3.5%	1.4%	1,305

Betting over when the expected goals say there should have been more goals provides a slightly positive return if you have access to the highest odds available on the market. Similarly, betting under when the expected goals say there should have been fewer goals provides a positive return.

It is also more interesting to bet in favour of the teams that should have a better goal balance than the other way around. It is better to bet in favour of the team that, according to the expected goals, has had relatively "worse luck" than to bet in favour of the team that has had relatively "good luck".

	BET YIELD	MATCHES
ACTUAL GOAL DIFFERENCE< EXPECTED GOALS DIFFERENCE	-0.5%	2,961
ACTUAL GOAL DIFFERNCE > EXPECTED GOALS DIFFERENCE	-3.0%	

In conclusion, expected goals are a metric that provides value both, when assessing the level of the teams and when betting, since it allows the level of play to be measured more reliably with a reduced number of matches. However, when it comes to evaluating the level of the teams in the long term, their predictive capacity does not exceed that of the real goals.

---

[33] Betting over consists of betting that during the match, at least a certain number of goals, usually 3 or more, will be scored between the two teams. Betting under consists of betting that during the match a certain number of goals will not be exceeded, usually 2 or less.

THE SWEET TASTE OF REVENGE

So far, we have tried to predict the outcome of soccer matches by analysing the performance of both teams in their respective previous matches. What about the head-to-head games between both teams in the past? Should we treat them as any other matches when predicting what will happen in the next game? Or do they have a special relevance that we must consider to make good forecasts?

In most leagues around the world every team faces all others twice during the season. The first face-off usually takes place in the first half of the league and a second showdown usually takes place in the second half of the championship.

The following table shows the probability that a second leg match ends in a home win, a draw, or an away win according to the final result between those same teams in the first leg:

FIRST LEG RESULT	MATCHES	SECOND LEG RESULT		
		HOME WIN	DRAW	AWAY WIN
VISITOR WON BY 6 OR MORE GOALS	447	26.2%	27.3%	46.5%
VISITOR WON BY 5 GOALS	1,129	32.7%	26.1%	41.2%
VISITOR WON BY 4 GOALS	3,308	36.9%	26.4%	36.8%
VISITOR WON BY 3 GOALS	8,517	39.3%	27.1%	33.5%
VISITOR WON BY 2 GOALS	18,146	42.4%	27.2%	30.3%
VISITOR WON BY 1 GOAL	31,072	45.2%	26.7%	27.9%
DRAW	36,338	48.3%	26.7%	25.0%
LOCAL WON BY 1 GOAL	20,490	51.5%	25.5%	23.0%
LOCAL WON BY 2 GOALS	9,558	54.2%	23.9%	21.9%
LOCAL WON BY 3 GOALS	3,556	58.4%	22.0%	19.6%
LOCAL WON BY 4 GOALS	1,272	60.8%	21.1%	18.2%
LOCAL WON BY 5 GOALS	307	71.7%	17.3%	11.1%
LOCAL WON BY 6 OR MORE GOALS	106	78.3%	13.2%	9.4%

If the away team won the first-round match by 6 or more goals, the probability that it will win the second-round match is 46.5%. If the home team won the first-round match by 6 or more goals, the probability that it will win the second-round match is 78.3%.

The away team in the second round played at home in the first-round match. That is why it is more common that the team that plays as a visitor in the second round won the previous direct confrontation.

Looking at this table, it is clear that there is a correlation between what happened in the previous match between the two teams and what will happen in the next one.

Let's think about two teams like Barcelona and Espanyol. The former is a much more powerful team than the latter. If we look at their head-to-head record, we will see an overwhelming percentage of victories in favour of Barcelona. If we build a model only with the information from their direct confrontations, it will tell us that Barcelona is the favourite to win the next derby.

However, the truly relevant question is, will this model have a greater predictive capacity than the models we have built so far? Or more precisely, can we use the information from the head-to-head record to enrich the information we have used so far?

If we run a regression using the result of the previous game between both teams as the explanatory variable, we obtain the following goodness of fit statistics:

ESTIMATED MODEL		
VARIABLE	COEFFICIENT	P-VALUE
GOALDIFPRE	0.1361	<0.01%

GOODNESS OF FIT	
CONCORDANCE	55.6%
ROC	56.1%

Clearly the goodness of fit of a model built solely with the previous face-off is very low and noticeably inferior to the models built so far. **What happened in a single match between two teams is not enough to accurately predict what will happen in their next match.**

If, instead of taking only the last direct confrontation, we take the last four head-to-head games, we obtain the following results:

ESTIMATED MODEL		
VARIABLE	COEFFICIENT	P-VALUE
GOALDIFPRE4	0.0882	<0.01%

GOODNESS OF FIT	
CONCORDANCE	58.5%
ROC	58.2%

Using a variable that considers the difference between the goals scored and conceded by each team in their four previous head-to-head games improves the indicators. However, they remain below those that we obtained with the models built in previous chapters. Expanding the time window further would not improve things much, as we would be forced to use information from games that took place a long time ago.

Therefore, **we completely rule out the possibility of building a model based solely on the head-to-head record between the two teams**.

There is still the option of developing a model that uses, simultaneously, both information from direct confrontations and information from the previous matches of each team against other squads. To try this option, we run a single regression using the following two explanatory variables:

- **GoalDif38**: difference between the goals scored and conceded by each team in their previous 38 matchdays.
- **GoalDifPre**: difference between the goals scored and conceded by each team in the match between them in the first leg.

These are the results obtained:

ESTIMATED MODEL		
VARIABLE	**COEFFICIENT**	**P-VALUE**
GOALDIF38	0.7560	<0.01%
GOALDIFPRE	-0.0102	2.4%

GOODNESS OF FIT	
CONCORDANCE	64.3%
ROC	64.6%

The goodness of fit indicators go up considerably. However, that is not the most relevant insight. The most relevant insight is that, **when the variable that measures the level of each team according to its previous 38 games is included in the model, then the variable of the previous face-off is no longer** significant[34]. All the predictive power of the model comes from the variable based on the 38 previous games. That means that **if we can correctly measure the level of each team, then the direct face-off does not provide any additional valuable information that allows us to make better predictions**.

This idea can be counterintuitive to many readers. In fact, it can even be disappointing.

Does this mean that I can ignore the previous results between both teams when I bet? Surprisingly, the answer is that **they should not be ignored. Although previous head-to-head matches may not have any special predictive power, many bettors believe they do. This generates a small bias in the odds that can be exploited by those who decide to bet in favour of the team that lost in the previous face-off**.

To measure this bias, we have simply calculated the profit or loss that would have been made by betting in favour of the home team in the second-round game. It is based on the result of the match between the same teams in the first round:

FIRST ROUND OUTCOME	MATCHES	SECOND LEG RETURN
LOCAL TEAM VICTORY	26,386	-3.7%
DRAW	25,279	-3.2%
VISITING TEAM VICTORY	42,909	-2.0%

Whoever had bet in favour of the home team when it won the previous head-to-head match would have lost an average of 3.7% of the wagered amount. Whoever had bet in favour of the home team when it lost the previous head-to-head game would have lost, on average, 2.0%.

A little warning before ending this chapter. All the analyses in this chapter have been done with information from leagues. That is, with information from relatively long tournaments in which all matches have similar importance when determining the final standings. The previous head-to-head game is likely to be

---

[34] As we mentioned in previous chapters, a p-value below 5% is normally required to consider that the variable is significant within a regression. Therefore, the 2.4% p-value that the GoalDifPre variable receives indicates that it is significant, but very weakly. So much so that if we remove it from the model, the concordance and the ROC drop only 0,1% to 64.2% and 64.5% respectively.

more relevant in play-off tournaments in which the result of the first match is used to determine what goal difference will allow one or the other team to qualify for the next round.

For example, Barcelona's comeback against Paris Saint Germain on March 8th, 2017 comes to mind when, after losing 4-0 in Paris two weeks earlier, they managed to win 6-1 in order to proceed to the next round. It was, without a doubt, a sweet revenge for the culés. In these cases, we could be looking at a clear increase in motivation because a team is on the verge of elimination. Therefore, the same effect that we saw in the case of teams that are about to be relegated occurs. However, I do not have enough historical information to analyse in detail this possible effect in knockout competitions.

THE PRICE OF A GREAT VICTORY

Imagine for a minute that you are a footballer. You play for an average team. Not the best, not the worst. The weekend is coming, a new matchday. But this time is special. It's not an ordinary game. This time it's your turn against one of the greatest teams. You are going to play against Real Madrid at Bernabéu.

In the training sessions you give your best. You want to be in the starting eleven at all costs. You know that there will be 80,000 fans in the stands and that millions of people from the five continents will watch the match. The goals and the best plays will be covered in all the news programs, viewed countless times on YouTube and discussed at length on the radio talk shows. If your team wins, your market value as a player could skyrocket. If you score a goal, it will be etched in the fans' memory.

And this time the dream comes true. After an epic match, your team is victorious. You and your companions have given everything and Goliath has bent the knee. Now it's time to celebrate and savour the victory. Who knows if you will win against a rival like Real again?

This situation is unusual but not unprecedented. In the last 20 years, Real Madrid and Barcelona have lost, in total, more than 50 league games at Bernabéu or at Camp Nou in games other than El Clásico. Away from home they have lost more than 140 times.

After a high of that magnitude, what can we expect from the motivation and performance of that mid-table team in its next match? Let's see what the numbers say:

BET NEXT MATCH AFTER BEATING REAL MADRID OR BARÇELONA	YIELD
DEFEAT	13%
WIN OR DRAW	-10%

Systematically betting that the team that just beat Real Madrid or Barça is going to lose its next game would have given us a 13% return. Big victories seem to come with a price and that is that they cause a performance slump in the next game. And, most interestingly, this phenomenon does not seem to be reflected in the odds.

Certainly, the sample we have is small, barely 200 games, so we are going to try to expand it. In order to do that we will see what profitability we would have obtained if we had systematically bet on the defeat of a team when it had just won a match against a significantly superior rival in any of the leagues in our database[35].

In this case the results would have been the following:

BET NEXT MATCH AFTER BEATING VERY SUPERIOR RIVAL IN ANY LEAGUE	YIELD
DEFEAT	3.2%
WIN OR DRAW	-9.9%

In the enlarged sample, the profitability obtained by systematically betting on defeat in the next match is lower. Still, it is clear that the alternative (expecting a good result after a great victory) is a much worse option.

---

[35] We consider that a team has just achieved a great home win if the odds were 5 or higher and that it has just achieved a great away win if the odds were 8 or higher. This allows us to have a sample of 1,000 games (500 after a great home win and 500 after a great away win).

KEEPING AN EYE ON YOUR RIVAL

There has been some discussion in recent years about whether it is better for Real Madrid or for F.C. Barcelona to play before or after their major rivals on each matchday. Let's see what the numbers say.

Since 2002, Real Madrid have played first 298 times. Barcelona have played first on 313 occasions. The rest of the matchdays they have played at the same time (against one another or not) or one of them did not play (because it had to attend the Club World Cup).

The team that played first, whether it was Madrid or Barça, won 73% of its matches. The team that played second won 67%. Part of the difference in these winning percentages may be due to the fact that the team that played later had Champions League or Cup during the week.

The really interesting thing is to analyse if the results of the team that plays before affect the results of the team that plays after. Is it better to play with the peace of mind of knowing that your greatest rivals failed to win or with the pressure of knowing that they won?

The data show that when the first team to play won its match, the second to play won 69% of its matches. When the first team to play tied, the second won 63% of its matches. Finally, when the first team to play lost, the second won only 59% of its matches.

In summary, although there may be several causes, it does seem that there is a certain relaxation effect - both at Real Madrid and at Barça - when they play knowing that their greatest rival has had a bad day.

Playing first would apparently provide two advantages: you are more likely to win, and, if you lose, your rival may relax and lose too.

It is possible that this correlation between the results of the two teams is due to a third factor. For example, if the league title has already been decided or if they have both played during the week, their motivation may drop. Consequently both teams may lose on the same matchday. In any case, it should be noted that only in half of the matchdays covered by this analysis the two teams won (308 out of a total of 611).

In penalty shootouts, whichever teams shoots first also has an advantage. This phenomenon has been studied in great detail by Professor Ignacio Palacios-Huerta who, using information from 1,001 penalty shootouts, observed that the first team to shoot from 11 meters won 60.6% of the time[36].

---

[36] Palacios-Huerta, Ignacio (2014), *Beautiful Game Theory,* Princeton University Press.

WHAT DID YOU EXPECT?

A team's most recent results may have been better or worse than those of its rivals simply because the different difficulty level of the matches it played. For example, if someone told us that a team had lost its last 3 games by 3 goals each, we would think that that team is pretty bad. However, if they later told us that that team had to face Real Madrid, Barcelona, and Atlético de Madrid on those 3 matchdays, we would think that perhaps it is not so bad, but that it had simply to face the most complicated rivals of the whole championship.

The fact that the level of the opponents varies is a factor that makes it difficult to build a good predictive model for any sport, including football.

The lower the number of matches used to construct an explanatory variable, the greater the risk that these oscillations in the difficulty of the rivals will add noise, both to the construction of the model and to its subsequent use.

A possible solution, therefore, is to use variables that consider a relatively high number of games. For example, to predict results of 20-team European football leagues, we could consider variables constructed with the previous 19 matchdays. This way we would be measuring the level of each team based on the results it has obtained when facing each of the remaining 19 teams that make up the competition.

This solution, however, is not perfect, because:

- We would be considering an odd number of matchdays (19). Therefore, we would be measuring the level of some teams with more home games than for others.
- Although we would be using a confrontation with each of the rivals in the competition, the level of these rivals is not stable over time. Using the 19 matchday variable, both team A and team B will have faced Real Madrid, Barcelona, and Atlético de Madrid, but perhaps team A faced them when they were in top form, and team B when they were experiencing a slump in their level of play.
- By constructing a single variable with such a long window, we are giving equal importance to very recent information (last 2 or 3 matchdays) and relatively older information (17, 18 or 19 matchdays ago).

In my experience these 3 drawbacks are relatively minor. The variables constructed with a number of games equal to the number of teams in the league (minus one) are usually quite predictive and robust[37].

There is another technique that allow us to contextualize the results of each team with respect to the difficulty of its matches. This technique consists of **using the odds of the previous games as an indicator of the difficulty that the matches had**.

Let's look at some simple examples:

- The odds offered for Team A's victory in each one of their last 6 games were 6. Out of those 6 matches, team A won 2. In other words, the market expected that out of the 6 matches, team A would win only 1, and yet it won 2.
- The odds offered for Team B's victory in each one of their last 6 games were 2. Out of those 6 matches, team B won 2. That is, the market expected team B to win 3 of the 6 matches, yet it only won 2.

In these examples both teams have won 2 of their last 6 matches. However, there is a very relevant difference. Team A has obtained more victories than expected, while team B has obtained fewer than expected. A bettor who had waged the same amount of money in favour of team A in each of its last 6 games would be winning money. A bettor who would have done the same with team B would be losing money.

Simply dividing the number of victories obtained by the number of expected victories we can construct a variable that tells us whether a team has recently done better than expected. In our example, Team A got twice as many victories as expected whereas Team B got only 66% of the expected number of victories.

Let's imagine that these two teams are going to face each other tomorrow. What should a bettor do with this information? Should he bet in favour of the team that is doing better than expected or in favour of the team that is doing worse than expected?

---

[37] As we saw in the chapter on the importance of the past.

To answer this question, we have calculated these variables for our entire historical sample and divided the games into four groups:

- Matches in which the home team and the visiting team face each other after having both been obtaining worse results than expected.
- Matches between a home team that has been performing worse than expected and a visiting team that has been performing better than expected.
- Matches between a home team that has been performing better than expected and a visiting team that has been performing worse than expected.
- Matches in which the home team and the visiting team face each other after having both been obtaining better results than expected.

These are the results obtained:

LOCAL TEAM PERFORMANCE	VISITING TEAM PERFORMANCE	MATCHES	YIELD HOME VICTORY BET	YIELD AWAY VICTORY BET
WORSE THAN EXPECTED	WORSE THAN EXPECTED	46,371	-2.6%	-6.3%
WORSE THAN EXPECTED	BETTER THAN EXPECTED	44,927	-1.8%	-9.0%
BETTER THAN EXPECTED	WORSE THAN EXPECTED	45,933	-4.9%	-5.3%
BETTER THAN EXPECTED	BETTER THAN EXPECTED	45,594	-4.0%	-8.9%

The best option is to bet in favour of the home team when it has been performing worse than expected and is facing a visiting team that has been performing better than expected.

If you want to bet in favour of the visiting team, it is better to do so also when it has been obtaining worse results than expected and is facing a local team that has been obtaining better results than expected.

The message is clear. **It is a bad strategy to bet in favour of the fashionable team. It is smarter to bet on teams that are on a losing streak**.

This conclusion is consistent with what we have seen in previous chapters. Bettors tend to place excessive importance on recent team results. This causes the odds to overreact. This bias can be exploited by those who assess the level of a team with a greater number of games. Obtaining worse or better results than expected in a set of 6 games does not mean that a team is getting worse or improving. These apparent drops or spikes in performance can be due to multiple factors (such as good or bad luck) and may not be significant going forward.

Another interesting insight from this table is that, obviously, **there are no teams that systematically make money to those who bet on them nor teams that systematically make lose money to those who bet on them**. Over a short period of time a team may perform better than expected, but it is not possible to beat expectations all the time. After each victory or defeat, expectations adapt.

For this reason, in general, it is worse to bet in favour of a team right after it has won than after it has lost. The following table contains the returns obtained by betting systematically in favour of the local team after having won, drawn or lost its previous match.

PREVIOUS RESULT	LOCAL BET YIELD
VICTORY	-3.6%
DRAW	-3.4%
DEFEAT	-2.3%

After a victory the odds paid for the next victory of a team may be reduced by the bookies or by the behaviour of the bettors themselves. Also, in some cases, the performance of the team may drop due to the distention of having won or even because of a hangover after a long night of celebration. This is something that some regressions point to. In some cases, it is observed that the result of the immediately preceding match has less predictive power than the second last game.

As we have seen in this chapter, taking into account if a team is beating expectations or not is a relevant factor in the profitability of bets. In section 3 of this book, we will study how to combine several biases discussed in these chapters to try to bet with the highest possible yield.

GOALSCORING AND GOALLESS GAMES

Do you like betting on the total number of goals that will be scored in a match? Would you rather bet that 3 or more goals will be scored (known as an over 2.5 bet) or that 2 or fewer goals will be scored (known as an under 2.5 bet)?

What do you think most bettors prefer to do?

Most of them prefer to bet over because it is a wager that:

- It can be won before the game is over.
- It is never totally lost until the referee blows the final whistle.

On the contrary, bets on under:

- Can be lost before the game is over.
- Are never won until the referee blows the final whistle.

These factors make it psychologically harder to bet under than over, and therefore most bettors prefer to bet over than under. This affects the odds offered by the bookies.

In addition, as spectators, we all tend to remember the most spectacular games, the big wins, the crazy comebacks..., and we tend to forget about the boring matches, with few goals, the dull 0-0 draws, etc.

This is why most non-professional gamblers overestimate the number of things that happen in a match. Being aware of this bias can help us bet better.

What would have happened if we had bet on over 2.5 goals or under 2.5 goals systematically?

In the long term, the same profitability is not obtained by betting over than under. For the reasons we have discussed, it is easier to find value in under bets than in over bets. Using all the available historical information (more than 95,000 matches) it is observed that a yield of -2.3% would have been obtained by systematically betting over and a yield of -1.4% by systematically betting under at the best available odds.

And what should we look at in order to select in which matches to bet over or under?

Most people look at the number of goals each team has scored and conceded in their previous games. **Normally this is not a winning strategy because the number of goals in the previous games is already considered in the odds**. Looking only at the historical number of goals, it will be very difficult to find value in the odds.

To bet over we must look for matches between teams that in their previous games scored and conceded few goals but in which there were many shots.

The few goals in the previous matches will make many people bet under when in fact the teams are generating and receiving many scoring chances.

To bet under we must look for matches between teams that in their previous games, with a low number of shots on target, have scored and conceded a lot of goals.

In this case, the high number of goals in the previous matches will make many people bet over when in fact these teams are generating and receiving few scoring chances.

As we know, in general, 1 goal is scored for every 3 shots on target. This is what would have happened to us with the following strategies:

- Strategy 1: bet over / under when both teams that are about to play scored and conceded less than 1 goal for every 6 shots on target in their previous matches.
- Strategy 2: bet over / under when both teams that are about to play scored and conceded at least 1 goal every 2 shots on target in their previous matches.

Using all available historical information, we observe that strategy 1 would have generated the following returns:

STRATEGY 1 YIELD	
OVER	-1.1%
UNDER	-2.3%

While strategy 2 would have provided the following results:

STRATEGY 2 YIELD	
OVER	-6.1%
UNDER	+2.8%

If you like to bet over, look for teams that generate and concede many chances but have recently scored and received few goals[38].

If you like to bet under, look for teams that generate and concede few chances but have recently scored and received a lot of goals. In general, you will find it easier to find value in the under odds.

Another factor that affects the number of goals is the moment of the season in which we find ourselves. In the final stretch of the season a higher number of goals are usually produced.

For example, from 2000 to 2018 in the major European leagues the following number of goals per game were scored:

	GOALS PER MATCH	GOALS PER MATCH LAST MATCHDAY
PREMIER LEAGUE	2.7	3.1
LA LIGA	2.7	3.1
SERIE A	2.7	3.4
BUNDESLIGA	2.9	3.6
LIGUE 1	2.4	2.9

In all of them, on the final matchday, approximately 0.5 more goals per game were scored than during the rest of the season. This phenomenon seems to be related to the fact that on the final matchday it is common that several teams have nothing at play. Therefore, they can take their games practically as if they were friendly matches. It does not seem to be related to other factors such as temperatures. At the beginning of the season the teams have travelled less and are more rested. This makes the matches more even and fewer goals are produced than in the final matchdays.

---

[38] These teams can be identified using information on shots on target or on expected goals as we saw in the chapter dedicated to this metric.

THE MYSTERY OF THE DRAW

Let's do a little mental exercise. Imagine a tennis match between two players of the same level. What would you expect to happen if those two tennis players faced each other a hundred times? Clearly each one of them could be expected to win roughly 50% of the matches.

Now let's go back to the world of football. What would you expect to happen if two teams of the same level faced each other a hundred times on neutral ground? What percentage of games would each team be expected to win? In this case we can no longer say that we expect each team to win 50% of the matches. The existence of the draw makes answering this question much more difficult. Initially the only thing we could say is that both teams will win the same percentage of matches, but we don't know if that percentage will be 30%, 35%, 40%, 45% ...

If we assume that both teams are equally good, on what depends the percentage of games that will end in a draw? The answer is that **it depends on the number of goals that we expect will be scored**.

Taking it to the extreme, let's think of a match in which we are confident that the number of goals that will be scored will be extremely low. If we think that there will be no goals, we are basically thinking that the final score will be 0-0, that is, a draw.

On the contrary, if we think that many goals will be scored in the match, the probability of a tie decreases, even if we continue to consider that both teams are of the same level.

To illustrate this point we have divided all available matches into over matches and under matches. Over matches are those in which more than 2.5 goals are expected to be scored and under matches are those in which less than 2.5 goals are expected to be scored. If the odds that the bookmakers offered for the over were lower than the odds offered for the under, the match is considered over. If the odds that the bookmakers offered for the under were lower than the odds offered for the over, the match is considered under.

As it can be seen, **29% of the *under* matches end in a draw while only 23% of the *over* matches end in a draw**.

MATCH TYPE	MATCHES	LOCAL VICTORY	DRAW	AWAY VICTORY	GOALS PER GAME
OVER	37,668	49%	23%	28%	2,91
UNDER	57,577	42%	29%	29%	2,43

Of course, for a match to end in a draw it is necessary, but not sufficient, that an even total number of goals is scored. 50% of matches in which 2 goals are scored end up in a draw (1-1, obviously), but only 36% of matches in which 4 goals are scored end in a draw (2-2, obviously).

TOTAL GOALS	MATCHES	LOCAL VICTORY	DRAW	AWAY VICTORY
0	7,692	0%	100%	0%
1	17,686	58%	0%	42%
2	23,925	32%	50%	19%
3	20,622	60%	0%	40%
4	13,795	41%	36%	24%
5	7,247	62%	0%	38%
6	3,261	46%	29%	25%
7	1,217	63%	0%	37%
8	415	50%	23%	27%

So, can we take advantage of the information on goal expectation to refine our predictions and improve our bets? The answer is yes.

The logistic regression models that we saw in the first chapters of this book captured the difference between the level of the teams very well but did not include variables on the **total number** of goals expected for the match.

In my experience, on the football games with an unusually high or unusually low goal expectation there are the greatest differences of opinion between bookies. The best bookies take the goal expectation correctly into account when estimating the probabilities of a home win, draw and away win while the worst bookies fail to do so.

The following table shows the profitability that would have been obtained by a bettor who had systematically bet on the home win, draw and away win in the over and in the under matches.

MATCH TYPE	MATCHES	LOCAL VICTORY YIELD	DRAW YIELD	AWAY VICTORY YIELD
OVER	37,668	-0.6%	-8.6%	-4.0%
UNDER	57,577	-3.2%	-2.5%	-4.8%

The yields speak for themselves. If you like to bet on a draw, always do it in under games. Some bookmakers do not correctly consider the goal expectation when setting their odds for 1X2.

Finally, let's imagine two matches. In the first one the highest over odds in the market are 1.67. In the second, the highest over odds are 1.43. With these data we know that more goals are expected in the second match than in the first one, but how many more?

The following table shows the relationship between the over odds and the number of goals that, on average, are scored in the matches:

OVER 2.5 ODDS	PROBABILITY OVER	GOALS PER GAME
5.00	20%	1.39
3.33	30%	1.82
2.50	40%	2.25
2.00	50%	2.67
1.67	60%	3.10
1.43	70%	3.53
1.33	80%	3.74

In matches in which the market tells us that the probability of over is 60%, an average of 3.10 goals are scored. When the market tells us that the probability of an over is 70%, an average of 3.53 goals are scored[39].

You can use this table to know how many goals to expect in a match from its odds or to know approximately from what minimum odds it could be interesting to bet depending on the number of goals you estimate will occur in the match. The latter only when, of course, you are sure that your prediction is more reliable than that of the bookie.

---

[39] For simplicity we are assuming here that the implied margin at the best odds is 0% so that the probability is just the inverse of the odds. Section 2 of this book explains how to calculate the probability from the odds if the margin is not zero.

COMPOSITION AND AGE OF THE SQUAD

Is it better to face a championship with a short squad in which most footballers can play minutes and be highly involved, or to face it with a long squad that allows the coach to make more variations and better cover injuries? Is it better to have a team made up of ambitious youngsters or one of crafty, battle-hardened veterans?

To answer these and other questions, we have compiled information on the composition of all the 2,042 squads that played in the 5 major European leagues from the 1999-2000 season to the 2019-2020 season.

The following information is available for each team and season:

- Total number of players, number of players included in any squad list and number of players fielded during the season.
- Number of foreigners in the squad.
- Average age of the entire squad, of the starting eleven and of the footballers fielded according to the minutes each one spent on the pitch.
- Market value of each team according to the Transfermark website from the 2009-2010 season onwards.

To analyse whether there is a relationship between total squad size and performance, we have created the following four groups, each one containing approximately 25% of the squads:

- Teams with 29 players or fewer in their squads.
- Teams with between 30 and 32 players in their squads.
- Teams with between 33 and 36 players in their squads.
- Teams with 37 players or more.

The high number of players may be surprising to many readers. This is because this figure considers all the players who were part of each club at any point during the season. This means, for example, that players who are traded in the winter market are part of two different clubs in the same season. The kids of the subsidiary / youth team that have been part of a squad list during the season are also included in the group.

The data shows that **there is little correlation between the size of the squad and the performance of the club in that season**. Teams with small squads got, on average, slightly more points per game than teams with large squads:

SQUAD SIZE	NUMBER OF SQUADS	POINTS PER MATCH
29 PLAYERS OR LESS	459	1.40
FROM 30 TO 32 PLAYERS	480	1.39
FROM 33 TO 36 PLAYERS	527	1.36
37 PLAYERS OR MORE	576	1.34

If we focus solely on the number of players fielded, we get much more interesting results:

PLAYERS FIELDED	NUMBER OF SQUADS	POINTS PER MATCH
25 PLAYERS OR LESS	607	1.56
FROM 26 TO 27 PLAYERS	493	1.38
FROM 28 TO 29 PLAYERS	461	1.31
30 PLAYERS OR MORE	481	1.18

Here the correlation is stronger. Teams that lined up a total of 25 players or fewer during a season got, on average, 0.4 more points per game than those that fielded 30 or more players.

Does this mean that having a small squad is better than having large one? Not necessarily. Several factors may be involved here. Teams that lined up more players may have been forced to do so because they suffered more injuries. Or it may be that they were teams that had a bad start to the season and resorted to a change of coach and several signings to try to turn the situation around.

Of course, it may also be that the teams with shorter squads are better at managing their financial resources: that **they sign selectively instead of signing excessively, and that by accumulating minutes these players improve their performance and are more motivated**.

Let us now look at the relationship between the percentage of foreigners and the performance of each club. If we divide the teams into four groups, we observe the following:

FOREIGN FOOTBALLERS	NUMBER OF SQUADS	POINTS PER MATCH
LESS THAN 35% (<)	452	1.25
FROM 35% (> =) UP TO 50% (<)	653	1.37
FROM 50% (> =) UP TO 60% (<)	521	1.41
MORE THAN 60% (> =)	416	1.46

For the purposes of this analysis, EU players who are part of a club outside their country of origin (for example, a Portuguese footballer on any Spanish team) are considered as foreigners. Also, Scottish, Welsh or Northern Irishmen playing for a team based in England are considered as foreigners. Taking this into account, it can be observed that **the squads with less than 35% of foreigners get on average 0.2 points per game less than the squads in which more than 60% of the players are foreigners**.

Looking at these results, it is not surprising that the percentage of foreigners in the five major European leagues has gradually increased from 39% in the 1999-2000 season to 52% in the 2019-2020 season[40].

Now let's look at the relationship between squad age and performance. As the average age of a team's footballers increases, the number of points per game that they get gradually falls.

AVERAGE SQUAD AGE	NUMBER OF SQUADS	POINTS PER MATCH
22 YEARS OR LESS	42	1.47
23 YEARS	260	1.44
24 YEARS	599	1.41
25 YEARS	600	1.36
26 YEARS	393	1.30
27 YEARS OR OLDER	148	1.27

On average, squads with a mean age of 22 got 0.2 more points per game than squads with an average age of 27 or older.

The most common average age of the squads in the five major leagues was 24 and 25 years, representing 59% of the total.

---

[40] Sometimes football clubs hire foreigners not only based on purely sporting criteria, but also seeking to increase their popularity in certain countries and thereby increase their income from the sale of t-shirts, merchandising, etc.

Of course, the total average age of a squad may differ from the average age of the players who are actually fielded and play the games. If we focus solely on the average age of the players that are lined up, we get the following figures:

AVERAGE AGE FIELDED PLAYERS	NUMBER OF SQUADS	POINTS PER MATCH
25 YEARS OR LESS	389	1.37
26 YEARS	589	1.37
27 YEARS	599	1.38
28 YEARS	351	1.36
29 YEARS OR OLDER	114	1.33

Here we observe that the players who actually jump onto the pitch are, on average, between 26 and 27 years old, that is, 2 years older than the average age of the squad to which they belong. In this case, the relationship between age and results is more complex. The teams that obtained the best results were those that fielded players that were, on average 27 years old. The teams that obtained the worst results were those who resorted to players with, on average, 29 years of age or more.

In summary, **the highest performing teams have been those that have brought together a young squad and have given the leading role to middle-aged players**.

In fact, teams have gradually lowered the average age of their squads from 24.9 years at the beginning of the century to 24.0 years just before the outbreak of the Covid-19 pandemic. Also, the average age of the fielded players has decreased slightly from 26.6 years to 26.4 in the same period.

Would you like your future son to become a professional footballer? The chances are always very low, but if you want to increase them, try to make sure that he is born in January, February, or March. Try to avoid that his birthday is in October, November, or December. The selection process in the lower categories of the clubs is strongly biased in favour of the older children born every year. This means that among professional footballers those born in the first trimester abound[41].

---

[41] To be fair probably this bias is not only due to the clubs themselves but to the kids and their parents as well. If, as a parent, I see that my kid wins every weekend I will spend more time and resources to help him become a professional. He will also be less likely to give up.

For example, if we analyse in which part of the year the 642 La Liga players of the 2019-20 season were born, we observe the following:

TRIMESTER OF BIRTH	NUMBER OF PLAYERS	PERCENTAGE OF PLAYERS
FIRST TRIMESTER	213	33.2%
SECOND TRIMESTER	169	26.3%
THIRD TRIMESTER	143	22.3%
FOURTH TRIMESTER	117	18.2%

This phenomenon occurs in other leagues such as the Premier League. For example, 33% of the footballers who played the 2019-20 Premier League were also born in the first quarter of the year. And it is not because there are more births in winter. On the contrary, both in Spain and in the United Kingdom, summer is the season in which there are more births.

Let's now imagine that your child is already kicking a ball and you want to advise him on which position to play. If the objective is to play as many minutes as possible, the following table could be useful:

POSITION	PERCENTAGE OF FOOTBALL PLAYERS	PERCENTAGE OF MINUTES PLAYED	DIFFERENCE
GOALKEEPER	11.4%	9.1%	-2.3%
DEFENDER	33.3%	37.7%	4.3%
MIDFIELDER	25.7%	26.0%	0.3%
FORWARD	29.6%	27.3%	-2.3%

11.4% of the members of La Liga squads in the 2019-20 season were goalkeepers. However, they only accounted for 9.1% of the minutes played[42]. This is not surprising, as each team fields only one goalkeeper.

The defenders (centre-backs, right-backs, and left-backs) are the most benefited from the distribution of minutes: they make up 33.3% of the squads, but they play 37.7% of the minutes. The midfielders (defensive midfielders, central midfielders, right midfielders, left midfielders and attacking midfielders)

---

[42] Considering that 380 games are played in a full season, that there are 22 players on the pitch (unless someone is sent off) and that the matches last 90 minutes (plus additional time), in total coaches must distribute 752,400 minutes in a season (380 * 22 * 90) among players. In the 2019-20 season of La Liga, the footballers totalled exactly 753,061 minutes on the pitch, of which 68,392 (9.1%) corresponded to the goalkeepers.

play the percentage of minutes that "corresponds" to them according to their presence in the squads. The forwards (centre forwards, right wingers, and left wingers) are the least used.

In the Premier League the same pattern occurs. The forwards are "underused" and the defenders "overused". On average, each defender plays approximately 1,350 minutes per season compared to 1,100 minutes for each striker. It's a 23% difference!

Now let's imagine that we are the owners of a club and we want to optimize our squad. We are, for example, doubting between signing the team's fourth central defender or the third centre forward. We can only choose one of them. Which one should we hire? Is the fourth centre back normally used more than the third centre forward or the other way around? The following table shows the percentage of minutes that each member of La Liga teams played in the 2019-20 season:

USE	POSITION	N.	MINUTES	USE	POSITION	N.	MINUTES
1	GOALKEEPER	1	85%	13	CENTRE-BACK	3	37%
2	CENTRE-BACK	1	81%	14	CENTRAL MIDFIE.	3	33%
3	CENTRAL MIDFIE.	1	74%	15	RIGHT-BACK	2	33%
4	CENTRE FORWARD	1	71%	16	ATTACKING MIDFIE.	1	30%
5	RIGHT-BACK	1	68%	17	LEFT-BACK	2	25%
6	CENTRE-BACK	2	67%	18	CENTRE FORWARD	3	24%
7	LEFT-BACK	1	67%	19	CENTRE-BACK	4	18%
8	RIGHT WINGER	1	57%	20	LEFT WINGER	2	17%
9	DEFENSIVE MIDFIE.	1	56%	21	RIGHT WINGER	2	16%
10	CENTRAL MIDFIE.	2	52%	22	DEFENSIVE MIDFIE.	2	16%
11	CENTRE FORWARD	2	51%	23	GOALKEEPER	2	14%
12	LEFT WINGER	1	46%	24	ATTACKING MIDFIE.	2	10%

The most used player was the starting goalkeeper. The starting goalkeeper played 85% of the minutes of the championship. The conclusion is clear: we would better have an excellent starting goalkeeper. The substitute goalkeeper, however, played only 14% of the minutes. The third goalkeepers, who do not appear in the table, played less than 1% of the minutes.

The second most used player by the coaches was the first centre-back. The best centre-back of each team plays more minutes on average (81%) than the best midfielder (74%) and the best forward (71%).

Answering the previous question, we see that the third centre forward usually plays approximately 24% of the minutes while the fourth centre-back only 18%. Considering the minutes that they spend on the field, it would be more interesting to hire a third centre forward than a fourth centre-back.

Therefore, taking into account the minutes played, a balanced squad of 24 players should be made up of:

POSITION	NUMBER
GOALKEEPERS	2
LEFT-BACKS	2
CENTRE-BACKS	4
RIGHT-BACKS	2
DEFENSIVE MIDFIELDERS	2
CENTRAL MIDFIELDERS	3
ATTACKING MIDFIELDERS	2
LEFT WINGERS	2
CENTRE FORWARDS	3
RIGHT WINGERS	2

The level of use of the footballers also depends greatly on their age. As the player matures, the number of minutes played per season increases, reaching its peak at the age of 27. From there onwards it begins to gradually descend:

	PERCENTAGE OF PLAYERS	PERCENTAGE OF MINUTES PLAYED	MINUTES PER PLAYER IN THE SEASON
19 YEARS OR LESS	11.4%	2.7%	274
FROM 20 TO 22 YEARS	25.5%	15.6%	715
FROM 23 TO 26 YEARS	23.5%	28.7%	1,429
27 YEARS	7.6%	11.2%	1,720
28 YEARS	5.9%	8.3%	1,646
FROM 29 TO 31 YEARS	17.1%	22.1%	1,516
FROM 32 TO 33 YEARS	6.5%	8.1%	1,444
34 YEARS OR OLDER	2.3%	3.4%	1,717
TOTAL	100%	100%	1,173

The high number of minutes (1,717) played by footballers aged 34 and over may be surprising. Although in the 2019-20 season, players aged 34 and over only accounted for 2.3% of the squads, they accounted for 3.4% of the minutes. This is due to the fact that in this age group there is an abundance of starting goalkeepers, who tend to be older than the rest of their teammates.

Finally let's talk about value variables. Transfermark provides two:

- Total value of the squad.
- Average value of the players in the squad.

The first one is the sum of the individual values of each player on the team. The second one is the total value of the squad divided by the total number of players in the club that season.

Out of the five leagues considered, it is in the Premier League and in the Spanish La Liga where both variables take the highest values. The Italian and German leagues take the intermediate values, and it is the French one the competition with the lowest values.

In general, from the 2009-2010 season, the first one with market values available on Transfermark, until 2019-2020, prices in football have increased. At club level, we can observe different trajectories depending on how each team performed during this time[43].

Within the same league there is a great diversity of valuations. The value of the biggest clubs within the same competition may be up to 25 times higher than that of the most modest teams. Here there are significant differences between countries, with the English and Italian leagues being the most equal in this regard. Over time the difference in valuations between large and modest teams has also gradually increased.

Which of these variables is more predictive: the total value of the squad or the average value of the players that make it up? To answer this question, given that the valuations are affected by the "inflation" that the world of football has experienced in recent years and differ between the leagues, we have transformed them into relative values so that they are comparable with each other.

---

[43] For example, the value of Atlético de Madrid has increased fivefold since 2009 while that of AC Milan has remained stable. The rise in valuations appears to have stopped in the wake of the COVID-19 pandemic.

The interpretation of the relative value is as follows:

- 50% indicates clubs with a value that, in the season in question, is half of its league average. That is, modest clubs.
- 100% indicates clubs whose value is exactly the average in their league. That is, intermediate clubs.
- 200% indicates clubs whose value is twice the average of their league. In other words, top-level clubs.

The results obtained for the variable of the total value of the squad are the following:

TOTAL SQUAD VALUE	OBSERVATIONS	POINTS PER MATCH
BETWEEN 12% AND 38%	212	1.05
BETWEEN 38% AND 50%	212	1.12
BETWEEN 50% AND 66%	213	1.19
BETWEEN 66% AND 97%	212	1.30
BETWEEN 97% AND 167%	213	1.57
BETWEEN 167% AND 577%	212	2.00

The results obtained for the average value of the player of each club are the following:

AVERAGE VALUE OF PLAYERS	OBSERVATIONS	POINTS PER MATCH
BETWEEN 13% AND 38%	212	1.04
BETWEEN 38% AND 51%	212	1.12
BETWEEN 51% AND 66%	213	1.18
BETWEEN 66% AND 95%	212	1.32
BETWEEN 96% AND 162%	213	1.56
BETWEEN 164% AND 566%	212	2.01

As it can be seen, both variables are very powerful. There is a strong correlation between the valuations and the points each team gets per game.

Both variables are very similar, but **the average value of the players is slightly more predictive than the total value of the squad** as shown by the greater difference in points obtained by the most modest clubs and the richest clubs when we classify them according to this criterion[44].

The bottom line is that **teams should not try to maximize the total value of their squads, but rather maximize the average value of their players.** In other words, having 25 players worth a total of 300 million (average value 12 million) gives better results than having 30 players worth a total of 300 million (average value 10 million). Again, we see that **relatively small squads give better results than relatively large ones**.

Of course, when using the valuation information, we must not only seek to increase the average value of our players, but above all, look for players that we consider are being undervalued by the market or that would cover a relevant need of our team.

It is clear that the higher the valuation, the better the results. However, this relationship is not linear, but decreasing. No matter how much a club spends, it is impossible for it to obtain more than 3 points per game. Let's imagine a team with players valued 5 million euros each and playing in a league in which that is exactly the average value of footballers (100%). That team could expect to obtain 1.43 points per game. If that club hired players valued 10 million, it could expect to get 1.86 points per game. That is, an additional 0.43 points per game. Now, if instead of doubling the value of its players it tripled it to 15 million each, it could expect to get 2.14 points per game, only an additional 0.28 points per game. Of course, this extra expense could be necessary depending on the objective of the club and the economic level of the rest of the teams participating in the competition[45].

---

[44] In more technical terms, the R^2 of the average value variable is 63% while the R^2 of the total value variable is 61%. The R^2 of both variables is even higher if it is calculated only with the most recent seasons, which may be an indication that Transfermark's valuations are increasing in quality. If both variables are included in the same regression as explanatory variables for the points obtained, the total value variable stops being significant.

[45] Sometimes the objective is to win a European title and not the national league. For example, Bayern Munich could probably transfer valuable players and probably continue to easily win the Bundesliga. Their squad is designed to be competitive in the Champions League. This creates a situation in which resources are "wasted" in the national championship.

The following table shows the points per game that a team can expect to get based on the average value of its players:

VALUE COMPARED TO THE LEAGUE AVERAGE	POINTS PER MATCH	VALUE COMPARED TO THE LEAGUE AVERAGE	POINTS PER MATCH
10%	0.90	250%	2.02
25%	1.00	300%	2.14
50%	1.15	350%	2.24
75%	1.30	400%	2.32
100%	1.43	450%	2.37
150%	1.66	500%	2.41
200%	1.86	550%	2.42

In the next chapter we will compare the predictive capacity of the composition of the squad with other variables related to the level of play. This will help us identify on what aspects clubs should focus in order to maximize their results in the medium term.

HOW DO THE BEST TEAMS PLAY?

The debate about the style of play in football is a passionate one. The discussions about the importance of possession, the number of passes, playing short, playing long, counterattacks, set pieces ... are endless.

Much of this debate is about beauty: what style is more pleasant, more entertaining, more attractive, in the eyes of the spectator. We are not going talk about beauty in this book. What we can try to study is **how the teams that obtain the best results play**, what ways of playing are the most effective when it comes to scoring and not conceding goals. We will also analyse if the playing style has evolved over the last 10 years.

To answer these questions, we have the following information on the five major European leagues from the 2009-2010 season onwards:

- Information about shots and goals:
  - o Area of the field from which the shots are taken (goal area, the penalty area, outside the area ...).
  - o Situation in which it is possible to score (open play, set pieces, penalty, counterattack ...).
  - o Part of the body used (right leg, left leg, head...).
- Information about passes and assists:
  - o Number of passes made and pass success rates.
  - o Type of passes (short, long).
  - o Passes that generate scoring chances.
- Information on the percentage of possession and playing area for each team.
- Information on offsides, tackles, turnovers, and aerial duels.

Let's start with the shots and the goals. The following table shows from which area of the field the teams shoot:

SHOTS BY AREA OF THE FIELD		
GOAL AREA	REST OF THE BOX	OUTSIDE THE AREA
6.0%	51.5%	42.4%

Only 6% of the shots are taken from the goal area. Most of the shots are taken from the rest of the box (i.e., without stepping onto the goal area).

Let's see now from where the goals are scored:

GOALS PER AREA OF THE FIELD		
GOAL AREA	REST OF THE BOX	OUTSIDE THE AREA
19.2%	66.6%	14.2%

Although 42% of all shots are produced from outside the area, only 14% of the goals are scored from that position. This is because the effectiveness of the shots varies enormously depending on the distance.

PERCENTAGE OF SHOTS THAT CONVERTED INTO GOAL		
GOAL AREA	REST OF THE BOX	OUTSIDE THE AREA
32.9%	13.4%	3.5%

1 in 3 shots from the goal area end in a goal. 1 in 7 shots from the rest of the box end in a goal. Finally, **a measly 3.5% of shots from outside the area are converted.** It's only 1 in 29!

The teams seem to be aware of this, as **the percentage of shots from outside the box has been gradually decreasing during the last decade**[46].

EVOLUTION OF THE PERCENTAGE OF SHOTS FROM OUTSIDE THE BOX	
SEASON	PERCENTAGE
2009-10	45.4%
2010-11	44.5%
2011-12	44.3%
2012-13	44.4%
2013-14	44.2%
2014-15	43.1%
2015-16	41.4%
2016-17	40.3%
2017-18	40.4%
2018-19	39.3%
2019-20	38.4%

The best teams have become especially reluctant to shoot from outside the box. As the following table illustrates, the best teams in the major European

---

[46] It is striking how, in parallel, in the world of basketball the percentage of 3-point shots has been increasing as teams have realized that they are more profitable.

leagues, in this case those that averaged more than 1.75 points per game, shot significantly less from outside the box than the worst teams.

SEASON 2019-2020	
POINTS PER MATCH	**PERCENTAGE OF SHOTS FROM OUTSIDE THE BOX**
LESS THAN 1.04	40.1%
BETWEEN 1.05 AND 1.33	40.0%
BETWEEN 1.34 AND 1.74	38.6%
OVER 1.75	35.0%

The guideline seems clear: **do not shoot from outside the box if it is possible to continue the play to try to shoot from within**. Of course, stepping on the rival penalty area is much easier for the good teams than for the bad teams.

Let's see now how the shots and goals are produced depending on the situation of the game:

PERCENTAGE OF SHOTS PER GAME SITUATION			
OPEN GAME	**COUNTERATTACK**	**SET PIECE**	**PENALTY**
72.4%	4.0%	22.4%	1.2%

Teams take 72% of their shots during "normal" plays. That is, in situations that are neither a counterattack nor a set piece (for example, a corner kick or free kick) nor a penalty shot.

The goals come as follows:

PERCENTAGE OF GOALS PER GAME SITUATION			
OPEN GAME	**COUNTERATTACK**	**SET PIECE**	**PENALTY**
62.9%	7.3%	18.2%	8.5%

It is worth taking your time looking at this table. In my opinion, it illustrates part of the beauty of football. Most goals come from standard plays, but more than a third are scored in other situations. Knowing how to run counterattacks, practicing set pieces, and having a good penalty taker are aspects that no team should neglect. For the same reason, it is essential to avoid counterattacks, to know how to properly defend set pieces and avoid committing penalties.

The 2019-2020 season was the one with the highest percentage of penalty goals in the major European leagues. 9.8% of the goals were scored from the spot. Only time will tell to what extent the introduction of the video assistant referee (VAR) will mean a structural increase in the number of penalties.

Almost 77% of penalty shots end in a goal. A very significant 20% of shots in counterattacks end in a goal. In open play situations or in set pieces, less than 10% of the shots end up in the back of the net.

PERCENTAGE OF SHOTS THAT END UP IN A GOAL			
OPEN GAME	COUNTERATTACK	SET PIECE	PENALTY
9.4%	19.7%	8.8%	76.6%

Finally, it should be noted that around 3% of goals are own goals. Given their nature it does not make sense to talk about the effectiveness of shots in this type of situations.

These are average figures that consider all teams (good and bad) in these competitions. If we focus on **the best teams, we see that they tend to score a higher percentage of their goals in open play situations,** while **the worst teams tend to score a higher percentage of their goals in set pieces, in penalty kicks or thanks to the opponent's own goals.**

PERCENTAGE OF GOALS PER SITUATION ACCORDING TO TEAM LEVEL					
POINTS PER MATCH	OPEN PLAY	COUNTER ATTACK	SET PIECE	PENALTY	OWN GOAL
LESS THAN 1.07	58.6%	6.4%	21.6%	9.2%	4.2%
BETWEEN 1.08 AND 1.26	59.8%	7.5%	20.0%	9.0%	3.7%
BETWEEN 1.27 AND 1.60	63.7%	7.7%	17.5%	8.4%	2.7%
OVER 1.61	65.9%	7.3%	16.3%	8.1%	2.3%

There is, however, no clear relationship between the level of the team and the use of counterattacks. Clearly every team uses the weapons at its disposal.

Throughout this book we have commented on several occasions that goal variables are more predictive than point variables when it comes to forecasting the future performance of a team. Given that we now have the breakdown of goals by type, it is worth asking: could we make the goal variable even more powerful by excluding, for example, the goals scored from penalties, or the own goals scored by the opponent?

Although it may seem counterintuitive, the answer is no. Goal variables reach their maximum predictive power when we consider all goals, regardless of how they were scored. Informally we can say that a team has won by luck because the rival scored an own goal or because the referee awarded a penalty, but, generally speaking, both situations are indicative of the level of play: to get penalties awarded or for the rival to score own goals, you have to step on the opponent's box and attack. Similarly, a team that is constantly under attack will be more likely to commit penalties or score own goals.

Another way to break down goals and shots is according to the part of the body with which they are scored or taken.

SHOTS PER PART OF THE BODY		
RIGHT FOOT	**LEFT FOOT**	**HEAD**
52.0%	31.4%	16.4%

52% of shots are taken with the right foot; 31%, with the left foot and 16%, with the head. A tiny 0.2% are taken with other parts of the body. Let's see now how the goals are distributed:

GOALS PER PART OF THE BODY		
RIGHT FOOT	**LEFT FOOT**	**HEAD**
52.9%	28.9%	17.5%

And the percentage of success depending on the part of the body:

PERCENTAGE OF SHOTS THAT ARE CONVERTED		
RIGHT FOOT	**LEFT FOOT**	**HEAD**
10.5%	9.5%	11.0%

As it can be seen, the level of effectiveness is somewhat lower when footballers shoot with the left foot. This is possibly because the left foot is not the natural foot for most of them, leading many to use it only when they have no other option. An astonishing 17.5% of goals are scored with the head. It's 1 in 6! Clearly, a team that wants to be balanced cannot ignore this type of offensive option. The importance of head goals is somewhat greater in modest teams than in top teams.

As it can be expected, in all areas of the field, in all types of play and with all parts of the body, the best clubs show a higher effectiveness in their shots than the modest clubs. Top teams not only generate more scoring opportunities, they also take better advantage of them. They are more lethal. Similarly, the best teams manage to reduce not only the number of occasions they are exposed to, but their effectiveness.

Let us now study the passing variables. Two of the main classifications of passes made by Who Scored and Opta are the following:

- Short / long pass: short passes are less than 25 yards long, that is, less than 22.86 meters. Long passes exceed that distance.
- Precise / imprecise pass: it is used to separate the well-executed passes from those that have not been well executed.

Pass accuracy is simply calculated as the sum of precise passes (whether short or long) divided by the total number of attempted passes.

The table below shows the types of passes used by teams according to their level.

NUMBER OF PASSES PER MATCH				
POINTS PER MATCH	LONG & PRECISE	LONG & IMPRECISE	SHORT & PRECISE	SHORT & IMPRECISE
LESS THAN 1.07	30	34	257	60
BETWEEN 1.08 AND 1.26	31	33	266	62
BETWEEN 1.27 AND 1.60	32	31	300	62
OVER 1.61	34	25	391	62

How are the best and worst teams different? The best teams:

- Make more passes per game.
- Achieve a higher pass accuracy.
- Use short passes proportionally more.

Out of the four columns in the table, the most striking is the third one. **The best teams make on average 50% more precise short passes than the worst teams.**

If we analyse the data season by season, we see that the short pass tends to be used more and more and we observe how the precision in its use has increased:

	PERCENTAGE OF PASSES PER MATCH					
TEMP	LONG & PRECISE	LONG & IMPRECISE	SHORT & PRECISE	SHORT & IMPRECISE	TOTAL SHORT	TOTAL PRECISE
2009	8%	8%	67%	17%	84%	75%
2010	8%	7%	68%	16%	85%	77%
2011	8%	6%	70%	16%	86%	78%
2012	8%	6%	71%	15%	86%	79%
2013	8%	6%	71%	15%	86%	79%
2014	7%	8%	71%	14%	85%	78%
2015	7%	8%	71%	14%	85%	78%
2016	7%	8%	72%	13%	85%	79%
2017	7%	7%	73%	13%	86%	80%
2018	7%	7%	73%	13%	86%	80%
2019	6%	7%	74%	13%	87%	80%

Additionally, passes can be classified into the following categories:

- Key pass: last pass made that allows a teammate to take a shot on the opponent's goal.
- Assist: last pass made that allows a teammate to score in the opponent's goal.

Both key passes and assists are assigned to one of the following groups. These are common concepts in the world of football, but it is worth reviewing them quickly:

- Cross: a pass from a wide position to a central attacking area.
- Corner: a pass from a corner kick.
- Through ball: a pass between the opposition players in their defensive line to find an onrushing teammate (facing the rival's goalpost).
- Free kick: a pass that comes from the service of a free kick.
- Throw-in: a pass that comes from a throw-in.
- Rest: passes that do not fit into any of the previous categories.

Let's see what kind of key passes the weakest and strongest teams resort to:

KEY PASSES PER MATCH ACCORDING TO TEAM LEVEL						
POINTS PER MATCH	CROSS	CORNER	THROUGH BALL	FREE KICK	THROW IN	REST
LESS THAN 1.07	2.33	0.77	0.27	0.47	0.08	5.37
BETWEEN 1.08 AND 1.26	2.40	0.79	0.39	0.49	0.09	5.54
BETWEEN 1.27 AND 1.60	2.51	0.85	0.42	0.48	0.07	6.08
OVER 1.61	2.71	0.97	0.67	0.44	0.06	7.73

Unfortunately, most of the key passes fall into the "rest" category. Nonetheless, some interesting conclusions can be drawn from this table.

The worst teams made a total of only 9.3 key passes per game while the best teams made 12.6, that is, 36% more. In relative terms, **the greater use that top teams make of the through ball to generate scoring opportunities is noteworthy**. They employ this technique almost 150% more than modest teams. Generally speaking, more than 90% of key passes are short passes.

Since we have the information on assists, we can see the level of effectiveness of each type of key passes:

PERCENTAGE OF KEY PASSES ENDING IN GOAL					
CROSS	CORNER	THROUGH BALL	FREE KICK	THROW IN	REST
11.2%	7.5%	25.3%	9.3%	3.5%	8.2%

The shots that are taken thanks to a through ball are the most dangerous. 1 in 4 ends in a goal. Second in danger are the crosses ending 1 out of every 9 shots taken thanks to this action in the back of the net.

Do these numbers mean that teams should try to attempt more through balls? Probably yes, but again you must take these data with caution. Clearly the best teams use more this type of pass when it comes to generating chances. When a shot is taken after this action the probability of scoring is high. However, since we have focused only on situations where a shot was taken, we are not being able to assess other factors such as the success rate per pass type, the percentage of them that end up in a shot or the risk of counterattack that each kind of play may generate.

On Who Scored you can also find positional statistics for each club. Two of the most interesting ones are the action zones and the attack sides.

Regarding the action zones, as it might be expected, the best teams play more in the midfield and the attack zone and less in the defensive zone of the pitch than the worst teams:

DISTRIBUTION BY SECTIONS OF THE PITCH			
POINTS PER MATCH	DEFENSIVE	MIDFIELD	ATTACK
LESS THAN 1.07	28.7%	45.0%	26.3%
BETWEEN 1.08 AND 1.26	28.2%	45.1%	26.7%
BETWEEN 1.27 AND 1.60	27.4%	45.3%	27.2%
OVER 1.61	25.4%	45.6%	28.9%

When attacking, teams can attack from the left, from the right or from the centre:

DISTRIBUTION BY SIDE OF ATTACK			
POINTS PER MATCH	LEFT	CENTER	RIGHT
LESS THAN 1.07	36.4%	26.4%	37.2%
BETWEEN 1.08 AND 1.26	36.1%	26.6%	37.3%
BETWEEN 1.27 AND 1.60	36.1%	26.5%	37.3%
OVER 1.61	35.9%	27.8%	36.3%

A couple of observations can be made about this table. The first is that **the best teams tend to attack proportionally more through the centre than the worst teams**. The second observation is that **clubs of any level have a slight tendency to attack more from the right side than from the left**.

Between 10% and 15% of the general population is left-footed. The percentage of left-footed professional footballers is higher, between 20% and 25%. While right-footed footballers tend to be more comfortable playing on the right wing, left-footed tend to prefer the left wing. This difference between right-footed and left-footed players also influences the direction of shots on goal, since shots to the left (the natural side to which right-footed players shoot) are somewhat higher than shots to the right (the natural side to which left-footed players shoot)[47].

---

[47] https://penaltyfile.com/left-footed-soccer-players-advantage/
https://www.lavanguardia.com/economia/management/20160615/402525074250/tandas-penaltis-futbol-loteria.html
https://as.com/futbol/2012/03/02/mas_futbol/1330673237_850215.html

One of the key debates in the world of football during the last decade has been about possession. Some coaches give enormous importance to this aspect. For others it is still a secondary element. Let's see what the numbers say.

First, clearly the teams that get the most points per game tend to have higher possession percentages than the worst-performing teams:

POINTS PER MATCH	POSSESSION PERCENTAGE
LESS THAN 1.07	46.8%
BETWEEN 1.08 AND 1.26	47.9%
BETWEEN 1.27 AND 1.60	50.0%
OVER 1.61	54.9%

But to really assess the importance of possession we must check if it is more or less powerful than other performance metrics when it comes to predicting the results of a team.

Let's imagine that the season has just ended, and we are asked what team we think is the favourite to win the next league. What variables should we look at?

In this comparison we are going to consider the following variables:

- Points per game.
- Goal difference.
- Shots on goal difference.
- Total shots difference.
- Possession.
- Pass success rate.
- Transfermark valuation.
- Who Scored rating.

To see which is the most powerful variable we have carried out two tests. In the first one we measure the capacity of each variable to predict the number of points that a team will get next season.

This is the result:

VARIABLE	PREDICTIVE CAPACITY [48]
GOAL DIFFERENCE	0.58
TRANSFERMARK VALUATION	0.58
SHOTS ON GOAL DIFFERENCE	0.56
POINTS PER GAME	0.54
TOTAL SHOT DIFFERENCE	0.48
WHO SCORED RATING	0.45
POSSESSION	0.45
PASS SUCCESS RATE	0.35

The most predictive variables are goal difference and the average value of the players (Transfermark valuation), while the least predictive are possession and pass accuracy.

As it can be seen, **although the best teams tend to have the ball more in their control and make fewer mistakes when passing, these are not the variables that best predict future performance**. Other aspects are much more decisive.

As we already knew, goal difference is a more powerful variable than points per game. On the other hand, the shooting variables, when only a reduced number of games are used to evaluate a team, are more powerful than goal difference[49], but when taking information from a complete season they are surpassed. That is, if shots are not converted for a few games, it may be due to bad luck. If shots don't get in throughout a season, the team simply isn't generating quality chances.

We have carried out a second analysis with these variables. When a team outperformed another according to a variable (for example, Who Scored rating) but was outperformed according to another variable (for example, in Transfermark valuation). What happened the following season? Which team came out on top, the one that is better according to Who Scored or the one according to Transfermark?

---

[48] Measured using the R^2 statistic. All R^2 have been calculated using linear regressions except for the valuation variables. For the valuation variables a polynomial regression has been used in order to capture their diminishing returns. The R^2 of these variables is lower than in the previous chapter because in this case we are measuring the power of each variable to predict the results of the next season and not those of the same season.

[49] As we saw in the chapter "Beyond goals".

VARIABLE	TRANSFERMARK FORECASTS BETTER
GOAL DIFFERENCE	50%
SHOTS ON GOAL DIFFERENCE	51%
POINTS PER GAME	53%
TOTAL SHOTS DIFFERENCE	55%
WHO SCORED RATING	53%
POSSESSION	57%
PASS ACCURACY	58%

This table tells us that in 53% of the cases, the team ranked higher by Transfermark performed better. In the rest of the cases (100% - 53%) = 47%, the team ranked higher by Who Scored ended up above. In other words, in the event of "disagreement" between both metrics, Transfermark is the one that is right in most cases. This is consistent with the fact that Transfermark obtained a higher R^2 than Who Scored on the first test.

A difference between 53% and 47% may seem small. This is because we are focusing here only on teams in which there was a discrepancy between both variables, that is, teams that are of a very similar level. In most cases, clubs that receive a higher rating from Transfermark also get a higher rating from Who Scored.

In the case of the possession variable, the difference is greater. In case of discrepancy, Transfermark wins possession 57% of the time.

These are the results for all pairings of the goal difference variable:

VARIABLE	GOAL DIFFERENCE FORECASTS BETTER
TRANSFERMARK VALUATION	50%
SHOTS ON GOAL DIFFERENCE	52%
POINTS PER GAME	59%
TOTAL SHOT DIFFERENCE	56%
WHO SCORED RATING	56%
POSSESSION	56%
PASS ACCURACY	57%

When the goal difference and average value of the players (Transfermark) variables do not agree on which is the best team, neither tends to get it right more than the other. Both are just as powerful. Half of the time (50%) the team with the best goal difference performs better in the future and the other half the team with the best valuation does[50].

Could these variables be used together to make better forecasts? The answer is yes. **When predicting the performance of the teams with a multivariate regression, only the goal difference and the average value of the players variable are significant.** Adding the other 6 candidate variables does not provide additional predictive power.

The model obtained is the following:

POINTS PER GAME EXPECTED NEXT SEASON										
		GOAL DIFFERENCE								
		-0,7	-0,4	-0,2	-0,1	0	0,3	0,7	1,0	1,5
AVERAGE VALUE OF PLAYERS	3,90	1,65	1,74	1,80	1,83	1,85	1,94	2,06	2,15	2,30
	2,37	1,44	1,52	1,58	1,61	1,64	1,73	1,85	1,94	2,08
	1,71	1,38	1,46	1,52	1,55	1,58	1,67	1,79	1,87	2,02
	1,17	1,24	1,33	1,39	1,42	1,44	1,53	1,65	1,74	1,89
	0,83	1,14	1,23	1,29	1,32	1,35	1,44	1,56	1,64	1,79
	0,65	1,07	1,16	1,22	1,25	1,28	1,37	1,48	1,57	1,72
	0,54	1,05	1,14	1,20	1,23	1,25	1,34	1,46	1,55	1,70
	0,44	1,03	1,12	1,18	1,21	1,23	1,32	1,44	1,53	1,68
	0,30	1,01	1,09	1,15	1,18	1,21	1,30	1,42	1,50	1,65

For example, a team with an average value of its players 17% higher than its league average and that got a goal difference per game of +1 this season would be expected to obtain 1.74 points per game next season[51].

This model tries to represent the two main aspects on which a club must focus to obtain good results in the medium term:

- A coach and a squad that strive to achieve the largest possible difference between goals scored and goals conceded.

---

[50] The results of this test for the rest of the pairs of variables are included in Annex 2. Additionally, Annex 2 includes information on offsides, interceptions, clearances, dribbles, and aerial duels, although these variables are poorly correlated with team results.
[51] The model achieves an R^2 of 64%. The average value of players has been included as a discretized variable to correctly capture its diminishing marginal return. This type of model could be used to try to evaluate the performance of a coach against "objective" expectations and considering the average value of the players available to him at the beginning of the season.

- A senior management that seeks to form a squad made up of players with the highest possible average value.

Regarding the first point, it is clear that **variables such as possession or passing accuracy are instrumental**. They are metrics that must be improved only to the extent that they allow the team to generate more or better scoring opportunities or to reduce or worsen the quality of the opponent's scoring chances. This is precisely what the multivariate regression tells us by giving them a weight of 0.

In this context, goal difference is the key variable that tells us whether a team's results are sustainable in the medium term. Shooting variables help in evaluating the level of play in the short term but not in the long term.

The average value of the players is the other key pillar. The evolution of this variable depends on multiple factors. One of these factors is the age of the footballers themselves. The following table shows how the market value of a club's squad evolves from one season to the next based on their average age.

RELATIONSHIP BETWEEN THE AVERAGE AGE OF THE FIELDED PLAYERS AND THEIR SEASON-ON-SEASON VALUE EVOLUTION		
AVERAGE AGE FIELDED PLAYERS	**OBSERVATIONS**	**VALUE EVOLUTION**
24 YEARS OR LESS	66	+34%
25 YEARS	182	+16%
FROM 26 TO 28 YEARS	858	+12%
29 YEARS OR OLDER	66	+5%

The 66 clubs that during a season lined up footballers with an average age of 24 years or less saw their value increase by 34% on average. The 66 teams that fielded players aged 29 and over had an average player value increase of only 5% from one season to the next.

What does this table tell us? As we saw in the previous chapter, the relationship between the current performance of a team and the age of its players is quite weak. However, **the team that fields young players is rewarded in the medium term: its squad tends to increase in value, and this makes it easier for it to achieve better results in the subsequent campaigns**. Interestingly, age is a variable that predicts better the future than the present. A squad with a high current valuation but with a high average age could mean problems down the road.

Another element that helps increase the value of a squad is to concentrate the minutes played on a small number of players. As we saw previously, teams that have behaved this way tend to get more points throughout the season and also usually see their squads go up in value more for the next one.

RELATIONSHIP BETWEEN NUMBER OF PLAYERS ALIGNED AND THE SQUAD SEASON-ON-SEASON VALUE EVOLUTION		
FIELDED PLAYERS	**OBSERVATIONS**	**VALUE EVOLUTION**
25 PLAYERS OR LESS	210	+17%
FROM 26 TO 27 PLAYERS	442	+16%
FROM 28 TO 29 PLAYERS	367	+10%
30 PLAYERS OR MORE	153	+9%

When analysing these tables, it must be taken into account that during this period the average value of the players increased by 14% per year for the teams of the five major European leagues. In other words, a club that did not keep at least that rate of revaluation of its players was weakening compared to its rivals.

FIRST AND SECOND HALVES

Until now we have always looked at the full-time results of the matches. We have focused on the total number of goals scored by each team and on who wins or loses when the referee blows the final whistle. In this chapter we are going to look at what happens within each game.

For this we have information on the goals scored at halftime by both the home team and the visiting team. This information will let us answer several questions that football fans usually ask themselves, such as:

- In which half are most goals scored?
- If there are many goals in the first half, can we expect many goals in the second half?
- How likely is my team to come back if it is losing at halftime?
- If I am a modest team versus a top one, should I try to score only in the final minutes to avoid "waking up the beast" of the opposing team with an early goal?
- Is it true that teams play at their true level in the second half?

We are going to answer these questions through data analysis. In this case we will work with the information of more than 135,000 matches of European leagues played between 1995 and 2018.

Regarding the number of goals in each half, these are the historical averages in our database:

GOALS FIRST HALF	1.15
GOALS SECOND HALF	1.49
TOTAL GOALS	2.64

As it can be seen, 44% of the goals are scored in the first half and 56% in the second half. In the second half, teams make more mistakes due to fatigue, they know that the time to score a winner is running out and there are also usually more minutes of injury time than in the first half.

These data are the averages of all the games in our database. If we breakdown the matches according to the number of goals scored in the first half, we can see what relationship exists between the goals in the first and second half.

GOALS FIRST HALF	PERCENTAGE OF MATCHES	AVERAGE GOALS SECOND PART
0	31%	1.40
1	36%	1.50
2	21%	1.53
3	8%	1.59
4	2%	1.60
5	1%	1.66
>= 6	0.1%	1.71

It is noteworthy that in 31% of all matches the score is 0-0 at halftime. Only in 11% of matches 3 or more goals are scored in the first half. What you will most frequently see is that only 1 goal is scored in the first 45 minutes.

As it can be observed, the higher the number of goals in the first half, the higher the number of goals we can expect in the second half. However, this relationship is quite weak. If we have watched a very entertaining first half with 4 goals, we can expect, on average, only 1.6 goals in the second half. If we have seen a goalless first half, we can expect 1.4 goals in the second half of the match.

To predict how many goals there will be in the second half, it is necessary not only to consider the number of goals that have been scored in the first half, but also other factors. For example, the scoring and defensive capacity of each team, whether the match is being played by teams of a similar level and who is leading at halftime.

In general, the more even the teams are, the fewer goals we should expect in the match, both in the first and in the second half. To illustrate this point, in the following table we have assigned the matches in our database to 8 different groups based on the difference in level between the home team and the away team.

GROUP	OBS	GOALS FIRST HALF	GOALS SECOND HALF	TOAL GOALS
1. VERY SUPERIOR LOCAL	6,258	1.37	1.74	3.11
2. SUPERIOR LOCAL	10,062	1.24	1.60	2.84
3. LOCAL SOMEWHAT SUPERIOR	19,731	1.19	1.51	2.70
4. LOCAL SLIGHTLYSUPERIOR	31,697	1.13	1.45	2.58
5. VISITOR SLIGHTLY SUPERIOR	30,398	1.10	1.43	2.52
6. VISITOR SOMEWHAT SUPERIOR	20,731	1.12	1.44	2.56
7. SUPERIOR VISITOR	10,817	1.16	1.49	2.64
8. VERY SUPERIOR VISITOR	6,927	1.20	1.60	2.80

In the first four groups are the games of local teams superior to the visiting team. In the last four groups are the games of local teams inferior to the visiting team. Groups 1 and 8 contain the matches with the most extreme level differences and Groups 4 and 5 contain the most even matches[52].

In closely matched games the number of goals falls. In particular, **the matches in which a home team faces a slightly superior visiting team see the lowest number of goals**. This is probably due to the fact that in these matches a draw may be considered a good result by both teams. By the home team because it is facing a slightly better team and by the visiting team because it is able to go back home after getting one point.

It can also be observed that **when a large team and a small team face each other, the goal expectation depends on whose pitch they play**. If they play at the big team's pitch, expect more goals than if they play at the modest team's ground. Due to home team advantage, the home games of a weak team are more even than the home games of the strong team. Perhaps the size of the stadium also has something to do with this difference, since the rules that regulate football allow, within certain limits, for the existence of grounds with different dimensions.

---

[52] In group 1, the goal average of the home team is at least 1.5 higher than that of the visiting team, considering the previous 19 games. In group 2 the difference in the goal average is between 1 and 1.5; in group 3 it is between 0.5 and 1; in group 4, between 0 and 0.5. Groups 5 to 8 consider the same goal average values but in favour of the away team. For example, a match between a home team that has scored 30 goals and conceded 15 in the last 19 games and a visiting team that has scored 14 and conceded 32 is in the first group because $((30 - 15) - (14 - 32)) / 19 = 1.74$.

The expectation of goals in the second half also depends on who is winning at halftime. In the following table we have divided the matches not only by the number of goals scored in the first half but also according to which team is leading after the first 45 minutes.

GOALS FIRST HALF	GOALS IN SECOND HALF ACCORDING TO RESULT AT HALFTIME		
	LOCAL TEAM LEADING	TIE	VISITING TEAM LEADING
0		1.40	
1	1.49		1.51
2	1.56	1.47	1.63
3	1.58		1.61
4	1.66	1.49	1.66
5	1.65		1.68

As it can be seen, it is not the same that, for example, a match with two goals in the first half reaches halftime being tied that being led by the home or away team. You can expect fewer goals in the second half if the match is tied at halftime. When one of the teams needs to come back, especially if it is the home team, more goals can be expected in the second half.

At this point it is worth asking to what extent it is important for a team to go into halftime losing or winning. The following table shows the percentage of matches that ended in a home win, draw or away win based on who was winning at halftime.

DIFFERENCE OF GOALS AT HALFTIME	PERCENTAGE OF MATCHES	RESULT AT THE END OF THE MATCH		
		HOME WIN	TIE	AWAY WIN
4 OR MORE	0.4%	99.8%	0.2%	0.0%
+3	1.7%	98.7%	1.2%	0.2%
+2	7.6%	92.7%	5.6%	1.7%
+1	24.6%	73.5%	19.3%	7.2%
0	42.7%	36.8%	38.8%	24.4%
-1	17.8%	13.1%	25.6%	61.3%
-2	4.3%	3.8%	9.9%	86.2%
-3	0.8%	0.4%	2.5%	97.1%
-4 OR LESS	0.1%	0.0%	1.2%	98.9%

In 24.6% of the games the home team reached halftime leading by 1 goal. In 73.5% of these matches the local team ended up winning. On the other hand, in 17.8% of the games it was the visiting team who reached halftime leading by 1 goal. In 61.3% of these matches the visiting team ended up winning when the referee blew the final whistle.

If either of the 2 teams reaches halftime with a 2-goal lead, the match is practically decided. The local teams end up winning 92.7% of the matches in which they lead by 2 goals at halftime. With a 2-goal lead at halftime visiting teams win 86.2% of the time.

The message is very clear: **coming back is tremendously difficult. The team that is leading at halftime has a high probability of winning the match**. Jumping onto the pitch being distracted and conceding an early goal has a heavy price.

Another striking fact in this table is that 42.7% of the games are tied at the end of the first 45 minutes. These draws can obviously be with goals or without goals. In these cases, the match remains much more open. The possibility of breaking the tie in the second half is 61.2% (36.8% + 24.4%). **In total, 59% of the matches end with the same result (1, X, 2) that they had at the end of the first 45 minutes**.

To understand these figures, we must not forget that we are analysing historical information on league matches. That is, in this sample there are no games between teams from different divisions. If the analysis were done with national cup matches, for example, we could expect a lower percentage of draws at halftime, since part of the matches would be between teams with a greater level difference.

Of course, not all teams have the same capacity to come back. The table on the following page shows the probability that each team has of being victorious based on its level before kickoff.

	RESULT AT THE END OF THE MATCH		
GROUP	HOME WIN	TIE	AWAY WIN
1. VERY SUPERIOR LOCAL	74%	16%	10%
2. SUPERIOR LOCAL	64%	22%	14%
3. LOCAL SOMEWHAT SUPERIOR	56%	26%	19%
4. LOCAL SLIGHTLY SUPERIOR	48%	28%	24%
5. VISITOR SLIGHTLY SUPERIOR	42%	29%	29%
6. VISITOR SOMEWHAT SUPERIOR	35%	29%	36%
7. SUPERIOR VISITOR	29%	28%	43%
8. VERY SUPERIOR VISITOR	21%	24%	55%

Now, if we focus only on the matches in which the visiting team is winning at halftime by 1 goal, we obtain the following probabilities:

LOCAL TEAM LOSES BY 1 GOAL AT HALFTIME	RESULT AT THE END OF THE MATCH		
GROUP	HOME WIN	TIE	AWAY WIN
1. VERY SUPERIOR LOCAL	28%	33%	39%
2. SUPERIOR LOCAL	24%	31%	45%
3. LOCAL SOMEWHAT SUPERIOR	19%	30%	51%
4. LOCAL SLIGHTLY SUPERIOR	15%	28%	58%
5. VISITOR SLIGHTLY SUPERIOR	13%	26%	61%
6. VISITOR SOMEWHAT SUPERIOR	10%	24%	66%
7. SUPERIOR VISITOR	7%	20%	73%
8. VERY SUPERIOR VISITOR	5%	17%	78%

As it can be seen, a much superior home team has, a priori, a 74% probability of winning the match. If it is losing by 1 goal at halftime, those odds drop to 28%. In that 28% of the cases, it will be able to come back in the second half and end up winning the match. In 33% of the occasions, it will equalize, and the match will end in a draw.

These are the probabilities when the home team is leading by 1 goal at halftime:

LOCAL TEAM WINS BY 1 GOAL AT HALFTIME	RESULT AT THE END OF THE MATCH		
GROUP	HOME WIN	TIE	AWAY WIN
1. VERY SUPERIOR LOCAL	89%	9%	2%
2. SUPERIOR LOCAL	83%	13%	3%
3. LOCAL SOMEWHAT SUPERIOR	79%	16%	5%
4. LOCAL SLIGHTLYSUPERIOR	75%	19%	6%
5. VISITOR SLIGHTLY SUPERIOR	71%	21%	8%
6. VISITOR SOMEWHAT SUPERIOR	65%	24%	11%
7. SUPERIOR VISITOR	60%	26%	14%
8. VERY SUPERIOR VISITOR	53%	27%	19%

If the home team manages to be leading at halftime, the chances that the visiting team will end up taking the victory are slim, even if it is a much superior squad[53].

Finally, these are the probabilities when the game is tied at halftime:

TIED AT HALFTIME	RESULT AT THE END OF THE MATCH		
GROUP	HOME WIN	TIE	AWAY WIN
1. VERY SUPERIOR LOCAL	61%	28%	11%
2. SUPERIOR LOCAL	53%	34%	14%
3. LOCAL SOMEWHAT SUPERIOR	45%	38%	17%
4. LOCAL SLIGHTLYSUPERIOR	38%	40%	22%
5. VISITOR SLIGHTLY SUPERIOR	35%	41%	25%
6. VISITOR SOMEWHAT SUPERIOR	30%	40%	30%
7. SUPERIOR VISITOR	26%	39%	35%
8. VERY SUPERIOR VISITOR	19%	35%	46%

---

[53] Groups 1 and 8 are made up of matches between teams with a difference in their goal average greater than 1.5. Therefore, the values in the table are representative for matches between teams with a level difference relatively close to that value. Sometimes, within the same league there may be teams with even greater level differences. In these cases, the values in the table would not be representative.

A great team should not worry too much if they go into halftime drawing against a weak team. They still have a 61% chance of winning if they are playing home and a 46% change if they are playing away.

In other words, if you are a humble team that has managed to reach halftime being tied against Real Madrid or Barcelona at the Bernabéu or at the Camp Nou, do not too excited just yet. Those 45 minutes of successful defence have only reduced your chances of being defeated from 74% to 61%.

To what extent does losing at halftime increase the performance of the teams that are forced to come back in the second half? Luckily, we can also measure it.

HOME GOALS - AWAY GOALS IN SECOND HALF	HALFTIME RESULT		
GROUP	LOCAL LEADING BY 1 GOAL	TIE	VISITOR LEADING BY 1 GOAL
1. VERY SUPERIOR LOCAL	0.85	0.89	0.84
2. SUPERIOR LOCAL	0.61	0.64	0.70
3. LOCAL SOMEWHAT SUPERIOR	0.41	0.45	0.50
4. LOCAL SLIGHTLYSUPERIOR	0.24	0.26	0.30
5. VISITOR SLIGHTLY SUPERIOR	0.10	0.15	0.19
6. VISITOR SOMEWHAT SUPERIOR	-0.08	-0.02	0.01
7. SUPERIOR VISITOR	-0.26	-0.17	-0.19
8. VERY SUPERIOR VISITOR	-0.45	-0.46	-0.45

This table shows the difference between the number of goals scored in the second half by the home team and the visiting team depending on the halftime result and the level difference between the teams.

Top teams score more goals than they concede. Modest teams concede more goals than they score. But the interesting thing is the difference between the figures in the three columns for the same row. **Teams that have to come back have an extra motivation in the second half. This is reflected in the higher goal difference they get when they are being led by the other team**.

For example, according to the table above, a superior home team that is leading at halftime scores, on average, 0.61 more goals than its rival in the second half. In contrast, when the superior team is losing at halftime, it manages to score 0.7 more goals than its rival in the second half thanks to the extra motivation[54].

However, **this extra motivation does not fully compensate the setback that is losing at halftime**. A goal is so valuable to the team that scores that you never have to fear waking up your opponent, even if they are a formidable squad. Although the enemy will probably see their motivation go up, in football **it is always worth hitting first**.

The extra motivation of losing instead of winning and, therefore, having to come back in the second half makes it possible to score approximately 1 additional goal every 10 second halves. Even if a team conceded a goal in the first minute of the game and therefore had 90 minutes to come back, it would clearly be at a disadvantage despite the additional motivation.

The fact that coming back is difficult does not mean, of course, that teams should not try. When a team is losing, it must score before time runs out. The leading team finds itself in the opposite situation: the clocks ticks in its favour.

The following table shows the average points obtained by the teams that are winning, drawing, or losing at halftime:

GOAL DIFFERENCE AT HALFTIME	EXPECTED POINTS HOME TEAM	EXPECTED POINTS AWAY TEAM
4 OR MORE	3.00	0.00
+3	2.97	0.02
+2	2.84	0.11
+1	2.40	0.41
0	1.49	1.12
-1	0.65	2.1
-2	0.21	2.69
-3	0.04	2.94
-4 OR LESS	0.01	2.98

In the games in which the home team reached halftime with a 1-goal lead, it ended up obtaining, on average, 2.4 points. When it was losing by 1 goal at halftime, it only got 0.65 points. If the game was tied at halftime, it got

---

[54] This effect of the increased motivation is observed in most cells of the table. However, it cannot be observed in those highlighted in grey.

1.49. The visiting team figures are similar. With a 1 goal advantage at halftime, it gets, on average, 2.1 points. With 1 goal against it only gets 0.41 points and when there is a tie at halftime, it gets 1.12.

Let's imagine that the home team takes the lead in the 30th minute of the first half. Should it go for the second goal or should it focus on defending its advantage? If it scored a second goal before halftime, its point expectation would go up from 2.4 to 2.84. However, if it conceded a goal its point expectation would drop from 2.4 to 1.49.

That is, scoring an additional goal before halftime, would increase its point expectation by 0.44 (2.84-2.4). Conceding a goal would decease it by -0.91 points (1.49-2.4). **Clearly, after taking the lead, it is worth focusing on defending, as conceding a goal would hurt more than what scoring a second goal would provide**.

The situation of the team that is losing by 1 goal in the 30th minute is just the opposite. It is interested in playing attacking football, since it gains more by scoring ((1.12 - 0.41) = **0.71**) than it loses if it concedes a second goal before halftime ((0.11 - 0.41)) = **-0.30**)).

To finalise this chapter, we must answer one of the questions we asked ourselves at the beginning of it: which variables are the best in order to measure the level of a team, those related to the first half or those related to the second half?

When trying to predict, using the information from a full season, what goal difference each team will achieve the following one, **the model does not improve when specific explanatory variables for each half are used**.

However, if instead of predicting the level of a team in the medium term, we are interested in predicting how it will do in its next game, it may make sense to use first half and second half specific variables.

As we have seen in previous chapters, the most recent result of a team affects the motivation with which it will face its next match and the bettors' behaviour. Generally speaking, we know that we will be better off backing a team if we do it consistently after a loss than if we do it after a victory.

Well, not all defeats hurt the same and the information on the result at halftime can help us identify those that caused especially intense suffering to both players and bettors.

Imagine that a team that has lost its last game 1-2. The psychological impact of that defeat is different if it was leading most of the match than if it was never ahead. Defeat will probably be more painful if it slipped through the players' fingers in the final minutes.

Similarly, the joy that a victory provides will be more or less intense depending not only on the scoreboard at the end of the 90 minutes but on how the game unfolded.

To analyse this effect, we have calculated the profitability of backing the local team immediately after two different types of defeats in its previous match:

- Assumed: already at halftime the team was losing.
- Painful: at halftime the team was drawing or winning. The defeat was due to a bad second half.

In these cases, the yields are as follows:

TYPE OF DEFEAT	MATCHES	NEXT LOCAL GAME YIELD
ASSUMED	26,147	-4.0%
PAINFUL	17,843	-2.1%

We can also separate the victories in the previous game into two groups:

- Assumed: already at halftime the team was winning.
- High: at halftime the team was drawing or losing. The victory was obtained thanks to a good second half.

In these cases, the returns are as follows:

TYPE OF VICTORY	MATCHES	NEXT LOCAL GAME YIELD
ASSUMED	18,428	-2.7%
HIGH	14,111	-4.1%

In both cases it is observed that what happens in the second half has more weight in the motivation of the players in the next game. A painful defeat increases the motivation to win the next match more than an assumed defeat. Similarly, a victory that gets the players high may have a price on the next game.

PROBABILITY OF NOT BEING RELEGATED

It is 21ST May, 2018. SD Huesca has just beaten Mirandés on matchday 40 of the Second Division. With this victory, Huesca is certain to finish the season in the second position of the table and, therefore, to be promoted directly to La Liga.

Tomás, a young fan of the team, is celebrating with his friends. They do not lack motives. It is the first time that their city will have a representative in the top tier of Spanish football. Tomás hopes that Huesca's adventure in Primera will not be short-lived. He wonders if, 1 year from now, his friends and he will be celebrating having avoided relegation or if, on the contrary, they will be suffering because of going down.

Let's see what history tells us. What is the probability of a team that is promoted for the first time to La Liga of remaining in the top tier of Spanish football?

63 different teams have taken part in the First Division since its creation in 1929 until the end of the 2019-20 season. 10 of them were part of the first edition of the championship. Another 53 were promoted at some later point.

Obviously, 53 cases are a small sample. In addition, the number of teams that compete each season in Primera and the number of teams that are relegated have changed over time. In any case, Tomás will be reassured to know that, of these 53 teams, only 18 were relegated at the end of their first season in the elite of Spanish football. Therefore, it can be estimated that Huesca has approximately a 66% probability of avoiding relegation in 12 months' time ((53-18)/ 53).

If the promoted team was, instead of a team that has never played in Primera like Huesca, a historic team that at some point in the past had already played in Primera. Would it be more likely that it remained in the top tier after one season?

In this second case, the available sample is much larger. A total of 189 promotions were starred by teams that had previously played in Primera, at least, on one occasion. In this sample, the same team may appear several times. Once for each time it was promoted[55].

In 65 of these 189 cases, the team went down after playing a single season in La Liga. This means that the probability of staying in Primera for the historical teams that return to the elite is (189-65) / 189 = 66%. It is, therefore, surprisingly the same that for the clubs that had never played in the top tier before.

Tomás is ambitious and, not only he wants his beloved Huesca not to go down at the end of the season, but he also hopes it will play many consecutive seasons in La Liga. How likely is it that Huesca will be able to go 3, 4, 5 or more seasons without being relegated?

The following table contains the historical probability of relegation based on the number of consecutive seasons played in Primera:

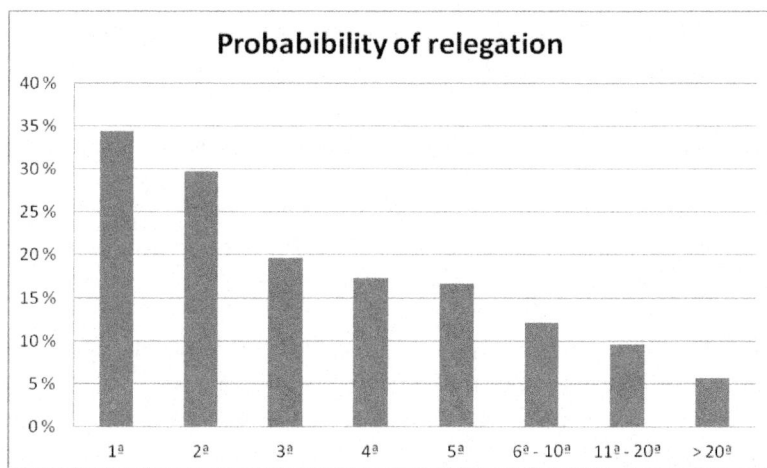

As we saw, a newly promoted team has, approximately, a 34% probability of relegation. If it manages to avoid relegation in its first year, it will face a nearly 30% chance of going down in its second season, 20% in the third, 17% in the fourth and fifth. In its sixth, seventh, eighth, ninth and tenth consecutive

---

[55] Real Betis is the team that has been promoted to First Division the most times with a total of 12. Its first promotion has been included in the first sample of 53 cases and the other 11 in the second sample of 189 cases. CD. Málaga, Celta de Vigo, Deportivo de la Coruña and Real Murcia have. each of them, been promoted a total of 11 times. Also, their first promotions are included in the first sample of 53 and the rest in the sample of 189.

seasons in Primera, it will face a 12% probability each year. A team that is between its eleventh and twentieth season in La Liga has a 10% chance of being relegated each year. Finally, a team that has been in La Liga for more than 20 consecutive seasons will only go down in 6% of the cases.

It is surprising how the probability of relegation at the end of the second season in the top tier is almost as high as the probability of relegation at the end of the first season. A newly promoted team is fully aware of the risk of relegation and that, in part, makes up for its lack of experience. The team that, after a promotion, went down after the highest number of consecutive seasons in La Liga was Atlético de Madrid at the end of the 1999-2000 season. By that time, they had been part of the elite of Spanish football for 63 years in a row. No other team has been relegated after such a long period in Primera.

5 of the 10 clubs that played the inaugural season of the league in 1929 played the 2020-21 season:

- Real Madrid, Barcelona, and Athletic de Bilbao, who have never been relegated. Therefore, they have played all 89 seasons in the First Division.
- Atlético de Madrid and Real Sociedad, who were relegated at some point, but later returned to the elite and are currently in it.

The remaining 15 clubs that took part in the 2020-21 season were clubs that reached the top tier at some point after its creation.

The following table shows how many consecutive seasons each team has stayed in Primera after each of the 242 promotions that have taken place since 1929. 14 of those cycles have not yet finished, so we do not know what their total duration will be:

TIME IN PRIMERA	TIMES	PERCENTAGE	PROBABILITY OF STAYING
1 SEASON	83	34%	66%
2 SEASONS	46	19%	46%
3 SEASONS	21	9%	36%
4 SEASONS	16	7%	30%
5 SEASONS	11	5%	25%
6 SEASONS	8	3%	21%
7 SEASONS	5	2%	18%
8 SEASONS	7	3%	15%

9 SEASONS	1	0%	15%
10 SEASONS	6	2%	12%
11 SEASONS	1	0%	11%
12 SEASONS	5	2%	9%
13 SEASONS	2	1%	8%
14 SEASONS	3	1%	7%
15 SEASONS	1	0%	6.5%
16 SEASONS	1	0%	6.1%
17 SEASONS	0	0%	6.1%
18 SEASONS	0	0%	5.6%
19 SEASONS	2	1%	4.3%
20 SEASONS	1	0%	3.9%
21 TO 63 SEASONS	8	3%	N / A
CONTINUE IN FIRST	14	6%	N / A

As we already know, a third of the teams went down after a single season in the elite. The right-hand column tells us that only after 46% of promotions the team managed to play at least 3 consecutive seasons in Primera. This table contains bad news for Tomás: it is more likely that not that Huesca will survive its first season in La Liga. But its stay in the top tier of Spanish football is expected to be less than 3 seasons. The probability that Huesca will not be relegated in the next 10 years is less than 13%. The median duration in Primera for a newly promoted team is only 2 seasons. The average duration is 4.7.

Do the probabilities in this table contradict the probabilities in the bar chart we saw earlier? They do not. The bar chart shows the probabilities of descending each year assuming that the club has managed to survive in the elite the previous seasons. The table contains the probabilities of remaining in the elite several years in a row that the club has when it has just been promoted.

And if a team is relegated, how long can it expect to spend in the misery of the Second Division before returning to Primera? To analyse this, we have a total of 235 relegations that have occurred since the league was created. The figures add up: If there have been 245 promotions by the start of the 2020-21 season and currently 10 teams more are part of the league than in 1929, necessarily there have been 235 relegations throughout its history.

In 29% of the cases, the relegated team managed to return to La Liga after spending only one season in the Second Division. 20% of the teams that failed to return to La Liga after a single season in the second tier managed to return to Primera at the end of their second season in Segunda. The teams that, after relegation, have played 2 seasons in Segunda also have approximately a 19% chance of returning to Primera in their third year in the silver division. If after 3 seasons in the Second Division the team has still not returned to the First Division, the chances of it being promoted again in any of the following seasons drop significantly. The following graph shows the historical probability of returning to Primera in the seasons following relegation[56]:

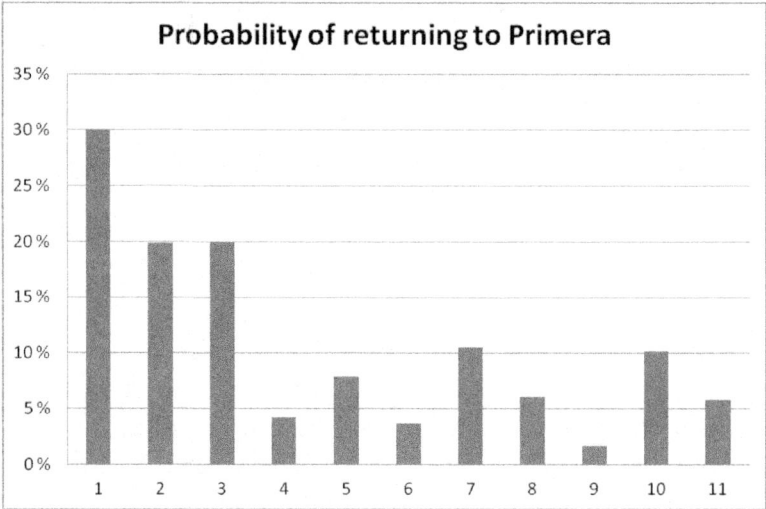

Probability of returning to Primera

A fan of a team that is relegated to Segunda should know that, historically, relegated teams were promoted back to Primera in 55% of cases after spending 3 seasons or less in the second division. 73% of the relegated teams managed to return to La Liga at some point during the 10 years after going down.

Only after 45 of the 235 relegations, the relegated team has not returned to Primera. Part of those relegations occurred many years ago and the teams that starred in them will hardly return to Primera[57]. Others are still very recent, and those teams do have a high probability of returning to Primera at some point in the next few years. The table on the following page shows after how many years each return to Primera has taken place.

---

[56] The volatile behaviour of the probability of being promoted when 4 or more years have passed since the relegation is due to the low number of available cases.

[57] Some of them have even disappeared such as U.D. Salamanca, CD Logroñés, S.D. Compostela, Burgos C.F., C.D. Malaga, CF Extremadura, C.P. Merida, A. D. Almería or E.U. Lerida.

DURATION OF STAY IN SECOND DIVISION OR LOWER	TIMES	PERCENTAGE[58]	CUMULATIVE PROBABILITY OF BEING PROMOTED[59]
1 SEASON	68	29%	29%
2 SEASONS	32	14%	44%
3 SEASONS	24	11%	55%
4 SEASONS	5	2%	58%
5 SEASONS	8	4%	61%
6 SEASONS	4	2%	64%
7 SEASONS	8	4%	67%
8 SEASONS	4	2%	69%
9 SEASONS	1	0.5%	70%
10 SEASONS	6	3%	73%
11 SEASONS	3	1%	75%
12 SEASONS	4	2%	78%
13 SEASONS	3	1%	79%
14 SEASONS	4	2%	82%
15 SEASONS	1	0.5%	82%
16 SEASONS	2	1%	83%
17 SEASONS	1	0.5%	84%
18 SEASONS	2	0.5%	85%
23 SEASONS	1	0.5%	87%
24 SEASONS	1	0.5%	88%
25 SEASONS	1	0.5%	89%
27 SEASONS	1	0.5%	90%
35 SEASONS	1	0.5%	92%
39 SEASONS	1	0.5%	93%
42 SEASONS	3	2%	95%
56 SEASONS	1	0.5%	96%
IT HAS NOT RETURNED TO PRIMERA YET	45	19%	N / A

[58] The percentages in this column do not add up to 100%, because in order to calculate the percentage of teams that have returned to Primera after spending 2, 3, 4, 5, etc., seasons in Segunda, we have excluded the relegations after which that number of years has not passed yet.

[59] For the same reason indicated in the previous note, it is compatible to affirm that after 45 of the 235 relegations (some of them very recent), the team has not yet returned to Primera with affirming that in the 35 years after a relegation, 92% of teams have been promoted back at some point.

Again, the probabilities of this table do not contradict the probabilities of the bar chart that we saw previously. The bar chart shows the probabilities of returning to Primera each year assuming that the club has remained in Segunda the previous seasons. The table contains the probabilities of playing several years in a row in Segunda before being promoted that a team has, a priori, the moment it has just been relegated.

The 4 teams that have managed to return to Primera after spending more years in misery are:

- Gimnàstic de Tarragona: They went down in the 1949-50 season and returned to the First Division for the 2006-07 season.
- UE Lleida: They went down in the 1950-51 season and got to play again in Primera in 1993-94.
- CD Alavés: They were relegated in the 1955-56 season and returned to Primera for the 1998-99 season.
- Córdoba CF: They were relegated in the 1971-72 season and got to play again in Primera in the 2014-15 season.

All this information gives Tomás more hope. Even if his beloved Huesca return to Segunda, there is a good chance that this will not be their only spell in Primera. In fact, considering both the probability of relegation and the probability of returning to Primera, the chances that a newly promoted team will find itself playing in La Liga several years down the road are the following:

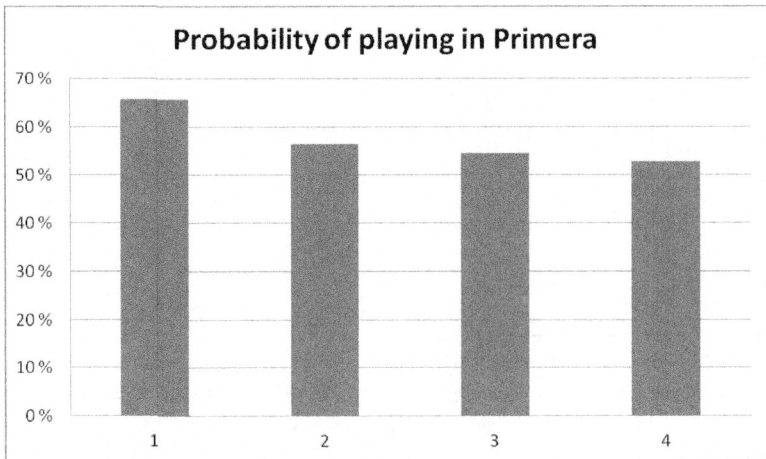

Probability of playing in Primera

In other words, Huesca has a probability of 52.2% of being in La Liga within 4 seasons, although only a probability of 30.7% of doing so without having stepped into Segunda at some point during that period[60].

To plot this bar chart, we have used the following flow chart. This flow chart represents all the possible promotions and relegations that a newly promoted team may go through in the following 4 campaigns. The probability that a team is playing in La Liga in 4 years' time is simply calculated as the sum of the probability of all the paths on which the team end ups in Primera.

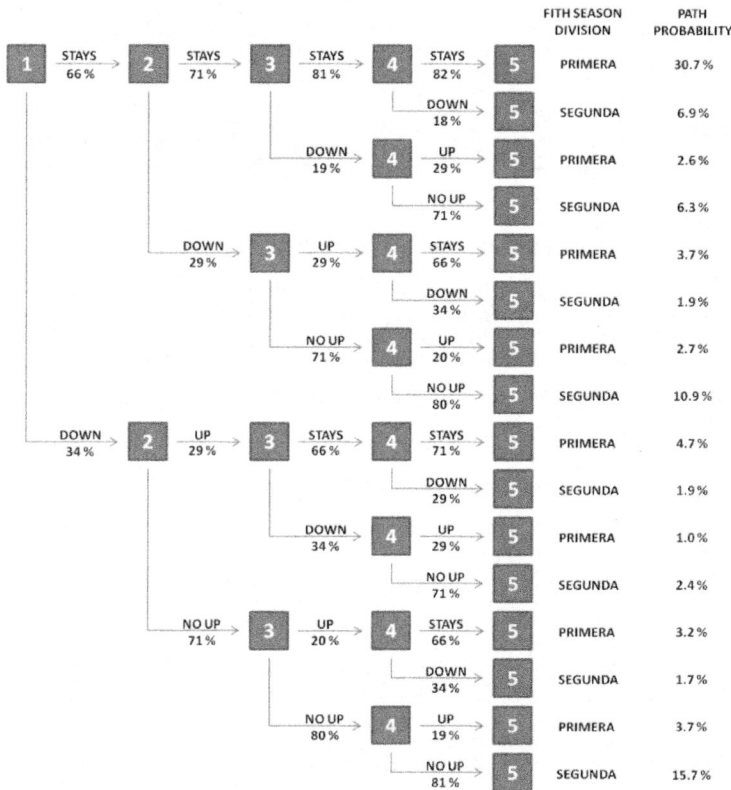

	FITH SEASON DIVISION	PATH PROBABILITY
1 → STAYS 66% → **2** → STAYS 71% → **3** → STAYS 81% → **4** → STAYS 82% → **5**	PRIMERA	30.7%
DOWN 18% → **5**	SEGUNDA	6.9%
DOWN 19% → **4** → UP 29% → **5**	PRIMERA	2.6%
NO UP 71% → **5**	SEGUNDA	6.3%
DOWN 29% → **3** → UP 29% → **4** → STAYS 66% → **5**	PRIMERA	3.7%
DOWN 34% → **5**	SEGUNDA	1.9%
NO UP 71% → **4** → UP 20% → **5**	PRIMERA	2.7%
NO UP 80% → **5**	SEGUNDA	10.9%
DOWN 34% → **2** → UP 29% → **3** → STAYS 66% → **4** → STAYS 71% → **5**	PRIMERA	4.7%
DOWN 29% → **5**	SEGUNDA	1.9%
DOWN 34% → **4** → UP 29% → **5**	PRIMERA	1.0%
NO UP 71% → **5**	SEGUNDA	2.4%
NO UP 71% → **3** → UP 20% → **4** → STAYS 66% → **5**	PRIMERA	3.2%
DOWN 34% → **5**	SEGUNDA	1.7%
NO UP 80% → **4** → UP 19% → **5**	PRIMERA	3.7%
NO UP 81% → **5**	SEGUNDA	15.7%

As it can be seen, the probabilities assigned to each pathway correspond to those shown on the previous pages. The probability of each path is calculated by multiplying the probability of the different nodes that make it up.

---

[60] In fact, SD Huesca were relegated to Segunda at the end of the 2018-19 season and were promoted back to Primera at the end of the 2019-20 season.

The probability of several pathways is the same. In fact, the goal of consolidating your team in the top tier of football is like a game in which the starting point is being promoted and if you go down, you have to start all over again.

The following diagram summarizes this situation:

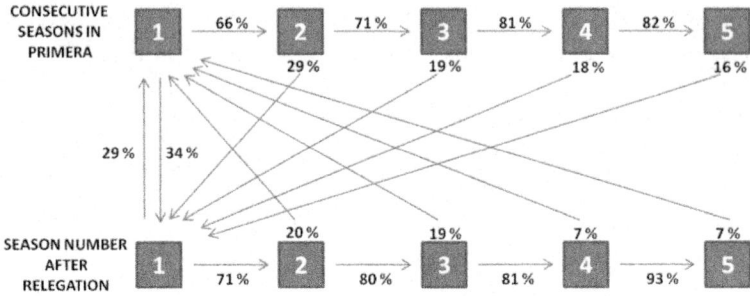

In recent years the Spanish Professional Football League (LFP) has established a relegation bonus system whereby clubs that to go down receive financial aid to help them in this transition. The creation of this system could increase the chances of returning to Primera for the newly relegated teams and make it more difficult for other clubs to join the elite of Spanish football[61].

[61] See the following article on this financial aid, the factors that influence its quantification, its advantages and disadvantages (in Spanish) :https://www.marca.com/futbol/primera-division/2020/07/15/5f0da454ca474155298b45c7.html

LOOKING FOR A SCORER

A week before the transfer market opens, the following conversation takes place in the offices of a football club in Seville:

—"We need to score more goals. We must find a striker who can make the difference, first-class, so we can find the back of the net more often next season", says the sporting director.

—"I have a candidate," says one of the scouts of the team. It's called Benoit. Benoit scored 10 goals in 19 games last season playing in Ligue 1.

—"I have another candidate," says another scout. His name is Trudeau. He scored 12 goals and played every game last season. He also plays in Ligue 1.

With this information, which player should the team sign, the player with the best goals-per-game ratio or the one that scored the most goals? Which one of them should we expect to score more goals next season?

Data analysis can help in this debate between the two scouts. To answer this question, we have compiled a database with the number of goals scored by every player in each of the last 5 seasons in each of the 5 major European leagues. Also, for every one of them we have information on their age, position on the field, assists, games played, and minutes played.

When we study the relationship between the number of goals that a footballer scores one season and the number of goals he scores the season after, we observe that historically there is a relationship of approximately 0.7. That is, for every 10 goals the footballer scores one season, we should expect that he will score 7 the next.

This value of 0.7 is the coefficient obtained in a linear regression in which the number of goals scored (explanatory variable) by each player in a season are used to predict the number of goals they will score the next (dependent variable). Unlike other chapters in this book, we use a linear regression in this case, since we do not want to assign a probability but to estimate the total number of goals to expect the following season. In addition, the regression has an intercept of 0.6. This means that those players who played during a season but did not score scored an average of 0.6 goals the season after.

To choose between Benoit and Trudeau, we also need to include in the model the variable of the percentage of minutes played by each player. This variable takes values between 0% and 100%. It will take the value 0% if the player has not played at all and 100% if he has played entirely all 38 games. The coefficient that the regression assigns to this variable is -0.5. In other words, being the number of scored goals equal, it can be expected that the footballer that has played for just a few minutes during the season will score 0.5 more goals the following season than the player that has played every minute.

In summary, with this model it is expected that the following season Benoit and Trudeau will score the following number of goals:

- Benoit = 0.6 + (0.7*10) − (0.5*50%) = **7.35 goals**
- Trudeau = 0.6 + (0.7*12) − (0.5*100%) = **8.5 goals**

The message is clear: **the total number of goals scored is a much better predictor than the number of minutes it takes to score every goal**. Trudeau can be expected to score more goals than Benoit next season even though Benoit has a better goals-per-game ratio.

Now let's imagine that Benoit is 24 years old and Trudeau is 31. We know that, in general, a 24-year-old footballer is still growing and developing his potential while a 31-year-old usually has already left his best years behind. Knowing that there is this age difference between the two, how should we adjust our goal expectation for the following season?

To answer this question, we add into the regression the variable with the footballer's age. Since the relationship between age and performance is not linear, we have to include it as a discretized variable. Once done, we observe that it receives the following weights:

- 25 years or less = +0.10
- 26 to 29 years = +0
- 30 to 33 years = -0.2
- 34 years or older= -0.7

Knowing that Benoit is 24, we must add one tenth to his goal expectation and knowing that Trudeau is 31, we must subtract two tenths from his. In summary:

- Benoit = 7.35 goals + 0.1 goals = **7.45 goals**
- Trudeau = 8.5 goals − 0.2 goals = **8.3 goals**

As it can be seen, the adjustment due to the age of the player is relatively small. Between a young player and a very veteran one it has the same importance as 1 goal scored the previous season.

In conclusion, to obtain a first estimate of how many goals a footballer can be expected to score next season, follow these steps:

1. Take the number of goals he scored last season and multiply it by 0.7.
2. Add 0.6 of the intercept.
3. Subtract the proportional part of -0.5 according to the percentage of minutes that he played during the season (for example, -0.25 if he played 50%)
4. Add 0.1 if he is 25 years old or younger and subtract -0.2 if he is between 30 and 33. If he is 34 years old or older, subtract -0.7.

Combining all these elements, the model achieves an R^2 of approximately 50% of which the vast majority corresponds to the variable of goals scored last season.

Let's imagine that, in the end, the club fails to sign Benoit and Trudeau. The scouts put two other possible candidates on the table, this time from Serie A:

- Luigi: he scored 15 goals last season and 10 goals two seasons ago.
- Mario: he scored 12 goals last season and 17 goals two seasons ago.

In this case, the scouts do not agree either. One of them thinks it's better to sign Luigi, as he scored more goals than Mario last season. The other thinks Mario is better, since he has scored a total of 29 goals in the last two seasons compared to 25 for Luigi. Who of them is right?

To answer this question, we develop a model in which, with the goals scored in each of the two preceding seasons, we predict the number of goals that each player will score the following one.

This model assigns a coefficient of 0.5 to the goals of the most recent season and 0.25 to those scored two seasons ago. The intercept is 0.4, which means that those players that did not score a goal in the previous two seasons scored an average of 0.4 goals the one after. This model has an R^2 of about 55%, making it more powerful than the one built using only the information from the previous season.

Therefore, the goal expectation for Luigi and Mario is as follows:

- Luigi: 0.4 + (15*0.5) + (10*0.25) = **10.4 goals**
- Mario: 0.4 + (12*0.5) + (17*0.25) = **10.65 goals**

In this case, Mario is better than Luigi. The interesting thing here is that we can conclude that the goals scored two seasons back also help predict how the footballer will do it in the future. However, their importance is approximately half that of the number of goals scored during the season that has just finished.

Given its higher R^2, we should use the model that considers the previous two seasons instead of the model with one season, whenever the available data on the footballer in question make it possible to do so. In case of relevant differences in age or minutes played, we can also apply the adjustment factors seen before[62].

Let's imagine that the club finally signs Mario with the expectation that he will score 10.65 goals next season. How likely is it that he will score, for example, 8 goals? Or what is the probability that he will score more than 13? To answer these questions we can use the Poisson distribution. The Poisson distribution is suitable for estimating the probability of a certain number of events (for example, goals) occurring during a time interval (for example, a season) from the mean of said variable (in this case 10,65), as long as we can reasonably assume that the events are independent of each other[63].

The Poisson distribution formula is available in Excel and is very easy to use. In this case, it indicates that the probability that Mario will score exactly 8 goals next season is approximately 9.7% and that he will score more than 13 goals is 27%.

---

[62] In the case of having information on the player's scoring record during the last three seasons, the coefficients that must be applied are 0.46 to the goals of the most recent season, 0.2 to the goals of 2 seasons ago and 0.15 to the goals of 3 seasons ago. The intercept of this regression is 0.16 and its R^2 is 59%.

[63] The assumption of independence is not fully met in this case (for example, a serious injury could get the played sidelined for the entire season). Even so, the Poisson distribution can give us a first idea about the probability of each number of goals. This technique can be used more appropriately with the total figures of a team or a tournament where the assumption of independence is satisfied to a greater extent.

In addition to the number of goals, there are many other variables related to the player's performance that we could find interesting to predict, such as his number of assists.

If we multiply the number of assists a player gave last season by 0.52 and add 0.76 (the intercept), we will obtain an estimate of the number of assists that he can be expected to give next season.

If we have information from the previous two seasons, we must multiply the number of assists from the most recent one by 0.39 and by 0.23 the number from two seasons ago. A 0.58 intercept must be added to the result.

It is noteworthy that the regressions to predict the number of assists perform worse than the regressions to predict the number of goals. Their R^2 are significantly lower. Who will provide the assist is more difficult to predict than who will score.

The relatively low correlation between the number of goals and the number of assists by a footballer in the same season is also striking. Although the relationship between both variables is positive, it is weak (R^2 of 27%). Clearly there are players that contribute to the attack by scoring goals and others by helping their teammates score them. **A player that both scores goals and gives assists is a rare treasure that must be taken good care of**.

Finally, let's try to predict how much time each player will spend on the pitch. To do this, **we must look at the number of minutes he was on the field and not at the number of games in which he participated**. If we have the data from the previous season, we must multiply the percentage of minutes played by 0.57 and add 0.18 of the intercept to calculate how much he will play the following season. **To forecast the number of minutes he will play, it does not make sense to include information from two seasons ago because the regression does not improve**. That is, to estimate how much time a footballer will play next season, in general it does not help to look beyond what he did in the previous season.

Intuitively this has a reason to be. **Depending on the characteristic of the footballer we want to study, we will need a longer or shorter time window to assess it correctly**. For infrequent events like goals or assists, it can be helpful to look beyond the previous season. If it is a more frequent type of action, such as the minutes played, the most recent season is all that is needed to forecast. This probably is also the case with other variables such as pass accuracy, distance covered or the player's top speed, which, given their nature, can be evaluated with a reduced number of matches[64].

Finally, it should be noted that any of the formulas presented in this chapter can be used in a sequential way to make predictions about how a footballer's performance will evolve beyond next season. For example, if a squad member played 90% of the minutes last season, we can expect that next season he will play 69% ((90% * 0.57) +0.18) and 58% two seasons from now ((69% * 0.57) +0.18).

---

[64] Something similar happens to us in our life when, for example, we begin a relationship with a person. The first date may be enough to find out, for example, how their manners are when eating or how they express themselves when speaking. However, we need much more time to get to know other aspects such as how they react to conflict situations or how they behave with their family.

SECTION 2: BETTING MARKETS

ODDS, PROBABILITIES AND MARGIN

Let's imagine a bet with two possible outcomes. For example, a bet on whether more or less than 2.5 goals will be scored in a match. In this bet there are only 2 possible outcomes:

- Outcome 1: 3 or more goals are scored in the match.
- Outcome 2: 2 goals or less are scored in the match.

In this situation, the bookmaker's profit is determined by the following equations:

If outcome 1 occurs, the bookie earns:

$$M_2 - M_1*(Odds_1-1)$$

Where:

- M_2 represents the total amount wagered in favour of outcome 2.
- M_1 represents the total amount wagered in favour of outcome 1.
- $Odds_1$ represents the odds offered by the bookie in European format[65] to whoever bets on outcome 1.

The interpretation of this formula is very simple and intuitive. With the money that the losers bet, the bookmaker pays the winners and makes its profit. If 3 or more goals are scored during the match, those who opted for outcome 1 will win the bet. In this case, the bookie obtains as a profit all the money that has been bet in favour of outcome 2 minus the profit that it has to pay to those who bet on outcome 1.

---

[65] The European format, also known as the decimal format, is the most common format in which bookmakers publish their odds in Europe, Canada and Australia. The odds shown in this book are in European format. Other odds formats are fractional and American. Most bookmakers allow the user to choose the format in which they want to view the odds. Additionally, there are odds converters available on the internet such as https://es.surebet.com/converter.

Similarly, if outcome 2 occurs the bookie earns:

$$M_1 - M_2*(Odds_2-1)$$

Where:

- M_1 represents the total amount wagered in favour of outcome 1.
- M_2 represents the total amount wagered in favour of outcome 2.
- $Odds_2$ represents the odds offered by the bookie in European to whoever bets on outcome 2.

The bookmaker will try to make money regardless of whether the final outcome is 1 or 2. More specifically, **the bookmaker will try that the relationship between the amounts wagered, and the odds is such that the profit is the same regardless of the outcome**. That is, mathematically the bookie wants:

$$M_2 - M_1*(Odds_1-1) = M_1 - M_2*(Odds_2-1)$$

From the previous formula you can arrive at the following equations:

$$M_2/M_1 = Odds_1/Odds_2$$

$$M_2 = (Odds_1/Odds_2)*M_1$$

$$M_1 = (Odds_2/Odds_1)*M_2$$

These equations indicate what conditions must be met for the bookmaker to make the same profit regardless of the outcome. The message they convey could be summarized as follows:

The bookmaker profit will be the same regardless of the outcome of the event as long as the amount bet in favour of outcome 1 is equal to the amount bet in favour of outcome 2 multiplied by the ratio between the odds.

In other words, even more clearly: The bookmaker will earn the same, whatever the result, when **the total wagered amount is distributed in the same proportion as the implicit probabilities of each outcome according to the odds**.

Let's see a numerical example:

- Odds if more than 2.5 goals are scored. $Odds_1$: 1.85
- Odds if less than 2.5 goals are scored. $Odds_2$: 1.95

Odds$_2$ has a numerical value that is 1.95 / 1.85 = 105.4% the value of Odds$_1$. Therefore, the bookie will want the amount wagered in favour of outcome 1 to be 105.4% the amount wagered in favour of outcome 2 (for example € 100 in favour of outcome 2 and € 105.4 in favour of outcome 1).

Let's verify that with the odds and amounts proposed, the profit of the bookie is the same regardless of the outcome.

If outcome 1 occurs, the bookie earns:

$$M_2 - M_1*(Odds_1-1) = 100 - 105,4*(1,85-1) = 10,4 €$$

If outcome 2 occurs, the bookie earns:

$$M_1 - M_2*(Odds_2-1) = 105,4 - 100*(1,95-1) = 10,4 €$$

The bookmaker always expects more money to be wagered in favour of the outcome for which it offers the lowest odds.

What if instead of a bet with 2 possible outcomes, it was a bet with 3 or more possible outcomes?

Let's see an example of a bet with 3 possible outcomes:

- Outcome 1: The match is won by the home team.
- Outcome 2: The match ends in a draw.
- Outcome 3: The match is won by the visiting team.

In this situation, the bookmaker's profit is determined by the following equations:

If outcome 1 occurs, the bookmaker earns:

$$M_2 + M_3 - M_1*(Odds_1-1)$$

If outcome 2 occurs, the bookmaker earns:

$$M_1 + M_3 - M_2*(Odds_2-1)$$

If the outcome is 3 the bookmaker earns:

$$M_1 + M_2 - M_3*(Odds_3-1)$$

In this case, for the bookmaker to earn the same amount regardless of the outcome, the following conditions must be met:

$$M_2 + M_3 - M_1*(Odds_1-1) = M_1 + M_3 - M_2*(Odds_2-1)$$

$$M_2 + M_3 - M_1*(Odds_1-1) = M_1 + M_2 - M_3*(Odds_3-1)$$

$$M_1 + M_3 - M_2*(Odds_2-1) = M_1 + M_2 - M_3*(Odds_3-1)$$

If we take, for example, the first of these three expressions to determine how the relationship between the amounts should be considering the different odds, we quickly observe that the variable M_3 appears with the same sign on both sides, so it can be eliminated. This means arriving exactly at the same equation as in the case of a bet with 2 possible outcomes:

$$M_2/M_1 = Odds_1/Odds_2$$

With the same reasoning, the following equations are obtained:

$$M_3/M_1 = Odds_1/Odds_3$$

$$M_3/M_2 = Odds_2/Odds_3$$

The bottom line is that, regardless of the number of possible outcomes, the bookmaker always earns the same profit when the amount wagered is proportional to the implicit probability of each result according to the odds.

The bookmaker manages to make money because there is an implicit margin in the odds. Next, we will see how to calculate this margin and how to calculate the probabilities of each result from the odds.

The bookmaker Betfair offered the following odds in European format for the Real Madrid - Barcelona match that was to be played two days later:

LOCAL ODDS (REAL MADRID)	DRAW ODDS	VISITOR ODDS (BARCELONA)
2.3	3.4	2.9

Observing these odds, two relevant questions arise:

1. What probability is implicit in them that each possible outcome will occur?
2. How much margin does the bookmaker earn?

As we will see, both questions are closely related.

To obtain the implicit probability in the odds, we must first calculate a factor called overround.

The overround is calculated as follows:

$$\text{Overround} = 1/\text{Odds}_1 + 1/\text{Odds}_2 + 1/\text{Odds}_3$$

In bets in favour of something happening, the overround will normally be greater than 100%. The higher the less efficient the market will be and the higher the margin the bookmaker is charging. An overround equal to 100% would indicate that the bookmaker is not charging any margin and an overround lower than 100% would indicate that it would be possible to secure a profit (green book) regardless of the result, if we bet the appropriate amount on each of them[66].

It goes without saying that situations in which the overround is lower than 100% are very unusual and usually only occur for very short periods of time when different bookies are offering significantly different odds for the same event. The behaviour of the betting market itself tends to eliminate these situations quickly.

In this example the overround is equal to:

$$\text{Overround} = 1/2.3 + 1/3.4 + 1/2.9 = 107.37\%$$

Once the overround has been calculated, the implicit probability that each result occurs is obtained as follows:

$$\text{Pimp}_1 = (1/\text{Odds}_1)/\text{Overround}$$

The implicit probability that a result will occur is calculated simply by **dividing the inverse of the odds in European format by the value of the overround[67]**.

---

[66] Just like a bookmaker, when building a green book, to ensure the same profit regardless of the result of the match, the wagered amounts must also be proportional to the odds. There are websites that specialise in arbitrage opportunities such as www.betburger.com and www.rebelbetting.com. In any case, this practice always involves some risks, since changes in the odds, fees or bookmaker restrictions mean that it is not always possible to take advantage of these opportunities in practice.

[67] We are assuming that the bookmaker margin in the odds is the same for all the possible outcomes of the match. In practice, the bookmaker could opt for a different pricing

The implicit probabilities of each result in the Real Madrid - Barcelona match in the example are therefore:

$$Pimp_1 = (1/2.3)/107.37\% = 40.49\%$$

$$Pimp_2 = (1/3.4)/107.37\% = 27.39\%$$

$$Pimp_3 = (1/2.9)/107.37\% = 32.11\%$$

The bookmaker estimates that the probability that Real Madrid win is 40.49%, that Barcelona win is 32.11% and that the game ends in a draw is 27.39%. Note how, by construction, the sum of all the implied probabilities equals 100% (the match has to end with one of the 3 possible outcomes). Note also that if the overround was 100% the implicit probability of each outcome would simply be the inverse of its odds in European format.

Although the overround is closely related to the percentage that the bookmaker earns, it is not exactly equal to it. The bookmaker margin is calculated as follows:

$$Margin = 1-(1/(1/(Odds_1)+1/(Odds_2)+1/(Odds_3)))$$

Taking the odds in the example, the bookmaker margin in this case is as follows:

$$Margin = 1-(1/(1/(2.3)+1/(3.4)+1/(2.9))) = 6.87\%$$

What does this 6.87% mean?

Let's imagine that the bookie has managed to ensure that the amounts wagered in favour of each of the results respect the proportions established by the odds and their implicit probabilities, as we saw at the beginning of this section. In that case, whatever the result, the bookie will make a profit of 6.87% of the total amount wagered. Let's see it with an example:

BET TYPE	ODDS	IMPLIED PROBABILITY	WAGERED AMOUNT	BOOKIE PROFIT
REAL MADRID WIN	2.3	40.49%	404.93	68.7
DRAW	3.4	27.39%	273.92	68.7
BARCELONA WIN	2.9	32.11%	321.15	68.7

---

methodology, for example, applying a higher margin to the less likely outcomes. On the following website you can download an Excel file that simulates other margin logics: www.football-data.co.uk/true_odds_calculator.xlsm.

In this example, the bookie has accepted bets for a total of € 404.93 + € 273.92 + € 321.15 = € 1,000 The amount wagered in favour of each result respects the necessary conditions so that, whatever the result, the bookmaker always earns **6.87%,** in this case € 68.7.

Evidently, if the amounts wagered in favour of each result had deviated slightly from the implied probability, the bookie could still have made money regardless of the outcome, although the exact amount of its profit would depend on the result of the match.

Let's now think from the bettor's perspective. A bettor that wages randomly would lose on average 6.87% of his bankroll. From a rational point of view, a bettor should only wage if, **in his opinion**, the actual probabilities of any of the outcomes occurring are greater than the implied probabilities in the odds. Specifically, the bettor should only wager if he considers that the probability of any of the results is higher than the inverse of the offered odds. Let's look at the following table:

BET TYPE	ODDS	IMPLIED PROBABILITY	MINIMUM REAL PROBABILITY TO BET
REAL MADRID WIN	2.3	40.49%	$1/2.3 = 43.48\%$
DRAW	3.4	27.39%	$1/3.4 = 29.41\%$
BARCELONA WIN	2.9	32.11%	$1/2.9 = 34.48\%$

If the bettor considers, for example, that the probability of Real Madrid winning is 50%, the 2.3 odds offered by the bookmaker will be attractive to him, since he will expect to obtain a positive return equal to:

$$\text{Expected Profitability} = (P_{win}*(\text{Odds}-1))-(1-P_{win})$$

Where:

- P_{win} represents the probability estimated by the player of winning the bet.
- Odds are the odds that the bookie pays if the bettor wins the wager.
- $1 - P_{win}$ is the probability that the bettor losses the wager.

In this example the wagerer expects to obtain an average return of:

$$(50\%*(2.3-1))-(1-50\%) = 15\%$$

At this point several observations should be made:

- The bettor only achieves positive expected returns when he considers that the probability of winning is higher than the inverse of the odds as shown in the previous table.
- The expected yield is the percentage that the bettor would expect to make on the wagered amount if he could place several bets with a similar theoretical return and the number of bets won in that series was as predicted.

If the odds correctly reflect the true odds of each outcome occurring, then the bettor will not be able to find value in them. **In most matches the bookmaker odds are correct and the most rational thing to do is simply not to bet on any outcome**.

In order for the bettor to make money in the long term, he must make **his predictions more accurately than those of the bookmaker.** If your predictions are worse, you will **NEVER** make money in the long run.

There are several factors that make it very difficult for a bettor to make predictions that are consistently more reliable than those of the bookie:

- The bookie has databases and software that allow it to make very accurate predictions.
- The bookie knows what each of the bettors are betting on. This is very valuable information to adjust the odds if necessary.

During the next few pages we will try to answer several questions:

- Do all bookies charge the same margins? To what extent can the margin charged be reduced by comparing the odds offered by different bookmakers?
- Do all bookies set their odds with the same level of reliability or are there bookies that are better than the others when it comes to estimating probabilities?

As in the previous section, to answer these questions, we will use real historical and statistical information from various leagues and bookmakers.

MARGIN CHARGED BY DIFFERENT BOOKIES

In this section we are going to compare the margin charged by different bookmakers in the full-time result market (1, X, 2) also known as moneyline. For this comparison we have historical information from 6 different bookmakers, 4 of them with a license to operate in Spain and 2 of them without this license. The bookmakers are the following:

- **Bet365 (B365)**: British company founded in 2000. It operates in more than 200 countries and has a Spanish license. Its parent company is taxed in the United Kingdom.
- **Bwin (BW)**: Formerly known as Betandwin. Company founded in 1997. From 2000 to 2016 it was listed on the stock market. It has a Spanish license. It currently has its headquarters in Gibraltar.
- **Interwetten (IW)**: Austrian company founded in 1990. It launched its online betting service in 1997. It has a Spanish license. It currently has its headquarters in Malta.
- **William Hill (WH)**: A British company founded in 1934. From 2002 to 2021, it was listed on the London Stock Exchange. It has a Spanish license. Most of its operations are taxed in Gibraltar, although its parent company continues in the United Kingdom.
- **Bet Victor (BV)**: A British company founded in 1946. In 1998 it moved its headquarters to Gibraltar. It does not have a license to operate in Spain. Formerly it was known as Victor Chandler.
- **Pinnacle (PS)**: Company based in Curaçao, Netherlands Antilles, founded in 1998. It does not have a license to operate in Spain.

The following table contains the average margin charged by these bookmakers in the 380 matches of the 2019-20 season of the First Division of the Spanish football league.

COMPETITION	LA LIGA
SEASON	2019-20
BET365	5.2%
BWIN	4.9%
INTERWETTEN	5.0%
WILLIAM HILL	4.8%
BET VICTOR	5.3%
PINNACLE	3.1%

The differences that exist in the pricing policies of these bookies are significant. Out of these 6 bookies, the most expensive one is Bet Victor with an average margin of 5.3%. 4 bookies (Bet365, Bwin, Interwetten and William Hill) charge margins between 4.8% and 5.2%. Finally, Pinnacle charges margins close to 3%.

The margin is very relevant. Let's imagine a bettor who places a €25 bet on each of the 38 league matchdays. During the league he will have wagered a total of 25 * 38 = €950. If the bettor does not have any type of edge over the bookie he uses, it could be expected that at the end of the season he would have lost the following amount:

COMPETITION	LA LIGA
SEASON	2019-20
BET365	-49.21
BWIN	-46.79
INTERWETTEN	-47.05
WILLIAM HILL	-45.75
BET VICTOR	-49.93
PINNACLE	-29.45

Betting on Bet Victor the bettor would lose on average €49.93 while betting on Pinnacle €29.45 only.

Obviously, a bettor does not have to bet always on the same bookie. Thanks to the internet and its odds comparators, it is relatively easy to check the odds offered for the same event by different bookmakers in order to place the bet on the one that pays the most. Let's see an example:

Bet365 and Bwin offered the following odds for the Sevilla - Valencia match on the last match day of the season:

	LOCAL ODDS (SEVILLA)	DRAW	VISITOR ODDS (VALENCIA)	MARGIN
BET365	1.9	3.4	4.0	6.6%
BWIN	1.9	3.6	3.8	6.3%

A gambler with this information who can bet on either bookie is actually facing the following situation:

	LOCAL ODDS (SEVILLA)	DRAW	VISITOR ODDS (VALENCIA)	MARGIN
ODDS	1.9	3.6	4.0	5.1%

As it can be seen, when comparing prices, the margin is reduced to 5.1%.

To what extent can a bettor reduce the margin he pays, by comparing across multiple bookmakers?

By always selecting the best odds offered by the 6 bookies for which we have historical information, the average margin in the 380 First Division matches of the 2019-20 season would have been reduced to 2.2%.

COMPETITION	LA LIGA
SEASON	2019-20
BEST ODDS 6 BOOKIES	2.2%

Of course, this margin is theoretical. To get this reduced margin we would need to be able to bet on any of the 6 bookies (as we have seen, not all of them have a license to operate in Spain[68]) and, in several cases, we would have to pay fees when depositing or withdrawing money. Still this analysis illustrates the relevance of comparing prices.

If, instead of taking the best odds offered by the 6 bookies, we take the best odds offered by the 4 bookies that operate in Spain, the margin is reduced to 3.1%.

COMPETITION	LA LIGA
SEASON	2019-20
BEST ODDS 4 BOOKIES	3.1%

---

[68] There are intermediaries or brokers that allow you to bet on bookmakers that do not have a license to operate in your country, although using their services may involve assuming additional risks.

In the case of the Spanish Second Division, the margins charged by each of these 6 bookmakers are as follows:

COMPETITION	SECOND DIVISION
SEASON	2019-20
BET365	6.3%
BWIN	5.9%
INTERWETTEN	6.1%
WILLIAM HILL	6.6%
BET VICTOR	4.8%
PINNACLE	3.7%
BEST ODDS 4 BOOKIES	3.8%
BEST ODDS 6 BOOKIES	2.3%

As it can be seen in this table, almost all bookies, charge higher margins for Second Division matches than for First Division matches. This is due to two reasons:

- The lower volume of bets that Second Division matches attract. This is a less efficient market than the First Division betting market.
- The greatest difficulty that bookies have when assigning correct probabilities to Second Division matches. Faced with this greater uncertainty, bookies protect themselves by charging a higher margin.

It should be noted that the cheapest bookie for First Division (Pinnacle) is also the cheapest for Second Division.

Do these margins mean that a wagerer should never bet on Second Division games? Not necessarily. It all depends on the level of knowledge of the bettor. A bettor with good knowledge of the Second Division, who believes that can make significantly better predictions than the bookies, should bet on this championship using the logic described above. A casual bettor should always bet on the competition with lower margins.

Both football and most bookmakers have their origin in England. Let's see below the average margin charged for Premier League matches during the 2019-20 season.

COMPETITION	PREMIER
SEASON	2019-20
BET365	5.0%
BWIN	4.8%
INTERWETTEN	5.0%
WILLIAM HILL	4.8%
BET VICTOR	4.0%
PINNACLE	2.8%
BEST ODDS 4 BOOKIES	3.2%
BEST ODDS 6 BOOKIES	2.1%

Four of the bookmakers analysed (Bet365, Bwin, Bet Victor and Pinnacle) charge lower margins in Premier matches than in La Liga matches. The other 2 bookies (Interwetten and William Hill) charge similar margins in both competitions. Always taking the best odds, the margin is 2.1% compared to 2.2% in the Spanish league.

It is also worth studying whether within the same competition the bookmarkers charge different margins depending on the type of match. Obviously, not all games attract the same interest or the same volume of bets. To analyse this aspect, we have divided the 380 matches of the 2019-20 season of the Spanish First Division into two groups:

- Matches in which Real Madrid and / or Barcelona played: 74 matches (36 matches played by Real Madrid against teams other than Barcelona, 36 matches played by Barcelona against teams other than Real Madrid and the 2 Clásicos played between them).
- Games in which neither Real Madrid nor Barcelona played: 306 games.

If we calculate separately the margins charged by the bookies for each group, we obtain the following results:

COMPETITION	LA LIGA	LA LIGA
SEASON	2019-20	2019-20
SUBGROUP	MADRID BARCELONA	REST OF GAMES
BET365	5.3%	5.2%
BWIN	4.9%	4.9%
INTERWETTEN	4.9%	5.0%
WILLIAM HILL	4.9%	4.8%
BET VICTOR	5.2%	5.3%
PINNACLE	3.3%	3.0%
BEST ODDS 4 BOOKIES	2.8%	3.2%
BEST ODDS 6 BOOKIES	2.1%	2.3%

The differences between the two subgroups are relatively small. In general terms, the margins charged in the Real Madrid and Barcelona matches are somewhat lower than those of the rest of the matches.

If we analyse the margins charged only in the two Clásicos between Real Madrid and Barcelona, the results are as follows:

COMPETITION	LA LIGA
SEASON	2019-20
SUBGROUP	CLÁSICOS
BET365	5.0%
BWIN	4.8%
INTERWETTEN	5.0%
WILLIAM HILL	4.4%
BET VICTOR	5.4%
PINNACLE	3.0%
BEST ODDS 4 BOOKIES	2.5%
BEST ODDS 6 BOOKIES	1.9%

It can be observed that Bwin, William Hill or Pinnacle charge lower margins in this type of matches. In these cases, the bettor can manage to face very low margins if he compares prices across all the available bookmakers.

MARGIN CHARGED IN VARIOUS MARKETS

Until now we have focused almost all the analyses on the odds offered on the 1, X, 2 betting market. However, the bookies accept many other types of bets in relation to a certain match, such as:

- Total number of goals to be scored (for example, if more or less than 2.5 goals will be scored in the match).
- Whether both teams will score or not.
- Double chance bets (for example, the away team will not win (1X)).

What margins do bookies charge in these other markets? Are these margins the same as for the 1, X, 2 market? To answer these questions, we have calculated the margins charged by Bet365 and William Hill for matchday 20 of La Liga 2020-21 season for several of these markets. The following table summarizes the results:

MARKET	MARGIN BET365	MARGEN WILLIAM HILL
FINAL RESULT (1, X, 2)	5.1%	4.8%
DOUBLE CHANCE (1X, X2, 12)	5.9%	6.0%
MORE OR LESS 2.5 GOALS	5.2%	7.0%
BOTH TEAMS TO SCORE	6.8%	7.2%

It can be seen that the margins charged differ, not only between bookmakers, but also within the same bookmaker across different markets.

The double chance market deserves special attention. This market has several interesting features that are worth commenting on[69]. Let's take the following real situation. These are the odds that were offered for Atlético - Valencia on matchday 20 of the 2020-21 season:

BOOKMAKER	FINAL RESULT			DOUBLE CHANCE		
	1	X	2	1X	X2	12
BET365	1.44	4.33	7.5	1.1	2.62	1.2
WILLIAM HILL	1.42	4.5	8.0	1.07	2.87	1.18

---

[69] Annex 3 explains how to calculate the overround, margin and implied probability for double chance bets.

Let's imagine that we are certain that the match is not going to end in a draw. What should we do?

If we look directly at the double chance market, we see that the best odds are on Bet365 which pays 1.2 in case the match ends in local or away victory. We can, however, try to get slightly higher odds for our bet. We can place two bets on the final result, one on local victory and another one on away victory, to build a double chance bet.

The following formula indicates which double chance odds can be obtained by placing two bets on the final result market:

$$\text{Double Chance Odds}_{ab} =$$

$$1/(1/\text{Odds Final Result}_a + 1/\text{Odds Final Result}_b)$$

In this example, to build our bet on 12, we take the best odds on 1 (1.44) and the best odds on 2 (8.0) and calculate:

$$\text{Doble Chance Odds}_{1x} =$$

$$1/(1/\text{Odds Final Result}_1 + 1/\text{Odds Final Result}_x)$$

$$1.22 = 1/(1/1.44 + 1/8.0)$$

By placing two separate bets, one that Atlético wins at 1.44 and the other that Valencia wins at 8.0, it is possible to build a double chance 12 bet at 1.22 odds, which are higher than the double chance odds that either of the two bookmakers are offering directly[70].

Although it may seem surprising, this situation actually occurs quite frequently. For the gambler interested in betting 1X, X2 or 12 it is usually worthwhile to build its own double chance bet than to accept the one offered directly by the bookmaker[71]. On other occasions, you will see that the double-

---

[70] Note how in this example with the odds for 1 and for 2 of William Hill, a 12 bet can be built that is higher than the double chance 12 odds offered by William Hill itself. In other words, this technique can be interesting even if it is only possible to bet on a single bookmaker.

[71] In this example, to build a bet on 12, the bettor places independently (on the same bookmaker or on two different bookmakers) a bet on 1 and a bet on 2. This practice should not be confused with the so-called multiple bets, in which a wagerer bets that he will win several bets from different matches, in order to multiply the odds

chance odds offered by the bookie are higher than the ones that could be obtained by betting on 1, X and 2, although this situation is much less frequent.

When building the double chance bet by means of two simple bets, it must be calculated how much to bet on each one so that the profit is the same whether there is one result (1 in this case) or the other (2 in this case). That is, the amounts must respect the following relationship:

$$M_a*(Odds_a-1) - M_b = M_b*(Odds_b-1) - M_a$$

Does this formula look familiar? This is exactly the same equation that we saw when we analysed how the amounts wagered should be distributed so that the bookie earned the same regardless of the result. Therefore, when building the double chance bet, the amounts wagered on the two individual bets must respect the following relationship:

$$M_b = (Odds_a/Odds_b)*M_a$$

So far, we have seen how a double chance bet can be built from two bets on the final result. Is the opposite possible? Can a bet on the final result (1, X, 2) be built from double chance bets? The answer to this question is yes. In this case, the equation to calculate the odds that could be obtained for a final result bet, from double chance bets, is the following:

$$Final\ Result\ Odds_a =$$
$$(((DCO_{ab}-1)+(DCO_{ac}-1)*(DCO_{ab}/DCO_{ac}))/(1-(DCO_{ac}-1)*(DCO_{ab}/DCO_{ac})))+1$$

For example, by means of a double chance bet on 1X and another double chance bet on 12, a final result bet on 1 can be built. The amounts must respect the same relationship seen in the previous case.

Just as the final result and the double chance markets are related, there are other relationships between other markets. These relationships make it possible to compare the odds across them in more or less complex ways. For instance:

- Correct Score - Final Result.
- Both Teams to Score - Correct Score.
- Margin of Victory - Correct Score.
- Asian Handicap - Final Result.
- Asian Handicap - Double Chance.

Asian handicap betting consists of predicting which team will win the match taking into account a fictitious initial goal difference. This initial fictitious difference is added to the actual result of the match to determine the winner of the bet. For example, in the Asian handicap bet Real Madrid -2, Rayo Vallecano +2 if we bet in favour of Rayo Vallecano and the match ends with Real Madrid winning by a single goal difference, we will have won the bet.

When the Asian handicap of the home team is -0.5, placing that bet is identical to betting that the home team will win. For this reason, it is convenient to compare the odds offered in the Asian handicap markets with the final result markets to find the highest ones. Similarly, when the visiting team's Asian handicap is -0.5, placing that bet is identical to betting that the visiting team will win.

Exploring how these markets relate to each other can allow you to place smarter bets.

MARGIN ON MULTIPLE BETS

Placing a multiple bet consists of making predictions about two or more different matches as part of a single bet.

For example, a Galician fan may think that, on the next matchday, both Deportivo de La Coruña and Celta will win their respective games. If Deportivo's victory pays 3 euros for each wagered euro and Celta's victory pays 2.5 euros for each wagered euro, a multiple bet on these two outcomes will pay 7.5 euros per wagered euro (3 * 2.5 = 7.5), since the odds of a multiple bet are calculated by multiplying the odds of each of the outcomes that are included in it:

$$\text{Multiple Bet Odds} = \text{Odds Outcome}_a * \text{Odds Outcome}_b$$

To place the multiple bet, the Galician fan only has to go to his favourite bookmaker's website, select the two (or more) outcomes that he wishes to combine into a single bet and, automatically, the total odds for all his selections will be calculated.

Obviously, placing a multiple bet is riskier than placing single bets on each of the matches. If, for example, Deportivo win their match and Celta do not win, the Galician fan will lose his multiple bet and he will have to say goodbye to the entire amount he wagered. However, with 2 single bets of the same amount each, the Galician fan would make money only by getting right one of them, since both odds are higher than 2. Finally, if the two teams actually win their respective matches, the best situation for the bettor is that he would have placed the multiple bet since, in this case, he would obtain a greater profit than with the 2 single bets.

The following table summarizes all these possible outcomes:

	YIELD	
	SINGLE BETS	MULTIPLE BET
DEPORTIVO WIN, CELTA WIN	175%	650%
DEPORTIVO WIN, CELTA FAIL TO WIN	50%	-100%
DEPORTIVO FAIL TO WIN, CELTA WIN	25%	-100%
DEPORTIVO FAIL TO WIN, CELTA FAIL TO WIN	-100%	-100%

There are several reasons why bookmakers love that bettors place multiple bets.

When placing a multiple bet the wagerer has to make all his selections on a single bookmaker. This prevents the bettor from placing his bets on the bookie that offers the best odds for each individual event. If the Galician fan had an account with two different bookies and placed single bets, he could place each of them using the bookmaker that paid the most for each result.

When placing a multiple bet, the best the bettor can do is to see which bookie would offer the highest odds for his multiple bet. This is much more complicated and laborious than seeing which bookie pays the most for a specific match[72].

Another less obvious reason is that when placing multiple bets there is a multiplier effect on the margin that the bookmaker manages to charge the client. Let's see this with an example:

	ODDS MORE THAN 2.5 GOALS	ODDS LESS THAN 2.5 GOALS	MARGIN
MATCH 1	1.9	1.9	5%
MATCH 2	1.9	1.9	5%

In each of these games, the bookmaker considers it equally likely that less than 2.5 goals will be scored and that more than 2.5 goals will be scored. By setting the odds at 1.9 the bookmaker is charging a margin of 5% in each of these markets. Out of every €20 wagered, players would recover, on average, €19. That is 95%.

A bettor who thought, for example, that in both games more than 2.5 goals would be scored and decided to place a multiple bet, would obtain odds of 3.61 (1.9 * 1.9). In fact, by combining these two games, four different multiple bets could be placed, all of them with the same odds:

- **Multiple Bet 1:** In match 1 more than 2.5 goals are scored and in match 2 more than 2.5 goals are scored.
- **Multiple Bet 2:** In match 1 fewer than 2.5 goals are scored and in match 2 fewer than 2.5 goals are scored.

---

[72] Some odds comparison sites can help on this task.

- **Multiple Bet 3:** In match 1 more than 2.5 goals are scored and in match 2 fewer than 2.5 goals are scored.
- **Multiple Bet 4:** In match 1 fewer than 2.5 goals are scored and in match 2 more than 2.5 goals are scored.

The probability of winning any of these bets, if the bookmaker has estimated the probabilities of each outcome correctly, is 25%. A bettor placing any of these 4 bets would win only 1 time out of every 4. The bookie would only pay € 36.1 out for every €40 wagered (90.25%). **This is a 9.75% margin in favour of the bookmaker instead of the 5% margin of the simple bets!**

To see more clearly the disastrous effect of multiple bets, let's check with real data what would have happened to two bettors with the following strategies:

- **Bettor A**: He bets every matchday that Athletic Bilbao and Valencia will win their respective matches by placing two simple bets. When these teams face each other, he does not bet.
- **Bettor B**: He bets every matchday that Athletic Bilbao and Valencia will win their matches by placing a multiple bet. When these teams face each other, he does not bet.

Each strategy from 2000 to 2020 would have obtained the following results:

	YIELD
BETTOR A (SIMPLE BETS)	-2.3%
BETTOR B (MULTIPLE BETS)	-6.6%

Bettor B would have incurred a significantly higher loss, given the higher margin he faces when placing multiple bets.

By placing a multiple bet, we are telling the bookie that, if we win the first selection, we want to reinvest the amount wagered plus our profits on the second selection. This in practice allows the bookie to charge us twice its implicit margin. It is a more aggressive way of betting that will make us lose our money more quickly.

HISTORICAL EVOLUTION OF THE MARGIN

All the margins presented in the previous chapters correspond to the 2019-20 season. How have the margins charged by the bookmakers evolved over time?

The following table contains the average margins charged by each bookie in the matches of the Spanish La Liga during the last fifteen years:

SEASON	B365	BW	IW	LB[73]	WH	BV	PS	BEST 5	BEST 7
2005-06	8.1%	9.3%	10.8%	10.9%	11.1%	10.9%		5.0%	4.9%
2006-07	7.4%	9.3%	10.1%	11.0%	11.1%	11.0%		5.0%	5.0%
2007-08	6.2%	9.3%	10.2%	10.9%	11.0%	9.3%		4.3%	4.1%
2008-09	6.1%	9.3%	9.2%	10.9%	10.2%	8.7%		3.5%	3.4%
2009-10	6.1%	7.5%	7.8%	10.7%	9.2%	7.9%		3.5%	3.4%
2010-11	6.2%	7.4%	9.2%	6.9%	6.3%	3.7%		3.0%	2.2%
2011-12	6.1%	6.1%	9.3%	6.7%	6.1%	3.3%		3.0%	1.9%
2012-13	6.0%	6.1%	7.8%	6.8%	6.0%	3.1%	2.0%	2.6%	1.0%
2013-14	6.0%	6.2%	7.5%	6.1%	5.9%	3.0%	2.0%	2.4%	0.9%
2014-15	5.2%	6.0%	7.5%	5.5%	5.9%	2.8%	2.0%	2.6%	0.9%
2015-16	4.9%	5.8%	7.5%	5.8%	5.8%	2.8%	2.0%	2.7%	1.0%
2016-17	4.8%	5.0%	5.6%	5.9%	4.7%	3.7%	2.0%	2.0%	0.9%
2017-18	5.0%	4.9%	5.3%	5.9%	5.8%	3.7%	2.2%	2.1%	0.9%
2018-19	5.0%	4.9%	5.0%		5.0%	3.7%	2.7%	2.7%	1.6%
2019-20	5.2%	4.9%	5.0%		4.8%	5.3%	3.1%	3.1%	2.2%

The data shows a clear trend. All the analysed bookies have reduced their margins in the last fifteen years.

However, this process of reducing margins seems to have stalled in recent seasons. Some bookies such as Bet Victor and Pinnacle seem to have increased their margins recently. Unfortunately, we only have information on Pinnacle for the last eight seasons.

---

[73] In addition to the bookies mentioned above, we have information on Ladbrokes for the seasons between 2005-06 and 2017-18.

Let's see this evolution graphically:

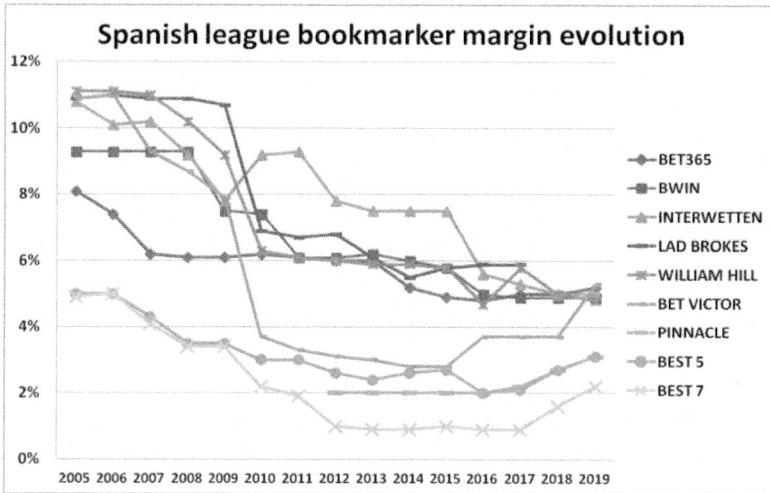

Spanish league bookmarker margin evolution

The vertical axis represents the margin charged by each bookmaker and the horizontal axis represents each of the last fifteen seasons, identified by its starting year. The reduction of margins in the last fifteen years has been considerable. The sports betting market is becoming more competitive and more efficient.

Imagine a situation in which two or more bookies charge margins very close to zero for a certain game. In this situation, it is **IMPOSSIBLE** for the odds offered by each of them to be very different, since any arbitrage opportunities (negative margins) would be exploited by the bettors that could wager on all of them. As bettors take advantage of this arbitrage situation, the odds would necessarily tend to converge.

An increasingly smaller margin in a betting market makes that market tend to adopt a single price (odds) for each event. The reduction of margins necessarily reduces the differences in the odds offered by the bookies.

This reduction in margins over the last fifteen years has been observed not only in the Spanish La Liga but in all competitions.

The following table and graph contain the figures for the Spanish Second Division.

SEASON	B365	BW	IW	LB	WH	BV	PS	BEST 5	BEST 7
2005-06	10.7%	10.9%	12.0%	10.9%	11.1%	11.0%		6.3%	6.1%
2006-07	10.1%	10.2%	11.9%	10.9%	11.1%	11.0%		5.5%	5.4%
2007-08	9.3%	10.1%	11.9%	10.9%	11.1%	10.0%		5.3%	5.0%
2008-09	8.3%	10.1%	11.9%	10.9%	11.1%	9.9%		5.0%	4.8%
2009-10	7.1%	10.1%	11.9%	10.9%	9.0%	9.3%		4.5%	4.3%
2010-11	6.8%	10.0%	11.8%	10.9%	8.8%	8.2%		4.4%	4.2%
2011-12	6.3%	9.1%	10.4%	10.9%	8.9%	5.1%		4.3%	3.4%
2012-13	6.1%	9.2%	10.2%	10.9%	8.5%	4.1%	2.9%	4.4%	2.2%
2013-14	6.0%	9.1%	10.2%	10.8%	8.4%	4.0%	2.9%	4.5%	2.1%
2014-15	6.1%	9.1%	10.1%	9.4%	8.4%	4.3%	2.9%	4.4%	2.1%
2015-16	6.2%	9.1%	9.5%	6.8%	8.2%	4.5%	2.5%	4.1%	1.8%
2016-17	6.1%	6.1%	9.2%	6.7%	7.8%	4.8%	2.5%	3.5%	1.6%
2017-18	6.2%	5.9%	7.5%	8.1%	7.7%	4.7%	2.8%	4.0%	2.0%
2018-19	6.1%	5.9%	7.5%		6.7%	4.8%	3.9%	3.8%	2.4%
2019-20	6.3%	5.9%	6.1%		6.6%	4.8%	3.7%	3.8%	2.3%

Let's see this evolution graphically:

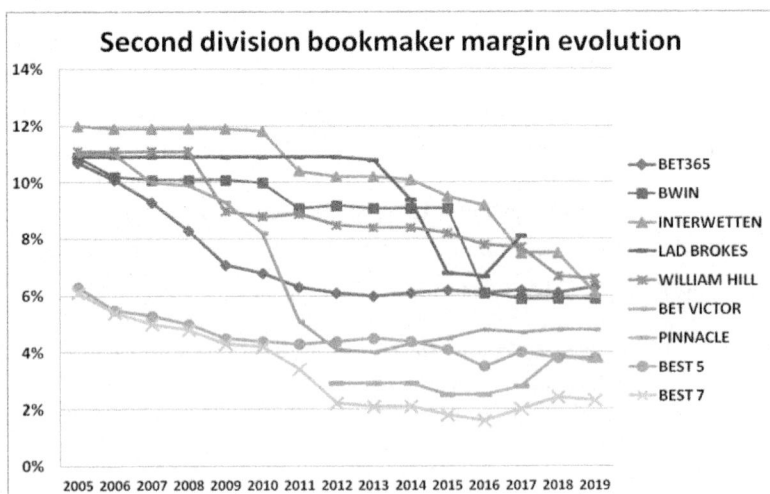

In 2005, most bookmakers charged margins higher than 10% on Second Division matches. Today most bookies charge margins between 6% and 7%. Below is the same information for the Premier League.

SEASON	B365	BW	IW	LB	WH	BV	PS	BEST 5	BEST 7
2005-06	7.3%	9.2%	11.0%	10.9%	11.1%	7.9%		5.0%	4.6%
2006-07	7.4%	9.2%	10.2%	11.0%	11.1%	8.0%		5.3%	5.0%
2007-08	5.6%	9.1%	10.2%	10.9%	11.0%	6.7%		4.4%	3.8%
2008-09	5.0%	9.2%	9.3%	8.4%	6.5%	6.2%		3.4%	3.1%
2009-10	5.2%	7.7%	7.7%	6.9%	6.8%	6.1%		3.4%	3.0%
2010-11	5.2%	7.4%	9.2%	6.1%	6.1%	3.5%		2.7%	2.1%
2011-12	5.2%	6.0%	9.2%	6.2%	6.3%	3.2%		2.7%	2.0%
2012-13	3.9%	6.0%	7.7%	6.3%	6.1%	2.8%	2.0%	1.9%	0.8%
2013-14	2.5%	6.2%	7.5%	5.6%	5.9%	2.7%	2.0%	1.6%	0.8%
2014-15	2.6%	5.4%	7.5%	4.4%	5.9%	2.5%	2.0%	1.5%	0.7%
2015-16	2.7%	5.7%	7.4%	4.9%	5.7%	2.5%	2.0%	1.6%	0.8%
2016-17	2.9%	4.8%	5.6%	4.6%	4.5%	2.7%	2.0%	1.4%	0.7%
2017-18	3.0%	4.8%	5.3%	5.8%	4.6%	2.7%	2.0%	1.4%	0.7%
2018-19	2.7%	4.8%	5.1%		5.0%	2.5%	2.3%	1.9%	1.1%
2019-20	5.0%	4.8%	5.0%		4.8%	4.0%	2.8%	3.2%	2.1%

Let's see this evolution graphically:

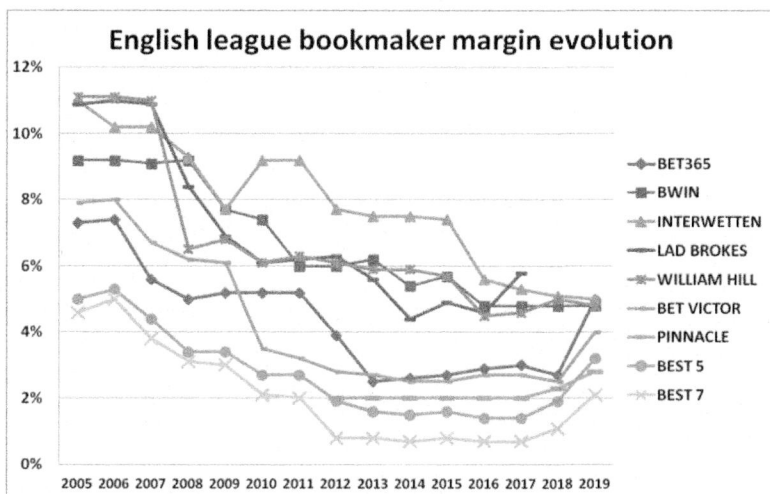

English league bookmaker margin evolution

BET365, BWIN, INTERWETTEN, LAD BROKES, WILLIAM HILL, BET VICTOR, PINNACLE, BEST 5, BEST 7

In case of the Premier League, fifteen years ago, by comparing prices, bettors could face margins of 4%, nowadays they can face margins of around 2%.

Similar tables can be found in Annex 4 for the following leagues:

- German Bundesliga.
- Italian Serie A.
- French Ligue 1.
- Dutch Eredivise.
- Portuguese Primeira Liga.

Now that we have seen how bookmaker margins have evolved over the last few years, it is also worth studying how the bookie margins evolve during the days leading up to a match. We will analyse this aspect in the next chapter.

EVOLUTION OF THE MARGIN BEFORE THE GAME

Typically, bookmakers start accepting bets for a match about a week before the match takes place. Market opening can happen more or less in advance depending on the following factors:

- The importance of the competition: in general, the market opens earlier for the most important competitions.
- The relevance of the match: in the case of highly relevant matches, the market opens even earlier. For example, for El Clásico between Real Madrid and Barcelona or the Champions League final, the market can open several weeks in advance.
- The date of the previous matchday: bookmakers will likely start, for example, accepting bets on games on matchday 4 if matchday 3 has already taken place.
- The policy of the bookmaker: some of them tend to start accepting bets earlier than others. Others wait to copy the odds from their peers.

In order to start accepting bets, the bookmakers have to set the initial odds[74]. During the days leading up to a game, these odds can be adjusted according to the bettors' behaviour. The odds offered just before kick-off can differ significantly from those initially offered.

And what happens to the margin? Do the odds move, but the margin charged by the bookmaker remains constant? Or does the margin also vary during the days leading up to the match?

To answer these questions, we have compiled a specific sample made up of more than 900 matches from 7 different European leagues played between March 2014 and June 2015. For each of these matches, the odds offered by the main licensed bookies in Spain were recorded (Bet365, Bwin, Sportium, Luckia, William Hill and Interwetten) at 3 different times.

- Initial odds: Between 70 and 90 hours (3 - 4 days) before kick-off.
- Intermediate odds: Between 10 and 14 hours before kick-off.
- Final odds: Between 1 and 3 hours before kick-off.

---

[74] This would not be the case in exchange-type markets where players bet against each other rather than against the bookie.

With this information it is possible to analyse multiple interesting aspects about the evolution of margins, trends, predictive capacity of the odds, etc. that we will cover in this and the following chapters. The next table indicates the margin that the bookies were charging at each moment, always considering the highest odds offered by the six bookmakers in the sample:

CHAMPIONSHIP	INITIAL MARGIN	INTERMEDIATE MARGIN	FINAL MARGIN
GERMANY	2.15%	2.07%	1.48%
FRANCE	3.16%	2.43%	1.71%
NETHERLANDS	3.68%	3.11%	2.61%
ENGLAND	2.76%	1.22%	0.69%
ITALY	3.13%	2.36%	2.17%
SPAIN LA LIGA	2.88%	2.16%	1.89%
SPAIN SECOND	5.53%	3.92%	3.45%

In the seven competitions it is observed how, as the match approaches, the margin of the bookies tends to go down. To confirm this phenomenon, we have generated a similar table analysing the behaviour of a single bookmaker, in this case Betfair[75].

CHAMPIONSHIP	MARGIN INITIAL	INTERMEDIATE MARGIN	MATCHES
GERMANY	5.72%	4.99%	105
FRANCE	6.52%	5.68%	94
NETHERLANDS	6.46%	5.67%	101
ENGLAND	5.75%	4.17%	109
ITALY	5.66%	4.62%	98
SPAIN LA LIGA	5.56%	4.65%	83
SPAIN SECOND	8.23%	7.75%	102

In this case, we only have recorded the odds at two different moments (between 70 and 90 hours before each game and between 10 and 15 hours before each game). The same phenomenon of margin reduction is clearly observed as the matches approach.

---

[75] Although these odds were compiled from the Betfair Spain sportsbook, a similar behaviour is observed in exchange-type markets. In exchange-type markets, bettors place bets against each other instead of against the bookie. In these markets it is clearly observed how as the match kick-off approaches, liquidity increases and margins are reduced.

All these margins have been calculated before the ball starts rolling. The margins charged by the bookmakers for live betting once a match has started are usually significantly higher than those charged in the hours prior to its start.

Do these data mean that a gambler should always place his bets shortly before the start of the match? If he doesn't have any kind of expert knowledge, the answer is yes, as, on average, he will lose less money. However, the exact answer depends, not only on the margin charged by the bookmaker, but also on the predictive capacity of the odds and on the bettor's own ability to detect opportunities in them. During the next chapters we will analyse in detail the predictive capacity of the odds offered by bookmakers.

PREDICTIVE CAPACITY OF BOOKIES

In the previous chapter we saw that bookmakers charge very different margins according to their pricing policies. We have also learned how to calculate the implied probabilities of each outcome from the odds. Calculating the implied probabilities means in practice "undoing" the impact of the margin on the odds so that the implied probabilities will always add up to 100%, even if the overround is higher and different across bookies.

By taking the sample used in the previous chapter and transforming all the odds into their corresponding implicit probabilities, we can analyse which bookies are better at estimating the probability of the different sport results, regardless of their pricing policies. Are all bookmakers equally good at forecasting results or are some of them better than the others?

To answer this question, we have built the following table with the average probability that each bookie assigned to the result (home win, draw or away win) of each match of the 2019-20 La Liga season.

COMPETITION	LA LIGA
SEASON	2019-20
BET365	40.91%
BWIN	40.87%
INTERWETTEN	40.76%
WILLIAM HILL	41.02%
BET VICTOR	40.91%
PINNACLE	40.95%

What do these data mean? Someone who could predict the future perfectly would assign a 100% probability to such event. If everyone knew with certainty that a team was going to win its next match, the odds offered for its victory would be 1 and the implied probability would be 100%. There would be no uncertainty and, therefore, there would be no betting market.

In the real world, of course, there is uncertainty. Bookmakers assigned an average probability of 40,9% to the outcomes (1, X, 2) that occurred in the 2019-20 season. The most predictive bookie was William Hill because, with 41.02%, it was the one that assigned the highest probability to the results that finally occurred. The worst forecaster was Interwetten since it only assigned a probability of 40.76% to those same results.

The difference between the most predictive and the least predictive bookie may seem small. This is because, as we have already seen, the odds offered by the bookmakers can only differ to a certain extent, since too large differences would generate arbitrage opportunities that would be quickly eliminated by bettors looking to place sure bets.

What happens in other leagues? What are the bookies that best predict the results of other European leagues? These are their results for the top leagues in the 2019-20 season:

COMP[76].	PR	SE	EN	FR	GE	IT	NE	PO
B365	40.9%	35.6%	42.8%	40.3%	42.7%	42.6%	45.2%	42.2%
BW	40.9%	35.5%	42.7%	40.2%	42.6%	42.5%	45.2%	42.2%
IW	40.8%	35.4%	42.5%	40.1%	42.2%	42.3%	44.7%	42.0%
WH	41.0%	35.5%	42.8%	40.3%	42.7%	42.6%	45.2%	42.1%
BV	40.9%	35.4%	42.8%	40.3%	42.6%	42.7%	45.3%	42.2%
PS	40.9%	35.5%	42.8%	40.4%	42.7%	42.7%	45.3%	42.4%

Two interesting phenomena can be observed in this table:

1. The difficulty of predicting the outcome of the matches in some leagues is significantly higher than in others. For example, Spanish Second Division matches are more disputed than La Liga matches. As the result is more uncertain, bookies assign in many of them similar odds to the local victory, the draw, and the visitor victory. There are no big favourites. In La Liga, however, there are quite a few games with a clear favourite (e.g., Barcelona or Real Madrid) to which, on occasions, bookies assign a victory probability greater than 90%.

   In this sense, this table not only tells us which bookmakers are the best forecasters, but also indicates which championships generally have more closely disputed matches. Those who consider La Liga a more exciting competition than the Premier League are likely to look at these numbers with satisfaction.

---

[76] PR: Primera División, SE: Segunda División, EN: England, FR: France, GE: Germany, IT: Italy, NE: Netherlands, PO: Portugal.

2. The bookies that best predict the results of the Spanish league are also those that best predict the results of other leagues. Likewise, the bookies that worst predict for La Liga are also those that worst predict the results of other leagues. There does not seem to be, therefore, "specialist" bookmakers in a certain football championship, but simply bookmakers that set their odds in a more accurate way.

To see this point more clearly, we have replaced the percentages in the table above with the position in which each bookie ranked when predicting the results of each league. We assign a 1 to the bookie with the highest predictive capacity for a given league, the second with the highest capacity is assigned a 2 and so on. The results are the following:

COMP.	PR	SE	EN	FR	GE	IT	NE	PO
B365	3	1	4	3	2	4	3	4
BW	5	2	5	5	5	5	4	3
IW	6	6	6	6	6	6	6	6
WH	1	4	3	2	1	3	5	5
BV	4	5	2	4	4	1	1	2
PS	2	3	1	1	3	2	2	1

Pinnacle is the most predictive bookie out of the 6 analysed. In second place is Bet Victor, closely followed by Bet365 and William Hill. Bwin occupies the penultimate place in terms of predictive capacity. Finally, Interwetten appears in last place as it was the least successful in all leagues.

If we compare these results with those obtained in the first edition of this book 4 years ago, we see that Pinnacle continues to be the bookie that forecasts the best. Similarly, Interwetten remains the worst one. For its part, William Hill has managed to improve positions by overtaking Bwin.

What does all this mean for a gambler? The bettor should be aware that **Pinnacle is less likely to make mistakes in setting its odds than, for example, a bookie like Interwetten**. If Pinnacle and Interwetten have different views on the same game, it is more likely that Pinnacle is right and Interwetten is wrong than the other way around.

The ideal bookie for a gambler should meet two conditions:

- Make mistakes in its predictions that can be exploited.
- Offer high odds with low margins.

To see which bookies have these characteristics, we have placed them in the following scatter plot, ordering them, on the vertical axis, from lowest to highest predictive capacity and, on the horizontal axis from lowest to highest margin.

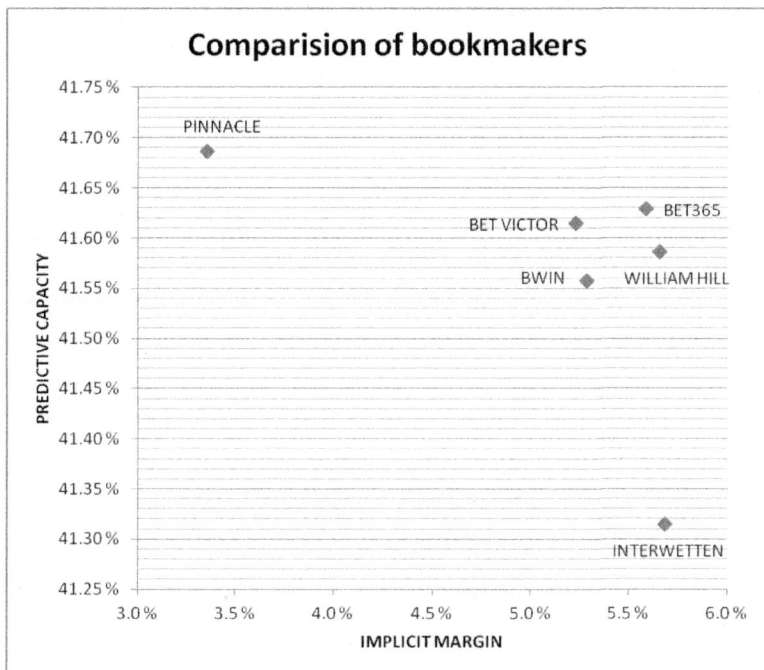

Comparision of bookmakers

It is clearly observed that those bookies that charge lower margins are those with the most predictive odds[77]. This should not surprise us. **By charging lower margins, the bookies attract a greater volume of bets and therefore have more information to adjust their forecasts in a more refined way than their competitors**.

In addition, **the bookies that charge lower margins are forced to modify their odds more frequently due to changes in the market**, since otherwise they would be easily exposed to possible arbitrage situations.

---

[77] Although this analysis has been carried out with only 6 bookmakers, we think that its conclusions can be extrapolated to the betting market in general. There are, of course, many other bookmakers on the market. For a comprehensive and up-to-date list of bookmakers that operate internationally, we recommend checking www.oddsportal.com. A complete list of the licensed bookies that operate in Spain can be checked at the General Directorate for the Regulation of Gambling website www.ordenacionjuego.es.

The ideal bookmaker for the bettor, one that makes mistakes in its forecasts and charges low margins, does not exist. The lower left quadrant of the diagram is empty. **Simple market logic prevents such a bookie from existing. A bookie with these characteristics would be a bargain for bettors, but it would be a terrible business for its owners and would be doomed to closure.**

Less predictive bookies "defend" themselves by charging higher margins and in many cases by restricting the amounts bettors can place on a certain event. This is clearly the Interwetten model.

What about those bookies in which the bettor bets against other bettors instead of against the bookie itself? Theoretically, in this case, the odds offered could be absurd without placing the continuity of the bookmaker itself in danger. However, it is possible to think that the absent-minded player or players who offered those wrong odds would not do so for a long time, given the money they would lose, without a doubt, in the medium term. From time to time there may be manifestly erroneous odds, but it will never be something systematic or continuous over time.

Additionally, it is not possible for large differences to arise between the odds offered by traditional bookies and exchange bookies, since these differences would also lead to the generation of arbitrage opportunities that would be quickly eliminated as well.

Given the higher predictive power of some bookies, a potentially interesting strategy may be to calculate the implied probabilities of an event from their odds and then bet on another less predictive bookmaker when it offers odds for the same event that compensate for that probability. Let's see it more clearly with an example. Let's imagine that for the same match Pinnacle and Interwetten are offering the following odds:

BOOKMAKER	ODDS			IMPLIED PROBABILITIES		
	1	X	2	1	X	2
PINNACLE	2.0	3.7	4.0	49.01%	26.49%	24.50%
INTERWETTEN	2.05	3.5	3.6	45.80%	27.48%	26.72%

In this case, Pinnacle considers a local win more likely than Interwetten. What bookie is right? A priori we do not know, but what we do know is that, historically, Pinnacle has predicted better the results of sporting events than Interwetten.

As Interwetten pays 2.05 for the home win and these odds more than compensate Pinnacle's implied probability (2.05> 1 / 49.01% = 2.04) we would bet that the home team will win at Interwetten.

If Interwetten paid 2.02 it would still pay more than Pinnacle, but in this case we would not bet, as the odds would not fully compensate Pinnacle's implied probability.

This situation occurs with some frequency. Although Pinnacle typically charges lower margins than Interwetten, as it is the case in this example, that does not mean that for certain results Interwetten may not offer better odds than Pinnacle.

Would you be interested in betting that the match will end in a draw or an away win, taking advantage of Pinnacle's higher odds? No, it would not be interesting for two reasons:

- Pinnacle is normally the most predictive bookie so we will assume those odds are correct. Even though those odds cover Interwetten's implied probability, we trust more Pinnacle's implied probabilities.
- If, as we have seen, it is interesting in this game to bet on the local victory, it would not make sense to bet on the draw or on the away victory at the same time since in this example it is not possible to build a green book. We are not facing an arbitrage situation, since, even taking the best odds from both bookies, the bettor continues to pay a margin.

Will this strategy work? Obviously, nothing guarantees that this particular match will end in a home win, but if we repeated this strategy multiple times, we should make a small profit in the long run.

Interestingly enough, in order to execute this strategy, we would not need to open an account at Pinnacle, since we would never place our bets at this bookmaker. What we would be doing would be to take advantage of its greater predictive power to detect possible errors in the odds of other bookies.

Based on information on odds from the 2012-13 season to the 2015-16 season, if we had followed this strategy, we would have obtained the following results:

LEAGUE	SEASON	MATCHES	BETS	WON	EARNINGS
GERMANY	2012-13	306	173	66	-232.20
	2013-14	306	156	71	-16.09
	2014-15	306	175	74	-234.39
	2015-16	306	185	83	262.93
FRANCE	2012-13	379	196	80	156.61
	2013-14	380	223	98	322.45
	2014-15	380	249	93	-136.90
	2015-16	380	225	89	-217.83
NETHERLANDS	2012-13	284	108	37	332.49
	2013-14	302	108	28	-137.46
	2014-15	304	126	47	408.83
	2015-16	305	115	33	-138.84
ENGLAND	2012-13	380	249	107	10.81
	2013-14	380	266	115	161.74
	2014-15	379	273	117	-182.97
	2015-16	380	246	104	307.60
ITALY	2012-13	377	192	98	435.42
	2013-14	379	212	89	-91.16
	2014-15	380	277	123	597.47
	2015-16	380	260	100	-91.63
PORTUGAL	2012-13	232	83	23	-149.23
	2013-14	238	75	26	94.88
	2014-15	301	120	39	-359.39
	2015-16	305	128	46	-110.53
PRIMERA	2012-13	380	208	77	-276.91
	2013-14	380	228	90	-85.97
	2014-15	378	229	84	171.68
	2015-16	379	216	77	-288.61
SEGUNDA	2012-13	460	115	41	-39.20
	2013-14	461	105	36	-35.07
	2014-15	451	121	34	-196.99
	2015-16	459	139	53	40.78
TOTAL		11,397	5,781	2,278	282.34

Out of a total of 11,397 games for which we have the information on the odds offered by Pinnacle, we would have bet on 5,781. In these 5,781 games, one of the other six bookies offered higher odds for one of the results (1, X, 2, 1X, 12 or X2) that more than compensated the implicit probability.

Out of these bets, we would have won in 2,278 of them and we would have lost in 3,503. In total, if we had paced €10 bets, we would have earned, after the four years, a total of € 282.34. That is, a small return of 0.4% (282.34 / 5,781 * 10).

This small return is consistent with the greater predictive power that Pinnacle has with respect to other bookies. This edge was around that percentage on average during that period, as we previously saw.

By betting randomly on the 11,397 games that make up this sample, we would have obtained a negative return of approximately -1%, which is the average margin considering the best odds offered by the seven bookies.

In the subset of 5,781 games that we would bet on, the margin is only -0.5%. This is because in these games some bookmakers are offering unusually high odds that represent value relative to Pinnacle's implied probabilities and, in turn, are lowering the margin of the market as a whole.

This means that this strategy would allow us to compensate that margin and also obtain a small profit. Of course, in the real world, we would also have to consider any fees that the bookies may charge us when depositing and withdrawing our money, and the value of the time spent analysing and placing all the bets.

As seen in the table, in several years and in several leagues, we would have lost money. Only, after a very high number of bets, this method would be profitable. Graphically the evolution of the accumulated profit / loss of this series of 5,781 bets would have been the following:

Accumulated profit

It is obvious how volatile the earnings path would have been. After practically two years placing bets we would not have made any kind of profit. While Pinnacle's greater predictive power is an interesting element, it does not provide substantial gains by itself.

HISTORICAL EVOLUTION OF THE PREDICTIVE CAPACITY

It is also worth analysing how the predictive capacity of the bookmakers has evolved over the years. In this book we have already seen that, over time, margins have gone down. Has the predictive power of the odds been increasing in parallel?

To try to answer this question, we have expanded the predictive capacity table to include information from all seasons since 2005.

SEASON	B365	BW	IW	LB	WH	BV	PS	BEST 5	BEST 7
2005-06	38.4%	38.5%	37.8%	38.2%	38.1%	38.3%		38.5%	38.5%
2006-07	39.2%	39.0%	38.6%	39.0%	38.8%	38.9%		39.1%	39.1%
2007-08	39.5%	39.4%	39.3%	39.0%	38.5%	39.4%		39.5%	39.5%
2008-09	41.1%	40.7%	40.7%	40.4%	40.5%	40.8%		41.2%	41.2%
2009-10	43.5%	43.4%	43.1%	42.8%	43.2%	43.6%		43.8%	43.8%
2010-11	43.7%	43.6%	42.9%	43.5%	43.5%	44.0%		43.8%	44.0%
2011-12	43.5%	43.5%	42.8%	43.2%	43.2%	43.8%		43.6%	43.8%
2012-13	43.3%	43.3%	42.8%	42.9%	42.9%	43.5%	43.7%	43.4%	43.7%
2013-14	43.8%	43.7%	43.3%	43.5%	43.4%	44.1%	44.3%	44.0%	44.3%
2014-15	45.9%	45.4%	44.9%	45.5%	45.4%	46.2%	46.2%	45.9%	46.3%
2015-16	44.4%	44.1%	43.5%	44.3%	44.1%	44.7%	44.6%	44.5%	44.7%
2016-17	45.7%	45.6%	45.0%	45.3%	45.3%	45.6%	45.8%	45.7%	45.9%
2017-18	43.0%	43.0%	42.8%	42.8%	42.8%	43.1%	43.2%	43.1%	43.2%
2018-19	40.6%	40.6%	40.4%		40.6%	40.6%	40.7%	40.6%	40.7%
2019-20	40.9%	40.9%	40.8%		41.0%	40.9%	40.9%	41.0%	41.1%

It can be seen how, since 2005, gradually the bookies have got better at predicting the winners of the Spanish La Liga matches. However, this trend seems to have stopped since the 2017-18 season. Until that date the champion and the runner-up used to exceed 90 points per season, something that has not happened again since then.

The predictive capacity of all bookies has evolved evenly. This makes perfect sense since, as we already mentioned, the market does not allow the odds to differ excessively across bookmakers.

As when we were analysing the margins, we have added two more columns to the table. The column called "Best 5" indicates the level of predictive capacity that a hypothetical bookie would have had if it had always offered the highest odds among Bet365, Bwin, Interwetten, Lad Brokes and William Hill. The column "Best 7" indicates the level of predictive capacity that a hypothetical bookie would have had if it had offered the highest odds of all seven bookies, that is, including Bet Victor and Pinnacle too. As it can be seen, every year the column "Best 7" takes higher values than the column "Best 5", given the greater predictive capacity of these last two bookmakers.

For any bettor who uses statistical models, this table will help them to know the minimum predictive capacity that their model must reach, in order to be more predictive than the bookies.

The information in the previous table is graphically shown below:

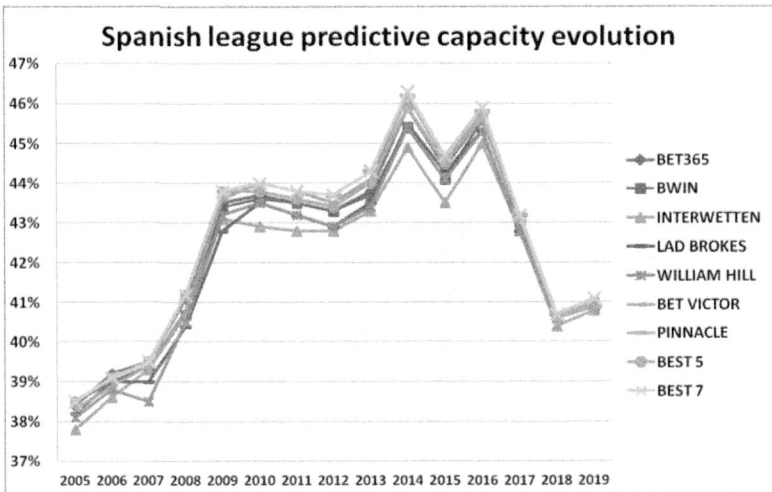

It is possible to wonder if this upward trend, observed from 2005 to 2016, is due to the fact that the odds are increasingly predictive, and therefore more difficult to beat, or if it is due to the fact that the Spanish league has become increasingly "boring".

Indeed, this trend could be showing that in the Spanish league there is a growing number of games with a very clear favourite that wins most of the time. It is therefore very difficult to know how much of this upward trend is due to the fact that the Spanish league is increasingly unequal, and what part could be due to a greater predictive capacity of the bookies.

To try to investigate this point further we have generated the same table for the English Premier League:

SEASON	B365	BW	IW	LB	WH	BV	PS	BEST 5	BEST 7
2005-06	42.5%	42.4%	41.6%	42.3%	42.2%	42.7%		42.5%	42.6%
2006-07	41.2%	41.1%	40.6%	40.9%	40.8%	41.2%		41.3%	41.3%
2007-08	43.7%	43.1%	42.5%	42.6%	42.7%	43.5%		43.6%	43.7%
2008-09	42.0%	41.6%	41.3%	41.3%	41.8%	41.8%		42.0%	42.0%
2009-10	44.2%	43.7%	43.5%	43.7%	43.9%	44.0%		44.2%	44.3%
2010-11	40.4%	40.2%	39.6%	40.2%	40.1%	40.4%		40.4%	40.4%
2011-12	41.9%	41.7%	41.2%	41.7%	41.5%	42.1%		41.9%	42.1%
2012-13	42.1%	42.0%	41.7%	41.6%	41.5%	42.0%	42.3%	42.1%	42.3%
2013-14	44.2%	43.9%	43.4%	43.6%	43.3%	44.1%	44.4%	44.2%	44.3%
2014-15	42.1%	41.4%	41.2%	41.8%	41.3%	42.0%	42.2%	42.0%	42.1%
2015-16	39.2%	39.0%	38.7%	39.0%	38.8%	39.2%	39.3%	39.2%	39.2%
2016-17	45.1%	44.8%	44.3%	44.8%	44.5%	45.1%	45.1%	45.0%	45.1%
2017-18	44.3%	44.1%	43.5%	44.0%	43.9%	44.4%	44.3%	44.2%	44.4%
2018-19	46.3%	46.0%	45.6%		46.0%	46.3%	46.2%	46.2%	46.3%
2019-20	42.8%	42.7%	42.5%		42.8%	42.8%	42.8%	42.8%	42.9%

If we graphically represent the information above, we obtain the following diagram:

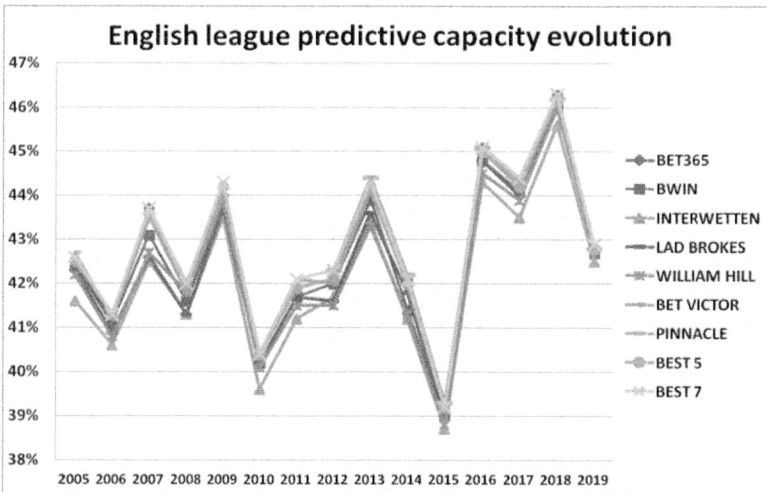

In the case of the Premier League there is no clear trend. It is observed that in some seasons (2007, 2009, 2013, 2016, 2018) the bookies predicted much better than in others. The 2015-16 season shows the lowest level of accuracy in the last fifteen years. This was probably due, not to the fact that the bookies suddenly became worse forecasters, but to the fact that the 2015-16 season was extremely unusual in England: A team that had been promoted two seasons earlier, Leicester, won the championship, while the previous season's winner, Chelsea, came in 10[th78].

It is clear, therefore, that these series serve to measure the extent to which there has been a high or low number of unexpected results in each season. We have not clarified, however, whether or not during the last fifteen years the odds have become more predictive.

What would happen if we plotted the graph above for several leagues? If we observed an upward trend in most of them, we would have an indication that, in general terms, the odds have become more predictive and therefore more difficult to beat.

If we calculate the level of accuracy of the odds of these eight leagues, the previous six plus the Spanish First Division and the English Premier League, over the last fifteen years, we obtain the following table:

SEASON	B365	BW	IW	LB	WH	BV	PS	BEST 5	BEST 7
2005-06	40.0%	40.1%	39.5%	39.9%	39.9%	40.1%		40.2%	40.2%
2006-07	39.9%	39.8%	39.4%	39.7%	39.6%	39.8%		40.0%	40.1%
2007-08	39.9%	39.7%	39.3%	39.4%	39.3%	39.7%		39.9%	39.9%
2008-09	40.6%	40.3%	39.9%	40.1%	40.2%	40.2%		40.6%	40.6%
2009-10	41.7%	41.4%	41.1%	41.2%	41.5%	41.6%		41.8%	41.8%
2010-11	40.5%	40.3%	39.8%	40.2%	40.3%	40.6%		40.6%	40.7%
2011-12	41.7%	41.6%	41.0%	41.3%	41.4%	42.0%		41.8%	41.9%
2012-13	41.3%	41.2%	40.8%	40.9%	40.9%	41.4%	41.3%	41.3%	41.5%
2013-14	41.7%	41.6%	41.2%	41.4%	41.3%	41.8%	41.9%	41.7%	42.0%
2014-15	41.6%	41.1%	40.8%	41.3%	41.1%	41.7%	41.7%	41.6%	41.8%
2015-16	41.3%	41.0%	40.6%	41.1%	40.8%	41.4%	41.4%	41.3%	41.5%
2016-17	42.3%	42.2%	41.6%	42.1%	41.9%	42.3%	42.4%	42.3%	42.4%
2017-18	43.1%	43.1%	42.5%	42.8%	42.7%	43.2%	43.1%	43.1%	43.3%
2018-19	43.0%	42.9%	42.6%		42.9%	43.1%	43.1%	43.1%	43.2%
2019-20	41.6%	41.6%	41.3%		41.6%	41.6%	41.7%	41.7%	41.8%

[78] To put into context the unusualness of the 2015-16 season, it should be remembered that at the start Leicester's victory as Premier League champion was paid 5,000 to 1.

This information is graphically represented below:

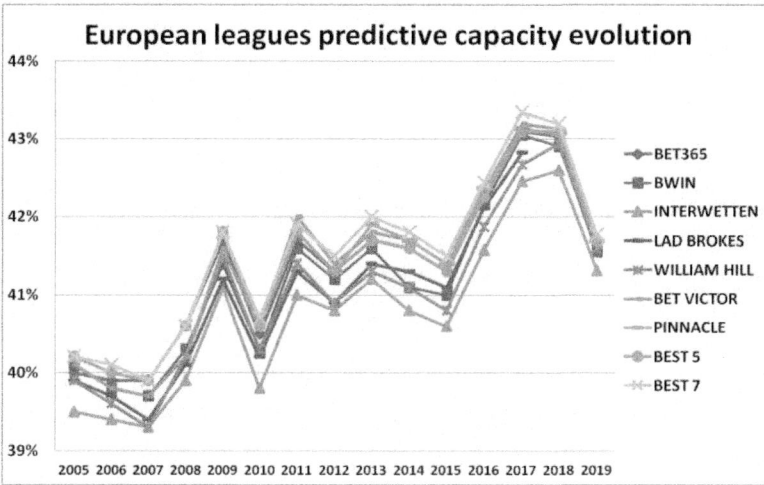

European leagues predictive capacity evolution

Legend: BET365, BWIN, INTERWETTEN, LAD BROKES, WILLIAM HILL, BET VICTOR, PINNACLE, BEST 5, BEST 7

Years: 2005 2006 2007 2008 2009 2010 2011 2012 2013 2014 2015 2016 2017 2018 2019

Clearly the margins charged by bookmakers have dropped significantly since 2005. Probably the predictive capacity has also increased, although the trend is less clear. It is possible that the predictive capacity of the odds has a certain limit and that they are already close to it. Therefore, the remaining room for improvement would be small[79].

Annex 5 of this book includes the same tables and graphs for the following championships:

- Spanish Second Division.
- German Bundesliga.
- Italian Serie A.
- French Ligue 1.
- Dutch Eredivise.
- Portuguese Primeira Liga.

---

[79] In this sense, Joseph Buchdahl, in his book Squares & Sharps, Suckers & Sharps, shows how the probabilities assigned by the bookmakers reflect, already with high precision, the real probability of occurrence of each result.

PREDICTIVE CAPACITY PRIOR TO THE MATCH

It is also interesting to analyse what happens to the predictive capacity of the odds, from the moment the bookies begin to accept bets, until the moment the match begins.

In the chapter on margin evolution before the match, we saw how the margin tended to decrease, from the moment a bookie begins to accept bets until kickoff. We can use the same sample to also analyse how the predictive capacity of the odds evolves during the same period.

The following table shows the level of accuracy of the initial odds, intermediate odds and final odds offered for a group of matches from various European leagues:

LEAGUE	INITIAL ACCURACY	INTERMI. ACCURACY	FINAL ACCURACY
GERMANY	41.23%	41.39%	41.53%
FRANCE	40.43%	40.66%	41.05%
NETHERLANDS	41.88%	42.05%	41.98%
ENGLAND	42.91%	43.15%	43.33%
ITALY	41.04%	41.11%	41.16%
SPAIN LA LIGA	45.45%	45.53%	45.87%
SPAIN SECOND	37.89%	37.65%	37.57%
TOTAL	**41.38%**	**41.48%**	**41.61%**

Although we only have information on about 130 games for each league, it can be seen how, in most cases, the odds tend to better reflect what will happen in the game as kickoff approaches[80]. This phenomenon occurs for several reasons:

- As the start of the game approaches, specific aspects that may influence its outcome (for example, probable line-ups, injuries or sanctions, weather, tactical scheme that each team will use, etc.) are disclosed. As this additional information is known, it is possible to make more accurate forecasts, both by bettors and by bookmakers.

---

[80] The purpose of this table is to show how, in general terms, odds tend to be more and more predictive over time. The fact that this phenomenon is not observed for a specific league does not mean that this league behaves differently. This exception is probably due to the small number of observations.

- From the moment the bookies begin to accept bets for a match, the behaviour of the market allows them to fine-tune their odds. If the offered odds, in the opinion of many bettors, are especially generous, the bookmaker will be forced to reduce them, so as not to become excessively exposed.
- Several days or weeks before the start of a match only a few bookmakers offer odds for that event. As the game approaches, more bookies start offering odds for the same match. This forces bookies that are not aligned with the market, and therefore with a greater probability of error, to adjust their odds to avoid being exposed to possible arbitrage situations. This phenomenon also allows bookies to observe what odds their competitors are offering and adjust theirs with this new information[81].

The percentages in the previous table have been calculated considering the highest odds offered by several bookmakers for each match. The highest odds for each outcome tend to change (increasing or decreasing) thus becoming more and more accurate. Also, the predictive capacity of the odds offered individually by each bookmaker tends to increase as the match approaches. The following table shows this phenomenon for the odds offered by Betfair:

LEAGUE	INITIAL ACCURACY	INTERMI. ACCURACY
GERMANY	39.43%	39.55%
FRANCE	40.89%	40.94%
NETHERLANDS	40.62%	40.87%
ENGLAND	41.39%	41.59%
ITALY	40.70%	40.61%
SPAIN LA LIGA	45.93%	45.89%
SPAIN SECOND	37.26%	37.24%
TOTAL	**40.75%**	**40.82%**

---

[81] When a single bookmaker offers bets for a certain match, there should be no possibility of arbitrage, since that bookie will have incorporated its margin into the published odds. It is only as other bookies publish their own odds that arbitrage opportunities may temporarily arise, while the market resettles through the movement of odds. On the other hand, it is common practice among bookmakers, when exposed to a certain result, to resort to exchange markets to balance their positions. This rebalancing will be much less expensive if the odds at which they accepted bets are not significantly misaligned with the market.

In short, grossly erroneous odds will tend to disappear as kickoff approaches. **A bettor who succeeds in placing the majority of his bets at higher odds than the final odds offered by the market will be well on his way to making a profit in the medium term**.

Let's imagine a situation in which three bookies are offering the following odds for the same game:

	LOCAL ODDS	DRAW ODDS	VISITOR ODDS	OVER-ROUND	MARGIN
BOOKIE 1	2.00	3.20	4.25	104.78%	4.56%
BOOKIE 2	2.00	3.10	4.50	104.48%	4.29%
BOOKIE 3	2.00	3.30	4.00	105.30%	5.04%
BEST ODDS	2.00	3.30	4.50	102.53%	2.46%
IMPLIED PROBABILITY	48.77%	29.56%	21.67%		

Let's imagine that, 12 hours later, the odds offered have changed and now are:

	LOCAL ODDS	DRAW ODDS	VISITOR ODDS	OVER-ROUND	MARGIN
BOOKIE 1	1.95	3.25	4.45	104.52%	4.33%
BOOKIE 2	1.90	3.30	4.70	104.21%	4.04%
BOOKIE 3	2.00	3.30	4.00	105.30%	5.04%
BEST ODDS	2.00	3.30	4.70	101.58%	1.56%
IMPLIED PROBABILITY	49.22%	29.83%	20.95%		

What happened in those 12 hours? Bookie 1 and Bookie 2 have moved their lines. In both cases they have reduced the odds offered for the local victory and have increased the odds offered for the draw and for the away victory. They probably did this because they received more bets than they expected in favour of the home victory, and less than they expected, in favour of the draw and the away victory.

For its part, Bookie 3 has not changed its odds. Maybe it did not move them simply because it did not receive more bets in favour of the local victory than it expected or simply because it is a slower bookie to react, that prefers to adjust its odds less frequently.

In this new situation, although the best odds offered in the market for the local victory remain at 2.00, the implicit probability that this result will occur has

190

changed. Before it was 48.77%, and now it has increased to 49.22%. Why? The implied probability of the home win has changed because the market overround has changed thanks to the higher odds now offered for the away win (it is now 4.7 compared to 4.5).

In this new situation there is no possibility of arbitrage, and no bookie offers odds that compensate the implicit probability. However, something interesting has happened. Apparently, there is greater interest in the local victory than the bookies had initially anticipated. How will the odds continue to evolve in the next few hours? Obviously, it cannot be known for sure, but one thing is clear. Initially, the bettors interested in a home win could get the best available odds by betting at any of the three bookies (all offered the same odds). Now the situation has changed. The bettors looking for the best odds for a local victory have to go necessarily to bookie 3. It is likely, therefore, that, once bookie 1 and bookie 2 have moved their odds, bookie 3 will shortly have to move them as well, given the increased action it is likely to experience.

This phenomenon makes the movement of the best odds in the betting markets have a certain inertia. **After a movement in a certain direction, the odds are more likely to continue moving in the same direction, than in the opposite direction**. The movement of the odds is not a purely random walk, but rather, the past behaviour provides relevant information about the possible future trend.

To illustrate this point more clearly, we are going to analyse in detail the trend of the odds using the sample that we have. Given that the odds have been recorded in 3 different moments, it is possible to see how they moved between the initial moment and the intermediate moment, and study if that movement foretold, in any way, the movement between the intermediate moment and the final moment.

Out of 932 matches, in 401 of them, the odds evolved in such a way that the probability of local victory was greater according to the intermediate odds than according to the initial odds. Out of these 401 cases:

- In 212, the final odds indicated an even greater probability of home victory than the intermediate odds.
- In 145, the final odds indicated a lower probability of home victory than the intermediate odds.

- In 44, the final odds indicated a local victory probability equal to that of the intermediate odds.

That is, in 52.87% of the cases (212/401), the trend in the movement of the odds in favour of the local victory continued. Only in 36.16% of the cases (145/401) the trend in the movement of odds reversed. In the remaining 10.97% of the cases (44/401) there were no changes in the implicit probabilities, between the intermediate moment and the final moment.

This phenomenon of inertia in the odds is also observed when the probability of away victory increases. From the same sample of 932 games, in 389 of them, the probability of away victory was higher according to the intermediate odds than according to the initial odds. Out of these 389 cases:

- In 202, the final odds indicated an away win probability even higher than the intermediate probability.
- In 140, the final odds showed a lower probability of away victory than the intermediate odds.
- In 47, the final odds indicated a probability of visiting victory equal to the intermediate odds.

Clearly, when the highest odds available on the market are moving in favour of a specific outcome, the move is more likely to continue than to reverse itself. The following table summarizes the information analysed:

	TOTAL	IT CONTINUES	IT REVERSES	SAME PROBABILITY
LOCAL VICTORY TREND	401	212	145	44
AWAY VICTORY TREND	389	202	140	47

When bettors perceive that the odds for a given outcome are generous, it is normal that, as the match approaches, they will shorten, thus reflecting the perception that the real probability of that result is higher than the probability initially estimated by the bookmakers. In the case of a tie, given its more ambiguous nature, it is more difficult to observe this phenomenon clearly.

As we have seen, as a general rule, as the odds offered for a match evolve, they will tend to better reflect the real probabilities of each outcome. **Not only the odds themselves, but the trend observed in their movement, help to predict what will happen during the match.**

192

Can this inefficiency be exploited to achieve better results as a bettor? To answer this question, let's imagine 2 players with the following strategies:

- Player 1: always bets in favour of the local victory following the trend observed in the odds. That is, he bets in favour of the home team, using the best available intermediate odds, when he sees that the probability of victory has increased since the publication of the initial odds.
- Player 2: uses the opposite strategy. Bets in favour of the visiting team, using the best intermediate odds, when the probability of a local victory has increased.

Player 1 bets in favour of outcomes for which the odds are shortening, while Player 2 bets in favour of outcomes for which the odds are lengthening[82].

With these strategies each player would have obtained the following results:

	TOTAL BETS	WON	EXPECTED WON	WON / EXPECTED WON
PLAYER 1	401	204	191.81	106.35%
PLAYER 2	401	118	121.87	96.82%

Player 1 would have placed 401 bets in favour of the local victory and would have won 204 of them. His number of bets won would have been 6% higher than expected according to the probabilities assigned by the bookies.

Player 2 would have placed 401 bets in favour of the away win and would have won 118 of them. His number of bets won would have been 3% lower than expected according to the probabilities assigned by the bookies.

Obviously, Player 1 wins more bets than Player 2 because he is betting on a more likely outcome (home wins are generally more likely than away wins). However, this is not the point. The point is that player 1, **when betting**

---

[82] Most bookmakers do not show how the odds offered for a given match have evolved over time. This could mean, in practice, the need to check their website several times to track them, and thus see what their trend is. Fortunately, there are websites like www.oddsportal.com where it is recorded how the odds offered for a match have been moving since the publication of the initial odds. This makes it possible to conveniently see what the trend has been.

according to the market trend, wins more bets than expected while player 2, **when betting against the market trend, wins fewer bets than expected**.

Do these results mean that it would be enough to see what the market trend is and follow it in order to make money gambling? Unfortunately, this is not the case for several reasons:

- The sample used in this analysis, with only 401 bets, is small, so the results obtained must be taken with caution.
- The analysis does not consider the possible commissions for deposits or withdrawals and assumes that both player 1 and player 2 have open accounts at all bookies.
- The simulation assumes that the bookie that is offering the best intermediate odds would always accept the bet. This assumption is too optimistic since, as we previously mentioned, the bookie that offers the best odds for an outcome for which the other bookies have already been shortening their odds is probably, precisely, a bookmaker that usually imposes significant restrictions and limits on its users[83].

This last point is the most important of the three. When analysing what results we would have obtained with a certain strategy, it is always necessary to consider that historical odds may not have always been available odds in practice to all bettors.

In any case, it is clear that, as a general rule, a bettor will do better in the long run going in favour of the market than going against it.

There is a type of bettor that tries to make money by trading on betting exchange markets like Betfair. His strategy consists of trying to place 2 bets: one of them in favour of a result and the other against that same result, in such a way that the different odds allow him to ensure a small profit regardless of the actual outcome of the game. This type of trading bettor does not directly benefit from arbitrage opportunities, which are based on odds offered at the same time by different bookies in order to lock in a profit, but instead takes advantage of the volatility of the odds to try to place his two bets in two

---

[83] It is a common practice among certain bookmakers to publish generous odds from time to time to try to attract new clients. A new user of one of these bookies will normally be able to take advantage of these odds for a few occasions. Unfortunately, soon after, he will discover that, if he has made a profit with this strategy, the bookie will only allow him to place very small bets or that his account has been cancelled.

different moments. The existence of inertia in the behaviour of the odds can be a hazard for this type of bettor, since it increases the risk that he will not be able to place his two bets in a profitable way.

A good trading bettor should therefore also take the market trend into account when placing his bets.

Let's see what would have happened if we had tried to take advantage of the market trend by following the next strategy. We observe the intermediate odds:

1. If we see that the probability of local victory is increasing, we place a bet in favour of that result hoping that the movement of the odds will continue so that later on two additional bets can be placed, one in favour of the away victory and another one in favour of the tie. All this in order to generate a risk-free green book.
2. Similarly, if we saw that the probability of a visiting victory was increasing, we would first place the bet in favour of the visiting team and later try to ensure a profit by betting in favour of the local victory and the draw

Would this strategy have paid off?[84]

In the case of the sample of 401 games in which the probability of local victory is increasing, only in 80 cases the movement of the odds would have been intense enough to be able to achieve a green book by taking advantage of the final odds paid for the tie and for the visiting victory. The average yield in these 80 games would have been 1.76%.

In the remaining 321 games we would not have been able to close the green book. Therefore, we would have had to choose between two options:

1. Placing the bets in favour of the draw and the visitor victory to avoid being exposed to the result of the match. This would have meant incurring in a small loss (red book).
2. Maintaining the bet in favour of the home team and running the risk of winning or losing money depending on the result of the match.

---

[84] To perform this analysis we use the best odds offered by the different bookmakers as an approximation of the different odds offered by the exchange markets at different times before a match.

With the first option, we would not have been able to make money with the sample of 401 games. The small winnings from the 80 green book games would not be enough to make up for the small losses from each of the 321 red book games. On average we would have lost 1.89% of the total wagered amount. In any case, the yield of this strategy (placing the bet in favour of the local victory with the intermediate odds and always placing the bets in favour of the draw and the visitor victory with the final odds) would be better than the intermediate odds margin and the final odds margin. We would therefore have incurred a lower loss thanks to the fact that we would be following the trend:

INTERMEDIATE MARGIN	FINAL MARGIN	STRATEGY YIELD
2.32%	2.01%	1.89%

With the second option, in the 321 games with a bet in favour of the local team, we would have obtained the following results:

TOTAL BETS	WON	EXPECTED WON	WON / EXPECTED WON
321	151	151.41	99.72%

In these 321 bets we would also incur a small loss. This result is very interesting. De facto we have once again divided the 401 games with a tendency in favour of the local team, but this time into two groups:

- 80 in which the local team odds continue to shorten. These matches generate a profit whether we use them for trading or if we simply bet in favour of the local victory.
- 321 in which the trend in favour of the home team is softer. In these matches there is no value in the local victory odds, regardless of whether we use a normal trading strategy or actually bet.

By observing the intermediate odds, we can know what trend they have followed up to that moment. We also know that the trend is more likely to hold than to reverse. What we do not know is in what games in particular the trend will continue and in which ones it will not. If we could identify which ones are going to keep it, we could make money with them through normal bets or through trading. Matches that change trend will also generate a loss regardless of the strategy used.

When there is value in the odds, this value can be exploited in various ways. If we consider that the line has not yet moved enough to represent the real probabilities of the results, we will try to take advantage of it. On the other hand, if we think that the line has overreacted, the correct strategy would be to not take any risk. If there is no value in the starting odds, there is no possible strategy to obtain a recurrent profit.

Something similar occurs with the sample of 389 games in which the probability of away victory is increasing. Only in 78 of them would the movement of the odds had been intense enough to lock in profit of 1.61%. The strategy, as in the case of the sample with the shortening local odds, would have meant in the 389 games a reduction in margin, but not a profit:

INTERMEDIATE MARGIN	FINAL MARGIN	STRATEGY YIELD
2.41%	1.90%	1.78%

In the 78 green book games, a profit would also have been obtained by keeping the risk open.

TOTAL BETS	WON	EXPECTED WON	WON / EXPECTED WON
78	35	27.62	126.70%

In the remaining 311 games, if the risk had been kept open, the following results would have been obtained:

TOTAL BETS	WON	EXPECTED WON	WON / EXPECTED WON
311	83	94.25	88.06%

In summary, it can be concluded that **the trend of the odds is an interesting and relevant factor when forecasting or betting, since it allows to marginally improve the return. The trend is relevant for strategies based on normal bets but also for trading strategies. However, by itself, it is not enough to ensure profits on a regular basis.**

EUROPEANS VS ASIANS

Many of us are used to placing bets on who will win the game. Due to the influence of the old football pools, we usually think in terms of 1, X, 2. We think that the match will end with a local victory, a draw, or a visitor victory.

In matches between even teams, having to choose between 1, X, 2 can be interesting. In unequal matches, such as those played by Real Madrid or Barcelona in their turf against teams in the middle or lower zone of the table, there is little doubt about who is going to win. It is much more interesting to ask yourself **by how many goals they are going to win**.

The odds offered for the victory of Real Madrid or Barcelona can be less than 1.1 in many games. The probabilities that they win are around or exceed 90% so the reward for winning the bet is small. But what is the probability that they will win by at least 2 goals or at least 3 goals or at least 4 goals….? Obviously, the more goals the bet demands, the riskier it will be and the higher the odds.

This type of bets is called handicap bets.

Let's see a real example. For the match between Barcelona - Ath. Bilbao on January 31, 2021, the following odds were offered:

1X2 ODDS		
1	X	2
1.47	4.73	6.61

ASIAN HANDICAP ODDS			
BARCELONA -2.5	4.02	ATH. BILBAO +2.5	1.26
BARCELONA -2.25	3.76	ATH. BILBAO +2.25	1.29
BARCELONA -2	3.31	ATH. BILBAO +2	1.35
BARCELONA -1.75	2.69	ATH. BILBAO +1.75	1.50
BARCELONA -1.5	2.29	ATH. BILBAO +1.5	1.67
BARCELONA -1.25	2.05	ATH. BILBAO +1.25	1.83
BARCELONA -1	1.76	ATH. BILBAO +1	2.14
BARCELONA -0.75	1.59	ATH. BILBAO +0.75	2.45
BARCELONA -0.5	1.47	ATH. BILBAO +0.5	2.75

To figure out the winner of an Asian handicap bet, the number of goals scored by each team during the match must be added to the handicap coefficients. If, after applying the handicap, the team we have bet on gets a number greater than 0, we have won the bet. For example, if we bet Barcelona -2.5 and the match ends 4 - 1 we will have won, since 4 - 1 - 2.5 = 0.5. However, if we bet Barcelona -2.5 and the match ends 2 - 0 we lose, since 2 - 0 - 2.5 = -0.5. Finally, if we bet Ath. Bilbao +1.5 and the match ends up with a victory for Barcelona by just one goal we will have won the bet, since 0 - 1 + 1.5 = 0.5.

If, when applying the handicap, the result is exactly 0 the bet is considered void. For example, if we had bet Barcelona -2 and the match had ended 4 - 2 we would recover the wagered amount without any gain or loss[85].

If we bet Barcelona -0.75, we actually place 2 bets. Half of the amount we bet will be treated as a bet on Barcelona -1 and the other half will be treated as a bet on Barcelona -0.5. Likewise, if we bet Ath. Bilbao +1.75 we will be betting half of our money on Ath. Bilbao +1.5 and the other half on Ath. Bilbao +2.

For all intents and purposes, betting Barcelona -0.5 is the same as betting that Barcelona will win the match by placing a moneyline bet. Equally betting Ath. Bilbao +0.5 means betting that the match will end up in a draw (X) or with a visitor victory (2). As surprising as it may seem, the same bookmaker may be simultaneously offering different odds for the same outcome in its 1X2 market and in its Asian handicap market, so it is always a good idea to check.

Out of all the possible Asian handicap markets for a given match, the one that tends to concentrate the highest volume of bets is the one in which the odds are closer to 2. For example, in the previous case it would be Barcelona -1.25 at odds 2.05 and Bilbao +1.25 at 1.83. In this market in which the handicap balances the probabilities of home win and away win, it is in which more bookies operate, there is, therefore, more competition and the bettor faces, consequently, lower margins[86].

As we have seen on several occasions throughout the book, lower margins and higher volume of bets are usually synonymous with more predictive odds. This means that **if, for the same match, there are different odds in the 1X2 market and in the Asian handicap market, the correct opinion is more likely to be that of the Asian handicap market than the other way around**.

---

[85] There is another less known type of handicap called European handicap. In European handicap, you bet on the local victory, draw or away victory applying a predetermined number of goals. Unlike in Asian handicap, in European handicap there are no void bets.
[86] Normally, these markets also allow bets of a larger amount than the 1X2 markets.

Let's see this with a practical example. For a match between Celta and Real Sociedad the following odds are offered:

1X2 ODDS		
2.58	3.2	3.0

ASIAN HANDICAP ODDS			
CELTA -0.5	2.55	R. SOCIEDAD +0.5	1.59
CELTA +0.5	1.45	R. SOCIEDAD -0.5	3.05

With these odds, if we wanted to bet in favour of Celta's victory, our best option would be to take the 2.58 odds offered by the 1X2 market. If, on the contrary, we wanted to bet in favour of the victory of Real Sociedad, the best option would be the 3.05 odds offered by the Asian handicap market.

In this example the 1X2 market thinks that Celta's win is less likely than the Asian handicap. The 1X2 market thinks that the Real Sociedad's win is more likely than the Asian handicap market. Well, since the 1X2 market makes mistakes more often than the Asian handicap market, we should bet in favour of Celta's victory.

To put it in another way, if we see that the 1X2 market offers higher odds for the home win or for the away win than the Asian handicap market, it may be interesting to take those higher odds.

The following table shows the results of betting in favour of the home win in the following three situations:

- When the highest odds are in the 1X2 market.
- When the highest odds are in the Asian handicap market.
- When both markets offer the same odds for a home win.

SITUATION	GAMES	1X2 MARGIN	AH MARGIN	WON / EXP. WON	YIELD LOCAL WIN BET
HIGHEST ODDS IN 1X2	8,285	2.7%	3.9%	102.7%	0.1%
HIGHEST IN HANDICAP	10,187	3.2%	1.8%	99.0%	-2.1%
SAME ODDS IN BOTH	3,284	2.9%	2.9%	99.1%	-4.0%
TOTAL	21,756	2.9%	3.1%	100.9%	-1.4%

If the highest odds are in the moneyline market the yield is +0.1%, but if the highest odds are in the Asian handicap market the yield is -2.1%.

One of the most interesting features of the Asian handicap is that it allows you to bet on any match without assuming an excessive level of risk. For example, let's consider again the match between Barcelona and Bilbao described at the beginning of this chapter. We may think that Bilbao are going to do better than expected, that they are going to stand up to Barcelona. We do not know if Bilbao will get points at the Camp Nou, but our opinion is that the game is significantly more even than what the market thinks. In this case we could, for example, bet on Bilbao +1.5 at odds 1.67. We would win the bet if Bilbao manage to win, tie, or if they lose by just 1 goal against Barça. Using this technique, we can bet in favour of the underdogs controlling our risk and reducing the volatility of our profits and losses. We avoid betting long shots.

Likewise, if we think that a favourite team is going to win its next match by a landslide, we can use the handicap to bet at higher odds than those of a simple victory.

Always betting at similar odds has the advantage of being able to know a priori what hit rate we need to make money. If I place all my bets at odds close to 2, I know that I need to hit at least 50% in order not to lose money. If I place them at odds close to 3, I will need to get 1/3 right, etc.

If I use very different odds in my different bets, my winnings will depend, not only on my hit rate, but also on which specific bets I win. For example, if you place several bets at low odds and some at high odds you can make a profit in the short term even losing the low odds bets, if you are lucky enough to win the high odds bets. However, if your hit rate is lower than expected, sooner or later you will end up losing money. It is, therefore, essential to track, not only your yield, but also to calculate whether the number of bets won is lower or higher than expected.

In summary, the bettor who is not familiar with the Asian handicap market should familiarize himself with it, being aware of its greater predictive capacity. In order to be able to quickly compare the odds offered in the moneyline (1X2) and Asian handicap markets in the different bookies, it is essential to use a website or application that collects this information and updates it continuously[87].

---

[87] At the time of writing these pages, as we have previously mentioned, the www.oddsportal.com website is an excellent comparator for this task.

PREDICT BETTER THAN THE BOOKIE

It has happened to all of us. At some point, as we bet, we find ourselves on a good streak. At that moment a hope begins to grow in our minds. Maybe I'm good at this, maybe I've found a way to make money.

How can we know that the results we are obtaining are not the product of just luck? Again, statistics have the answer.

Let's imagine that we normally bet at odds 2 and that in our last 100 bets we have obtained a return of 10%. Do I have the right to think that I am good?

The reality is that 1 out of every 6 times that we place a sequence of 100 bets at odds 2 we will obtain a yield of 10% or higher **by pure randomness**. For the same reason, 1 out of 6 times we will obtain a yield below -10%. 100 bets are not a long enough series to know if the results we are obtaining are the product of chance or due to our expertise.

If we were able to maintain a 10% profitability after 1,000 bets at odds 2 then we could have full confidence in our abilities. Such profitability after such a long sequence only occurs by sheer luck 1 out of every 1,309 times.

The following table shows the possibility of obtaining a return of 5%, 10%, 15% or 20% by pure randomness after a series of 100, 250, 500 or 1,000 bets at odds 2:

ODDS 2	NUMBER OF BETS AND YIELD			
	100	250	500	1.000
5%	3	4	7	17
10%	6	17	79	1.309
15%	15	116	2.675	1.081.374
20%	45	1.411	316.628	$12*10^9$

Who is better? A tipster that has obtained a 10% yield after 500 bets or another one that has achieved a 20% yield after 100? This table provides us with the answer. The first tipster is better because the probability that their results are exclusively a product of luck (1 in 79) is less than that of the second (1 of 45).

If we bet at average odds of 1.5 or 5 the tables would be the ones on the next page.

202

ODDS 1.5	NUMBER OF BETS AND YIELD			
	100	250	500	1.000
5%	4	7	19	92
10%	14	111	2.478	932.786
15%	99	8,701	10.725.277	$12*10^{12}$
20%	1.655	6.780.429	$49*10^{11}$	$19*10^{23}$

ODDS 5	NUMBER OF BETS AND YIELD			
	100	250	500	1.000
5%	2	2	3	4
10%	3	4	7	15
15%	4	7	17	81
20%	5	14	54	638

As it can be seen, the higher the average odds, the greater the number of bets that are necessary to tell if the yield obtained is the product of chance or not.

These tables can also be used in another way. Imagine that **you know** that your expected profitability **in the long term** is 10% betting at odds 2. What is the probability that in a series of 250 bets you will not make money? And that your yield will be 15% or more after a series of 500 bets? It is 1 in 7. That is, the percentages in the rows should be interpreted as deviations, positive or negative, on your expected profitability. If you do not have any type of advantage over the bookie, you must assume that your expected return is zero.

All these tables have been prepared assuming that the implicit margin charged by the bookie is close to 0%. In practice that will not be the case. If, for example, we have obtained a yield of 8% and we know that on average we faced an implicit margin of 2% then we should look at the 10% row to know our level of skill as forecasters even though our real profitability has been lower. In other words, if after a long sequence of bets, you have neither lost nor made money, it means that you know how to predict better than the bookie, but only so to compensate for the margin it is charging you[88].

---

[88] All calculations in this chapter are based on hypothesis testing for mean differences assuming a t-distribution. At the following website https://www.football-data.co.uk/blog/P-value_calculator.xlsx you can download a file created by Joseph Buchdahl to calculate these probabilities for other combinations of yield, number of bets and average odds.

THE PERFECT OFFICE POOL

In several countries, it is common, before a match or a particularly relevant tournament (World Cup, Euro, Copa América, Champions League, Copa Libertadores, etc ...), to make small bets between friends or colleagues to see who predicts better the result, the classified teams, the winners, or the scorers. In Spain the expression "hacer una porra" is used to refer to this type of game, while in Latin America the word "polla" is sometimes used. In English they are called "sweepstakes", "betting pools" or "office pools".

Each participant usually contributes a small amount of money. The money raised is used to pay the prize to whoever wins. Here we already observe a first difference between these games and how bookmakers work: in general, there is no implicit overround of any kind. All the money raised goes to prizes. No one keeps a margin.

Another big difference with betting on a bookmaker is that there are no odds. All results that are guessed correctly are usually equally relevant. For example, in a betting pool about the World Cup, you get the same points by guessing right that Brazil will beat Costa Rica than guessing right that Mexico will beat Germany.

What can be done to improve our predictions in these games? One possible strategy is to use **the odds of the bookmakers to guide us when making our predictions**. This is because these games do not consist in looking for possible errors in the odds but in **predicting better than the other participants**.

As we have seen in this book, the odds provided by the bookmakers are in most cases accurate and serve to approximate in a very reliable way the real probabilities of each result. If we complete our betting pool predictions following the betting market, we will be making better forecasts than most of the other participants in the game and will substantially increase our chances of winning.

Some people may think that mimicking bookmakers' forecasts on an office pool is cheating. In my opinion it is not. The forecasts of the bookies are public and it is not even necessary to open an account to be able to access them. It is therefore information that everyone can use if they wish. It is just as legitimate to use that information as looking at the results of previous matches to get a better idea of the level of each team or asking for an opinion to a football expert relative.

Some betting pools do not allow two participants to select the same score. For example, in an office pool about the next Boca - River once someone has picked that the result will be 2 - 0 no one else can select that same result. In these cases, it is always advisable to enter the game as soon as possible to avoid that the most probable outcomes have already been taken.

On the other hand, in other betting pools it is possible that several participants make the same predictions. In this case, the best strategy is to wait as much as possible until the deadline to participate since as we have seen in previous chapters, the odds that we will use as the basis of our prediction will be, as the event approaches, more reliable. Also, by waiting as much as possible until the deadline, we reduce the risk that a key player is injured after having chosen him, for example, as our favourite top scorer or golden ball of the tournament.

When making our forecasts according to the odds we will see that, in general, it is convenient to bet that just a few goals will be scored. This is due to the fact that, although in approximately 50% of the matches 2 goals or fewer are scored and in the other 50% 3 or more goals are scored, **the range of possible results is much more limited when 2 goals or fewer are scored**.

For example, in matches in which just one goal is scored there can only be two possible outcomes: (1 - 0, 0 - 1). In matches where two goals are scored, there can be three possible outcomes (2 - 0, 1 - 1, 0 - 2). In matches in which three goals are scored, up to four possible outcomes can occur (3 - 0, 2 - 1, 1 - 2, 0 - 3) and so on. Reviewing the entire historical database used for this book, we see that the most frequent results in football matches since 2000 have been:

FINAL SCORE FREQUENCY					
LOCAL WIN		**DRAW**		**VISITOR WIN**	
1-0	10.9%	1-1	12.3%	0-1	7.6%
2-1	9.1%	0-0	8.0%	1-2	6.5%
2-0	7.9%	2-2	5.1%	0-2	4.4%
3-1	4.3%	3-3	1.0%	1-3	2.5%
3-0	4.1%	4-4	0.1%	0-3	1.9%
3-2	2.5%	5-5	0.01%	2-3	1.8%
OTHERS	6.8%	OTHERS	0.001%	OTHERS	3.2%
TOTAL	**45.6%**	**TOTAL**	**26.6%**	**TOTAL**	**27.8%**

If someone asks us who will win a game and we have no idea of the level of the teams, the best thing to say is that the local team will win. However, if someone ask us what the exact score of a match will be, it is best to say that it will end up 1-1 since that is the most frequent result.

GOAL DIFFERENCE			
LOCAL WIN		AWAY WIN	
+1	22.9%	+1	16.2%
+2	13.2%	+2	7.5%
+3	6.1%	+3	2.8%
+4	2.3%	+4	1.0%
+5	0.8%	+5	0.3%
+6	0.2%	+6	0.1%
OTHERS	0.1%	OTHERS	0.0%
TOTAL	45.6%	TOTAL	27.8%

If someone asks what goal difference there will be in a game, it is best to say that it will be 0 since 26.6% of the matches end up in a draw. The second-best answer is to say that the home team will win by a single goal as this occurs in 22.9% of matches.

TOTAL NUMBER OF GOALS			
0	8.0%	6	3.5%
1	18.5%	7	1.3%
2	24.6%	8	0.5%
3	21.5%	9	0.1%
4	14.3%	10	0.04%
5	7.6%	OTHERS	0.01%

Finally, if someone asks you how many goals will be scored in the match, the best answer you can give by default is 2. In 24.6% of the matches 2 goals are scored and in 51.1% of the matches, 2 goals or fewer are scored.

Therefore, completing your betting pool with low scores increases your chances of guessing right not only the total number of goals in a game but also the exact score.

The expected number of goals in a match is usually somewhat higher when two teams of very different level face each other and lower when two more even teams face each other. This aspect can also be easily considered in your office pool by looking at the odds offered by the bookmakers for each result.

In general, in 1X2 betting pools it is never advisable to pick a draw since the home victory or the away victory are, in almost all matches, more likely than a draw.

In some countries like Spain, sports betting continues to coexist with the old 1X2 betting pools (quiniela) run by the public lottery. Given that the predictive capacity of the odds of the bookmakers is greater than that of the quinielistas, some specialists use the information of the former to try to make money in the latter[89]. It is a strategy, as we mentioned earlier, based on the idea, not of predicting perfectly, but of predicting better than the others.

---

[89] Watch, for example, this video: https://www.youtube.com/watch?v=ZWZxyjbyUCs (in Spanish)

SECTION 3: TIPS FOR BETTORS

The reader who gets here after having read all the preceding chapters will have by now a clear understating about how difficult it is to beat the market and make a profit by betting.

Therefore, the first thing to do is to seriously consider the possibility of not betting at all. Deciding **not to bet is an option that will ensure that you do better than the vast majority of bettors**. From a purely economic point of view, it is probably the most rational decision. It must also be borne in mind that the world of gambling is, in part, rigged: many bookmakers end up limiting or expelling systematic winners.

Not gambling is an obligation if you are a minor and it is good that it is this way. If you are under the legal age to do so, don't gamble. That prohibition has been put in place to protect you. Dedicate yourself to study in order to have a profession tomorrow. There are no shortcuts to economic prosperity[90].

Betting is also not an option if you are compulsive gambler or run the risk of becoming one. Betting can be very addictive. In the world there are millions of people hooked on various games, which leads them to put their financial resources at risk. If you are hooked, stop gambling immediately and seek help. Don't ruin your life.

If you are of legal age and decide to bet, please do so responsibly. This involves following a series of guidelines. Personally, I consider the following eight points to be essential:

1. Set a priori how much money you are willing to lose by betting and, if you reach that limit, stop wagering. That bankroll should consist of money that you don't need for other things. It should be an expense that you can afford.
2. Never stake more than 5% of your bankroll on a single bet. As interesting as a bet may seem, nothing is 100% sure. If it pays you money, there is the possibility that it will not happen. No matter how

---

[90] If you are a teenager, I recommend that you watch the film Gran Torino. In it, the character played by Clint Eastwood teaches the young protagonist two valuable lessons about life.

skilled you may be, by simple randomness, you will experience winning and losing streaks. Don't risk excessively.

3. Set in advance the criteria you will follow to decide on which matches you will bet. In this book we suggest several possible criteria. You may have other criteria, or you may use your own statistical model to calculate probabilities. When a match meets the criteria you have set in advance, go ahead and bet. If a certain day or a weekend no match meets the criteria you have set, do not bet. Don't bet just to bet, bet only when you think there is value in the odds. Remember that the vast majority of odds are correct. Only a small percentage of odds are wrong and can be exploited.

4. Never chase losses. If you have lost one or more bets, do not increase the amount of the next bet to try to get back to even. Any technique that promises that you can make money just by simply adjusting the stake (progressive staking) is extremely dangerous and inevitably leads to disaster. Run away from systems like Martingale, Fibonacci, D'Alembert, Labouchère and the like as if they were the plague.

5. Also, don't chase losses by absurdly increasing the odds you bet on. If you are not comfortable with long shots, do not use them to try to put an end to a losing streak. In general terms, those who bet at low odds are better off than those who bet at high odds given the higher implicit margin that bookmakers usually charge on the latter[91].

6. Use the odds comparison sites that are available on the internet. As we have seen in the chapters on margins, there can be substantial differences between what different bookmakers offer for the same outcome.

7. Do not resort to multiple bets as they increase the risk and the margin you face and, above all, they prevent you from betting at the best available odds for each selection.

8. Keep track of the bets you place. Writing down the bets you are placing and their results is the only way to know how your bankroll is going. It's your track record. You can use your own spreadsheet to store the information you need (for example, date of the bet, match, bookmaker, odds, result, probability provided by your model, etc.) or

---

[91] Personally, I never bet on anything that has odds greater than 5, that is, with a probability of occurring that is less than 20%.

use one of the websites that allow you to create a profile to save your forecasts[92].

The tips above are, let's say, operational in nature. Let's review below the different tips that we have seen throughout the book on how to select which bets can be interesting to place:

- The number of goals scored and conceded by a team is a better indicator of its level than the number of points it has obtained.
- A team's offensive level (goals scored) and a team's defensive level (conceded goals) are equally important when predicting its future results. Defence is as important as attack. There is, however, a bias that makes it more interesting to bet in favour of relatively defensive teams (that is, teams that tend to score and concede fewer goals than the average) than to bet in favour of relatively offensive teams (that is, that score and concede more goals than the average).
- If a team achieves better results one season than the previous one, it is likely that its results will worsen the next. If a team achieves worse results one season than the previous one, it is likely that its results will improve the next.
- In the final stretch of the league, the teams that are at risk of being relegated improve their performance and the teams in the middle zone of the table reduce their performance.
- The probability of a match ending in a draw is higher the lower the number of expected goals. In case you want to bet on a draw, it is significantly more interesting to do so when a low number of goals is expected since the 1X2 odds of some bookmakers do not correctly price this factor in.
- Better results are obtained by systematically betting on under than betting on over. The number of goals is usually higher on the final matchdays of the season than on the opening days, so bets on under and draw are more interesting in the initial part of the championship than in the final part.
- The level of a team should always be assessed considering its previous games both at home and away.

---

[92] Like for example www.pyckio.com. Many bookmakers allow you to see what bets you have placed in the past, but it is convenient to have your own list that brings together all the bets placed with different bookmakers.

- To correctly measure the level of a team, its performance in the current season and in the previous two must be considered.
- The number of shots a team takes and receives can be, in the short term, a better indicator of its level than the number of goals it scores or concedes. If, in the last matches, a team has scored few goals but shot a lot or if a team has conceded several goals while receiving few shots, it can be interesting to bet in its favour. The quality of the chances that a team generates or receives can be evaluated with the expected goals metrics.
- The last head-to-head match between two teams is not of special relevance to predict the outcome of their next direct confrontation. It can be interesting to bet in favour of the team that was defeated in the previous head-to-head match.
- When a team has got worse results than expected in its last few matches, it can be interesting to bet in its favour.
- In general terms, better results are obtained by betting on the local victory than on the visitor victory.
- In general terms, better results are obtained by betting on likely outcomes (low odds) than on unlikely outcomes (high odds).
- The probability of relegation goes down as a team spends more seasons in a row on the top division. However, the probability of relegation in the second season after being promoted is only slightly lower than the probability of relegation in the first season after promotion.
- Not all bookmakers are equally good at predicting the future. Depending on which bookmaker is the one that offers the highest odds for an outcome, it is more or less likely that there is value in those odds. The lower the margins a bookie charges, the more predictive its odds.
- As a general rule, odds get more accurate as the start of a match approaches.
- In general terms, better results are obtained by betting in favour of results whose odds are dropping (steamers) than in favour of results whose odds are lengthening (drifters).
- Not all markets are equally predictive. The Asian handicap market is typically more predictive than the 1X2 market.

In general, the previous points are due to the fact that in betting markets:

- Too much importance is given to recent team matches (and too little to older ones).
- Too much importance is given to the results obtained by the teams (and too little to their level of play).
- It is easier to measure a team's past performance than its motivation for the next game.

Individually these guidelines help detect small biases in the odds. Several of these guidelines can be followed together to try to improve your betting results. For example, you can decide to bet in favour of a team only when the following conditions are simultaneously met:

- It plays at home.
- It lost on the previous matchday.
- It has been obtaining worse-than-expected results recently, but its level of play has been good.
- It is facing a team that has been obtaining better-than-expected results recently and against which it lost the previous head-to-head game.
- The best odds are offered by a bookmaker that is not very predictive.
- The best odds are on the 1X2 market and not on the Asian handicap market.

By demanding that all these conditions are met, you will be reducing the number of possible bets, but you will be increasing the yield of the ones you place. In general, the various biases discussed in this book can be combined to achieve slightly positive returns. There are, however, two warnings to be made:

- Avoid focusing on matches with excessively high odds when combining the different criteria.
- Review the trend of the odds in the days and hours prior to the game.

As we saw at the time, in general, it is better to place bets when the odds are dropping. However, if the odds for a certain event have gone down too much, there may no longer be any value left in them. Also, at times, the trend that the odds are following can change. They can stop dropping to start lengthening or vice versa. These changes in trend may be due to the more professional bettors, who usually place their bets, of an average amount well above the casual bettor, when there are only a few hours left for the initial whistle.

In my experience, a bettor using a probability model based on each team's previous matches can follow one of the following two strategies:

1. Bet on a match when the two teams have just finished playing their respective previous matches and the initial odds have just been published. If the bettor's model is based on the previous matches of each team, it will be at this point that it will be more likely to find value in the odds. The model is already making its finest forecast and the possible errors in the odds have not yet been corrected by the market.

2. Bet just before the start of the match. In this case, it is essential to combine the information from the bettor's model, and the possible biases that he has identified, with the behaviour of the odds since their publication.

In short, if when betting there is information about how the odds have evolved, it is vital to consider it.

It is also relevant to consider the matches of other competitions (for example, European competitions, cup, etc.) that each team may have played during the week. From what I have been able to observe, the general principles in this book also apply in these cases. That is to say, in general it is better to bet in favour of a team in the league after a bad European or cup result than after a good result. Not all losses hurt the same. The extra motivation of the players after losing a match will be higher if that defeat was especially painful or recent. Similarly, the lack of focus after a victory will be more relevant if the triumph was especially significant.

The statistical literate reader who is willing to conduct his or her own analyses, develop models, or run regressions can find several free databases on the internet that can be downloaded[93].

I am aware that most of the inefficiencies and biases discussed in this book are primarily psychological in nature. They reflect errors in judgment that humans often make when evaluating the probability of something happening. The reflection of these biases in the odds may gradually disappear or diminish over time as more people become aware of them and exploit them. Statistics have served to detect, isolate, and quantify these biases. To try to make money by

---

[93] For example, at http://www.football-data.co.uk/downloadm.php.

betting, or in any other market, the important thing is not to predict perfectly, but to have more information and / or know how to take advantage of it better than the others. One of the most beautiful things about betting is precisely that: you can get to know if your prediction techniques are better than those of the rest.

It is not the objective of this book, but it is very likely that some of the biases discussed also affect the odds of other sports or markets. Without a doubt, this would also be a very interesting terrain to explore.

When estimating the probability that a match ends in a local victory, draw or away victory, we must not only consider the difference in level between both teams but also the number of goals that are expected for the match and the intensity of the home-field advantage. The intensity of the home-field advantage varies considerable across different leagues and countries. In general, it has decreased over the years, but it is still very relevant, even when the match is played behind closed doors. To make good predictions, try to measure these 3 elements as accurately as possible (level of the teams, goal expectation and intensity of the home advantage). If you build a model, check whether the variables you are using and the way you segment the data are correctly capturing these aspects for the matches you want to make predictions about.

There are also multiple other factors that affect football matches (for example tactics, weather, video refereeing, etc.) that are not covered in this book. The world of live betting is not addressed either. Knowing how to read the games as they unfold in front of your eyes clearly requires other skills. Not having covered them is simply because the statistical analysis of these factors is much more complex, mainly due to the lack of public databases of sufficient size with this information. Having not covered them in this book does in no way mean that they should be considered irrelevant factors.

The last piece of advice I can give a bettor is to have patience. A long series of bets is required to know if the results we are obtaining are due to chance or to our predictive ability. This is why prudent bankroll management is absolutely essential. In the short term luck dictates whether we win or lose, only in the medium term skill separates the good forecasters from the bad forecasters.

SECTION 4: TIPS FOR FOOTBALL CLUBS

Studying the performance of a football team is an exciting field. Many of the decisions made by club managers, coaches and players are public and accessible to all. Similarly, the results of these decisions can also be collected and analysed. It is therefore a very fertile field for learning by imitation.

The difficulty lies in the fact that it is not easy to determine how relevant each decision has been in the observed result, nor it is easy to know how much of that result is due to "luck", to the noise of the short term. Throughout this book we have tried to study each factor individually to try to deal with the first problem and we have used databases as large as possible to limit the second.

We have divided the tips for football clubs into four groups:

1. Management of squads and transfers.
2. Recommendations on the style of play.
3. Management of expectations and psychological elements.
4. Use of big data.

Let's start with the first one. Regarding squads and signings, it is observed that:

- Relatively short squads provide better results than relatively long ones. Between two squads of the same value, the one with fewer players tends to perform better. In addition, a smaller squad tends to increase in value more than a larger team. If you have 100 million to create a team, it is better to sign 22 players than 25.
- Teams with a higher percentage of foreigners perform better. Therefore, it is necessary to take advantage, as much as possible, of the legal possibilities that the club has to attract talent from abroad. You have to fish in the largest possible talent pool. In addition, signing foreign players can be an excellent marketing strategy.
- The performance of footballers increases as they age until it peaks when they are 26 - 28 years of age. After that, it gradually decreases. However, this relationship is weaker than many people think. A veteran player can provide excellent results in the short term. However, if the club wants to increase its squad's value over time, it must rely on young players. A young and small squad with several experienced

players may be the best option to achieve short-term results while increasing the future potential of the team.

- It is key to maintain a balanced squad. Coaches employ defenders far more than forwards and midfielders. The centre forwards of the 5 major European leagues, in the last 5 years, played each, on average 1,071 minutes, per season. Each central defender played 1,526 minutes. It is 42% more! The fourth centre back of a team plays twice as many minutes as the fourth centre forward. Don't sign a fourth centre forward! Every squad must have enough right-footed and left-footed players. It must have at least a couple of excellent penalty takers (this is how 8.5% of all goals are scored) and some players that are able to head the ball in (17.5% of the goals). It makes no sense to have 3 level B goalkeepers. You should have a level A starting goalkeeper, a level B substitute goalkeeper and level C third goalkeeper whose salary is as low as possible so you can afford other good players for other positions.

- Wage spending is a much better indicator of a team's future results than signing spending[94].

- Defence and attack are equally important. Raising the expectation of goals scored per game by, for example 0.5 will produce the same increase in expected points as reducing the expectation of goals conceded per game by 0.5. However, if a team has, for example, the sixth best offense in the league, but only the tenth best defence, it will possibly be more economical to improve the defence than to continue to improve its attack. When in doubt invest resources in strengthening the weakest link of your team. Most teams in the major leagues concede more goals than they score.

- Although it may be counterintuitive, empirically it is observed that a player that has scored 12 goals in 35 games during the season performs better in the future than another who has scored 11 goals in 20 games. When in doubt, sign the player who has played the most minutes.

- To compare two players that have scored a different number of goals in the last two seasons and see which one can be expected to score more next season, you can use the following rule of thumb: divide the number of goals scored two seasons ago by two. Whoever, after

---

[94] I take this from Soccernomics by Simon Kuper and Stefan Szymanski.

considering this factor, accumulated a higher number of goals in the last two campaigns, can be expected to score more in the next. This approach can also be used to predict who will provide more assists.

- When predicting which player will play the more minutes next season, it is only necessary to look at the previous campaign. The prediction does not improve when considering the minutes played two seasons ago. To predict the level of use of a footballer, do not look at the number of games in which he took part, but at the total minutes he was on the pitch.
- There are relevant biases in the youth player selection process. This bias means that those born in the first quarter of the year have an advantage over those born in the fourth quarter. Try that your club does not discard a possible future player simply because it is comparing him with other kids who are 10 or 11 months older than him.

Now let's move on to the recommendations on the style of play:

- During the last decade, teams have been reducing the percentage of shots they take from outside the box due to their low effectiveness. Take long shots only if there is no possibility to continue advancing towards the opposing goal.
- During the last decade, teams have been increasing the use of the short pass and reducing the number of long passes.
- The best teams make significantly more through-ball passes than the worst teams.
- 18.2% of goals come from set pieces. It is therefore essential to know how to take advantage of them and know how to defend these types of play.
- 7.3% of the goals are scored in counterattacks. It is therefore critical not to fall into these situations and know how to take advantage of them.
- Possession is a fairly weak indicator of the future results of a football team. To be useful, possession must translate into generating scoring chances and reducing those generated by the opposing team.
- Pass accuracy is also an unreliable indicator of a team's future results. The best teams are willing to try risky passes as long as the possibility of suffering a counterattack is limited.

- Distance covered is not a valid predictor of the results that a football team will obtain.
- In penalty shootouts, the team that shoots first has an advantage.
- Inward corner kicks have a greater probability of ending up in a goal than outward corner kicks[95].
- In general, coaches tend to substitute footballers too late into the game. They could improve their teams' results by substituting players earlier[96].
- In general, modest teams tend to play more from the wings, take a higher percentage of their shots from outside the box, and score a higher percentage of their goals on set pieces than the best teams.
- Teams of any level tend to play slightly more on the right side than on the left side of the pitch.

Regarding the management of expectations and psychological aspects, the following conclusions should be highlighted:

- When evaluating a team with a reduced number of games, it is much better to look at the variables related to the level of play (shots, expected goals, etc ...) than at the results. If the results have been bad but the variables related to the level of play are good, it is advisable not to rush, for example by firing the coach prematurely, especially if he continues to have the support of the squad. Similarly, analytics can be used to make our own players aware that an opponent is not as weak as their latest results may seem to indicate.
- When setting your goals for the following season, you have to be realistic. It is impossible that all teams improve their results over the previous season. If the results did improve last season, it is more likely that they will get worse the following season than they improve further. When setting goals, it makes more sense to look at goal difference than points. The previous two seasons must be taken into account.
- When the team squad changes, one way to set the objectives for the season may be to look at the historical relationship between squad

---

[95] According to the analysis carried out by Manchester City and reflected in the book Soccernomics by Simon Kuper and Stefan Szymanski.

[96] This idea is taken from the article by Brent Myers (2012), "A proposed decision rule for the timing of soccer substitutions" published in the "Journal of Quantitative Analysis in Sports" and reflected in the book "The Numbers Game" by Chris Anderson and David Sally.

218

value and the number of points obtained. This way, it is possible to estimate the number of points that a team should get according to the level of its squad. Another alternative may be to rely on the odds provided by the bookmakers. One possible way to detect good coaches may be to identify those whose teams consistently get better results than what would be expected based on the level of their squads (measured in terms of goal difference, their ratings or squad value).

- Motivation is an element with a huge influence on the results. Recent victories often make players lower their guard. Painful defeats often increase motivation in the short term. We must prevent players from relaxing excessively because they already beat next Sunday's opponent back in the first half of the season or because they are overconfident after defeating a great club. Motivation management is especially complex when the team is alternating matches from several tournaments. Winning during the week in European competitions or cup matches can lead to poor results in the weekend league match.

- The relevance of motivation is clearly shown in the home advantage. Home-field advantage weakens but does not disappear if the match is played behind closed doors. Home advantage is related with the concept of territoriality. No team should waste the opportunity to train in its opponent's ground.

- It is more difficult to measure the individual motivation of each player but probably situations such as facing a former team after an unfriendly exit, being in the presence of his national coach or playing a match against a rival from the same country of origin are situations that increase the footballer's desire to perform at his highest level.

- Trailing at the scoreboard increases the chances of scoring the next goal. However, the value of a goal is so high that it is always worth it to score first, even in the initial minutes of the game. A small team needs not fear "waking up the beast" of the opposing team with an early goal. Scoring is always good news.

- The higher the number of goals expected, the easier it is to equalize. For this reason, when a team is leading, it is interested in slowing down the game. It makes perfect sense to adapt the style of play according to the opponent and the match situation. The opposite is suicidal.

- The risk of relegation is practically as high for a team in its second season in the First Division as it is for a newly promoted team.

Maintaining the category should be the objective of any club facing its second season in the elite.

Finally, let's discuss some tips in relation to the use of big data by football teams:

- The availability of information in today's football can be overwhelming. To separate the useful variables from those that are not, the predictive capacity of each of them must be tested. What indicators will help the team achieve better results in the future? Are some variables redundant? The answer is that not all the information that is collected is useful and much of it is just noise. Properly selecting the metrics and working with a manageable list that the entire organization agrees on is key to success.

- If several data providers offer advanced metrics (for example, expected goals, expected assists, player ratings, etc ...) the way to choose one over the other should depend on the one hand on the level of transparency and understandability of its calculation and on the other on its capacity to predict future results. For example, not all "expected goals" metrics have the same predictive capacity. Stick with the one that best predicts future results.

- The same variable may be relevant for one purpose but not for another. For example, the distance covered by footballers during matches is a poor predictor of the outcome of the game but can be a useful variable to assess injury risk. In this book we have focused on the use of statistics to predict football results, but a club might be interested in using analytics for other aspects such as optimizing the price of tickets or merchandising sales.

- Some variables are relevant to improve the performance of a team but do not show a high correlation with results. For example, the number of offsides. It would be expected that the worst teams would be caught offside more often given their lower quality. However, as the best teams attack more, they tend to be caught offside more times per game. The fact that there is not a clear correlation between the number of offsides and the team results does not mean of course that teams should not train them (both in attack and in defence). The existence or not of an offside in a play can be absolutely decisive for the outcome of a match.

- Be wary of overly specific variables. In this book we have seen that to predict the results of home games it is better to consider both home and away games. Another example would be the number of first half goals: To predict the number of goals that will be scored in the first half, it is better to use 90-minute averages than 45-minute averages. When in doubt, put potential candidate variables to compete.
- The use of data analysis techniques should be a complementary tool to common sense and traditional methods. Just as no bank grants a 40-million-euro loan solely because of a positive automatic rating, no club should sign a player solely for what the numbers say. Data must always be put into context. Rely on multiskilled teams that combine people with deep football knowledge with people with deep knowledge on data processing and modelling.
- The analyses must be expressed in understandable terms so they can add value to the organization. If you tell a coach that the Pearson correlation between number of points and future results is 0.05 lower than the correlation between goal difference and future results, most likely he will not understand a thing. If you tell him that, when a team with better goal difference faces another that has more points, the team with better goal difference usually wins, he will understand.
- In general, a data analyst can provide value in two ways: by identifying variables that are more relevant than what most people think or precisely the other way around, by identifying variables that are less relevant than what most people think.
- When using statistics, try to answer each question separately. Trying to answer small questions little by little (e.g., what is the best way to take advantage of corner kicks) works better than trying to answer multiple questions at once. Don't isolate yourself in your ivory tower, talk to the rest of the organization and try to address their concerns.

If I were a data analyst at a club, I would initially focus on providing the coach with valuable information about each opponent. Making suggestions about your own team without first gaining the coach's trust could be counterproductive, making the coach himself feel criticized. Giving information about the rival team we do not run that risk.

I would try to provide very practical and specific information about, for example, which players from the rival team are in good shape, are good headers, tend to shoot from certain positions, generate more chances.... And also information about the rival's weak points: the player that tends to get dispossessed the most, the one that suffers the most when pressed upon, the one that misses more passes, the one that is slower, the one who is more likely to be sent off, the areas of the field that the opponent leaves uncovered, the types of shots that tend to cause more problems to their goalkeeper, etc... That analysis of the next match would of course also include the style of the referee that will be officiating.

Once the coach sees that as analysts we are capable of providing valuable information about the opponents, he will surely be more open to receiving information about his own players, the lineups that work best, the differences in performance between first and second halves, metrics in which the team is standing out both positively and negatively compared to the rest of the teams in the competition, etc... Of course, always prioritizing those aspects that the coach himself requests and including video images whenever possible.

All the analyses included in this book have been made using public information, freely available on the internet and working on it part-time. Imagine what is potentially possible if you have internal information from the club itself, using data providers and a team of fully dedicated professionals. Remember, it's not about doing it perfectly, it's about doing it better than everyone else.

To finalize, I can only thank the reader of these pages. I hope you have found this book interesting and that it has given you a different point of view on the world of football. If that is the case, I am fully satisfied[97].

Madrid, 2nd January 2022

---

[97] If you want to get more electronic or paper copies of this book, in English or in Spanish, you can buy them online. If you wish to send me any type of comment, you can write to the following address: metodospredictivosparafutbol@gmail.com, contact me on Twitter at @MetodPredFutbol or via LinkedIn. Finally, I really appreciate if you can rate this book in the store, app or website where you purchased it.

ANNEX 1: CALCULATION OF THE ROC

The ROC and the power stat are two different metrics that are used to measure the discriminating capacity of a model.

Imagine that we have a model that calculates the probability that a match will end in a local victory. We evaluate a sample of 1,000 football matches with it. Out of the 1,000 matches in the sample, 400 ended up in a local victory while the other 600 ended up in a draw or a visitor victory.

If our model were predictive, it would assign high probabilities of ending in a home victory to the matches that actually ended with that result. It would also assign low probabilities of ending in a home victory to those games that ended in a draw or away victory. If we scored and ranked the 1,000 matches in the sample from highest to lowest probability of home victory and our model was perfect, then the 400 matches that ended in home victory should have received the highest 400 probabilities. With a perfect model, the 600 matches that ended in a draw or away win should all have received lower probabilities than the matches that ended in a home win.

Graphically we can plot 3 lines that represent how a model orders when:

1. It has no discriminating capacity.
2. It has certain discriminating capacity.
3. It has a perfect discriminating capacity.

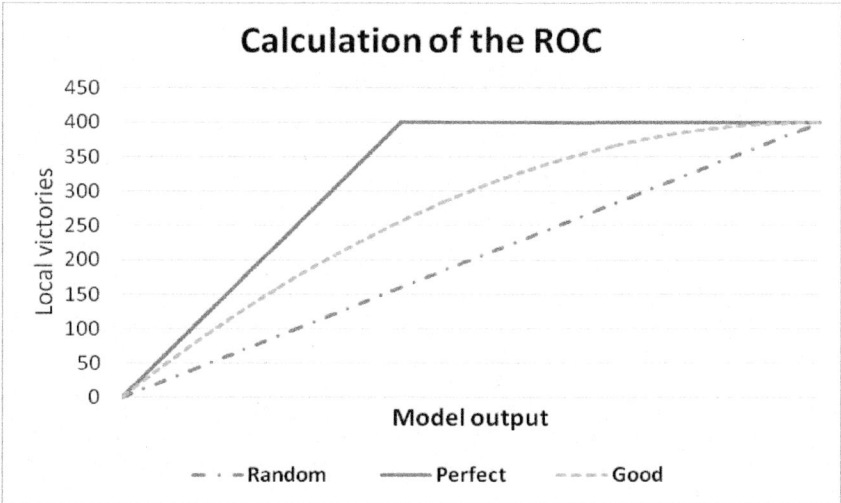

223

The lower diagonal line represents the model without any discriminating capacity. With this model, the matches that ended in local victory are distributed evenly across all the probability range. No relationship is observed between the probability assigned by the model and what actually happens in the game.

The curved line in the middle represents the model with a certain discriminating capacity. Most of the matches that, according to the model, were expected to end in a local victory did indeed end that way. There is a relationship between the model score and what actually happens.

The upper angular line represents the perfectly discriminating model. The model predicts, without error, which matches are going to end in a local victory. All matches that were assigned a high probability ended in a home victory. No game with a low probability ended in a home victory.

The bottom line and the top line respectively represent a useless model and a perfect model. Any model we build will normally lie in the middle. The closer to the top line the better it will be.

The power stat is calculated by dividing the area under the curve of our model by the area under the curve of the perfect model. The power stat can take values between 0% and 100%. The perfect model would receive a power stat of 100% and the non-discriminating model would receive a power stat of 0%. ROC can be calculated directly from the power[98]. Its formula is the following:

$$ROC = (Power\ Stat + 1) / 2$$

By construction ROC takes values between 50% and 100%. Like the power stat, the higher it is, the more discriminating the model is.

The predictive capacity of a model must be evaluated both on the construction sample and on a different sample. This is done to verify that it works correctly for populations other than the one used for its training.

---

[98] The calculation of the ROC can also be explained from the statistical concepts of sensitivity and specificity, but I prefer to explain it from the power stat because I consider this approach to be more intuitive. Instructions on how to estimate and run a logistic regression in Excel can be found on the internet.

ANNEX 2: SHOTS, GOALS, FOULS, CORNERS AND CARDS

The following tables show the number of goals, fouls, shoots on target, yellow cards, red cards, and corners per game for the main European leagues[99]:

PREMIER LEAGUE (ENGLAND)

SEASON	GOALS	SHOOTS	SHOOTS ON TARGET	FOULS	YELLOW CARDS	RED CARDS	CORNER
2000-01	2.61	22.2	10.69	26.9	3.14	0.17	10.94
2001-02	2.63	21.5	10.15	26.6	3.07	0.19	11.05
2002-03	2.63	22.4	11.87	25.4	3.01	0.20	11.59
2003-04	2.66	23.2	12.57	25.8	2.84	0.15	11.15
2004-05	2.57	22.2	11.76	26.1	2.71	0.16	10.78
2005-06	2.48	21.6	11.19	26.3	3.09	0.20	10.66
2006-07	2.45	22.5	11.45	25.1	3.22	0.14	11.28
2007-08	2.64	23.1	12.49	24.4	3.20	0.16	11.06
2008-09	2.48	24.4	13.16	23.2	3.15	0.17	11.10
2009-10	2.77	24.4	13.65	24.2	3.26	0.18	11.19
2010-11	2.80	24.9	13.61	22.4	3.25	0.17	11.04
2011-12	2.81	26.0	14.67	20.4	3.10	0.17	11.39
2012-13	2.80	25.1	14.24	20.9	3.12	0.14	11.15
2013-14	2.77	26.9	8.92	21.5	3.19	0.14	10.77
2014-15	2.57	25.9	8.41	22.7	3.59	0.19	10.69
2015-16	2.70	25.7	8.51	21.5	3.10	0.16	10.83
2016-17	2.80	25.5	8.67	22.7	3.63	0.11	10.41
2017-18	2.68	24.4	8.39	20.7	3.04	0.10	10.28
2018-19	2.82	25.3	8.71	20.5	3.21	0.12	10.26
2019-20	2.72	24.7	8.55	21.5	3.35	0.12	10.71
2020-21	3.14	23.2	8.67	22.9	3.10	0.13	9.73
TOTAL	**2.67**	**24.1**	**11.06**	**23.4**	**3.16**	**0.16**	**10.90**

---

[99] The 2020-21 season only considers the matches played until November 17, 2020.

LA LIGA (SPAIN)

SEASON	GOALS	SHOOTS	SHOOTS ON TARGET	FOULS	YELLOW CARDS	RED CARDS	CORNER
2005-06	2.46	25.1	8.76	39.0	5.23	0.39	9.77
2006-07	2.48	24.0	8.34	36.6	5.00	0.41	9.78
2007-08	2.69	24.7	8.81	34.7	4.93	0.38	10.20
2008-09	2.90	26.4	9.52	33.3	5.25	0.41	10.26
2009-10	2.71	26.0	9.36	31.8	4.99	0.40	10.88
2010-11	2.74	25.8	9.60	29.1	5.04	0.29	10.82
2011-12	2.76	26.0	9.34	29.4	5.60	0.34	10.93
2012-13	2.87	26.0	9.27	28.4	5.42	0.37	11.24
2013-14	2.75	25.3	8.86	27.9	4.91	0.30	11.15
2014-15	2.66	23.8	8.37	28.4	5.29	0.27	10.24
2015-16	2.74	23.8	8.62	27.2	5.27	0.29	10.11
2016-17	2.94	24.0	8.91	27.9	5.00	0.23	9.50
2017-18	2.69	24.0	8.56	27.7	5.02	0.19	9.81
2018-19	2.59	24.3	8.42	27.1	5.17	0.21	9.59
2019-20	2.48	22.6	7.85	27.5	5.13	0.23	9.24
2020-21	2.41	21.2	7.40	27.6	4.61	0.25	8.55
TOTAL	**2.69**	**24.7**	**8.82**	**30.4**	**5.14**	**0.31**	**10.21**

SERIE A (ITALY)

SEASON	GOALS	SHOOTS	SHOOTS ON TARGET	FOULS	YELLOW CARDS	RED CARDS	CORNER
2005-06	2.61	19.3	9.38	37.9	4.15	0.33	9.42
2006-07	2.55	21.0	9.94	37.2	4.44	0.38	9.84
2007-08	2.55	27.1	8.86	38.7	4.62	0.31	10.34
2008-09	2.60	27.2	9.33	36.8	4.36	0.31	10.50
2009-10	2.61	26.9	9.02	35.5	4.55	0.31	10.49
2010-11	2.51	27.4	8.82	31.0	3.94	0.28	10.75
2011-12	2.56	26.5	8.79	30.5	4.34	0.27	10.42
2012-13	2.64	26.2	8.83	30.5	4.79	0.32	10.39
2013-14	2.72	26.8	8.95	29.5	4.60	0.28	10.31
2014-15	2.69	26.3	8.65	30.3	4.80	0.31	10.49
2015-16	2.58	25.8	8.33	30.4	4.87	0.34	10.43
2016-17	2.96	26.5	9.33	27.9	4.40	0.25	10.84
2017-18	2.68	25.6	8.74	25.6	4.07	0.23	10.34
2018-19	2.68	20.4	10.47	26.1	4.65	0.24	10.69
2019-20	3.04	21.1	11.42	27.5	5.09	0.26	10.64
2020-21	3.40	19.2	10.61	27.4	4.16	0.19	9.53
TOTAL	**2.67**	**24.9**	**9.27**	**31.6**	**4.51**	**0.29**	**10.38**

BUNDESLIGA (GERMANY)

SEASON	GOALS	SHOOTS	SHOOTS ON TARGET	FOULS	YELLOW CARDS	RED CARDS	CORNER
2005-06	2.81	28.5		39.2	4.23	0.19	10.25
2006-07	2.74	27.7		37.4	3.67	0.20	10.38
2007-08	2.81	28.2	9.67	35.8	3.60	0.16	10.36
2008-09	2.92	27.8	9.56	36.1	3.81	0.20	10.89
2009-10	2.83	26.0	9.35	33.9	3.46	0.13	10.08
2010-11	2.92	25.6	9.21	32.7	3.39	0.19	9.84
2011-12	2.86	25.5	9.37	32.4	3.49	0.19	9.42
2012-13	2.93	25.2	9.33	31.5	3.68	0.21	9.75
2013-14	3.16	27.2	10.09	30.7	3.51	0.20	10.01
2014-15	2.75	26.0	9.43	30.5	3.62	0.17	9.72
2015-16	2.83	25.6	9.51	29.0	3.79	0.13	9.51
2016-17	2.87	24.9	8.84	28.6	3.74	0.18	9.12
2017-18	2.79	25.2	9.01	26.7	3.38	0.14	9.43
2018-19	3.18	26.8	9.67	22.4	3.45	0.14	10.07
2019-20	3.21	26.5	9.62	23.4	4.01	0.18	10.09
2020-21	3.21	25.2	9.49	25.1	4.00	0.10	9.43
TOTAL	2.92	26.6	9.44	32.2	3.73	0.17	9.94

LIGUE 1 (FRANCE)

SEASON	GOALS	SHOOTS	SHOOTS ON TARGET	FOULS	YELLOW CARDS	RED CARDS	CORNER
2005-06	2.13	19.4	8.53		3.49	0.21	
2006-07	2.25	19.1	8.41		3.47	0.20	
2007-08	2.28	25.1	8.42	34.9	3.27	0.19	9.58
2008-09	2.26	25.3	8.21	33.6	3.31	0.16	9.60
2009-10	2.41	25.3	8.48	32.5	3.49	0.23	9.65
2010-11	2.34	24.8	8.34	32.0	3.30	0.21	9.50
2011-12	2.52	24.8	8.52	31.3	3.64	0.28	9.94
2012-13	2.54	23.6	8.49	28.3	3.26	0.28	9.99
2013-14	2.46	23.5	8.26	27.5	3.13	0.24	9.63
2014-15	2.49	22.8	7.98	27.5	3.36	0.21	9.26
2015-16	2.53	23.0	8.23	26.7	3.76	0.31	9.57
2016-17	2.62	24.0	8.26	25.0	3.29	0.26	9.58
2017-18	2.72	24.8	8.60	26.1	3.83	0.23	9.85
2018-19	2.56	24.7	8.33	26.4	3.67	0.26	9.56
2019-20	2.52	24.3	8.34	26.0	3.80	0.25	9.71
2020-21	2.82	24.0	8.26	26.9	4.50	0.41	10.04
TOTAL	2.45	23.6	8.36	29.1	3.48	0.24	9.65

There are some interesting trends in these data:

- In all the leagues analysed, the number of fouls has been gradually decreasing over the last 15 years.
- The number of yellow cards per game differs across the different leagues. In England it is close to 3. In Germany and France it is around 3.5. In Italy it is 4.5 and in Spain an average of 5 yellow cards are shown per game.
- The number of corners per game is lower than 10 in France, close to 10 in Germany, slightly higher than 10 in Italy and Spain, and close to 11 in England.
- About 15 years ago approximately 10% - 11% of all fouls received a yellow card. Currently that percentage is 15%.

We have prepared the following tables to study the relationship between the level of a team and the number of goals, shoots, fouls, cards, and corners that occur in a match. These metrics are calculated by grouping the matches according to the odds offered for the victory of the local team.

LOC VIC ODDS	LOC GOALS	VISI GOALS	1H LOC GOALS	1H VISI GOALS	LOC SHO	VISI SHO	LOC SHO TAR	VISI SHO TAR
< 1.3	2.7	0.6	1.2	0.3	18.5	7.4	8.0	2.7
[1.3 - 1.5)	2.2	0.7	1.0	0.3	16.4	8.5	6.9	3.2
[1.5 - 2)	1.8	0.9	0.8	0.4	14.1	9.3	5.8	3.6
[2 - 2.5)	1.4	1.1	0.6	0.5	12.6	10.1	5.1	4.0
[2.5 - 3)	1.3	1.2	0.6	0.5	11.7	10.8	4.6	4.4
[3 - 4)	1.1	1.4	0.5	0.6	11.1	11.8	4.3	4.7
>= 4	0.9	1.9	0.4	0.8	9.8	13.8	3.7	5.8
TOTAL	1.5	1.2	0.7	0.5	12.7	10.4	5.1	4.2

LOC VIC ODDS	LOC FOULS	VISI FOULS	LOC YEL	VISI YEL	LOC RED	VISI RED	% YEL FOULS LOC	% YEL FOULS VISI
< 1.3	10.8	12.3	1.1	1.9	0.05	0.11	10.6%	15.7%
[1.3 - 1.5)	11.8	13.0	1.4	2.0	0.06	0.12	11.5%	15.6%
[1.5 - 2)	12.2	13.1	1.5	2.0	0.07	0.13	12.1%	15.4%
[2 - 2.5)	12.6	13.2	1.6	2.0	0.09	0.13	12.9%	14.9%
[2.5 - 3)	12.5	12.8	1.7	1.9	0.09	0.11	13.7%	14.8%
[3 - 4)	12.7	12.8	1.8	1.8	0.10	0.11	14.2%	14.2%
>= 4	12.9	12.2	1.9	1.7	0.11	0.09	14.9%	14.2%
TOTAL	12.4	12.9	1.6	1.9	0.09	0.12	13.1%	14.9%

LOC VIC ODDS	LOC COR	VISI COR	% RED FOULS LOC	% RED FOULS VISI	% LOC SHO TAR	% VISI SHO TAR	% 1H LOC GOALS	% 1H VISI GOALS
< 1.3	7.7	3.1	0.4%	0.9%	43.0%	36.8%	44.7%	43.4%
[1.3 - 1.5)	7.0	3.7	0.5%	0.9%	42.1%	37.4%	43.9%	42.8%
[1.5 - 2)	6.4	4.2	0.6%	1.0%	41.2%	39.2%	44.0%	44.0%
[2 - 2.5)	5.8	4.6	0.7%	1.0%	40.3%	40.1%	44.0%	43.3%
[2.5 - 3)	5.4	5.0	0.7%	0.9%	39.6%	40.6%	44.3%	43.7%
[3 - 4)	5.0	5.3	0.8%	0.8%	38.6%	40.3%	44.2%	42.9%
>= 4	4.3	5.9	0.8%	0.8%	37.4%	41.8%	44.0%	43.4%
TOTAL	5.7	4.7	0.7%	0.9%	40.3%	40.1%	44.1%	43.5%

Therefore, the first row of each of the three previous tables tells us what happens when the home team is much stronger than the visitor, and the penultimate row tells us what happens when the home team is worse than the visiting team[100].

It is observed that, in general, the better a team is:

- It scores more goals.
- It concedes fewer goals.
- It takes more shots.
- It receives fewer shots.
- It commits fewer fouls.
- It is fouled more.
- Gets more corners in favour.
- Receives fewer corners against.

Not only do the best teams take more shots and commit fewer fouls than their rivals. The best teams also direct a higher proportion of their shots on target and receive fewer bookings in relation to the number of fouls they commit.

In the previous tables it can also be observed that when teams play as visitors their performance worsens in all these variables compared to when they play at home.

---

[100] LOC VIC ODDS: local victory odds, LOC GOALS: local goals, VISI GOALS: visitor goals, 1H LOC GOALS: local goals in first half, 1H VISI GOALS: visitor goals in first half, LOC SHO: local shoots, LOC SHO TAR: local shoots on target, LOC FOULS: local fouls, LOC YEL: local yellow cards, LOC RED: local red cards, % YEL FOULS LOC: local yellow cards per foul, LOC COR: local corner kicks, % RED FOULS LOC: local red cards per foul. % LOC SHO TAR: percentage of local shoots on target, % 1H LOC GOALS: percentage of local goals in first half.

Regarding goals, it is worth highlighting that:

- Approximately 44% of all goals are scored in the first half.
- In 54% of matches at least 1 goal is scored in both halves.
- In 51% of matches both teams score at least 1 goal.
- Only in 5% of matches do both teams score in both halves.
- In 44% of matches, more goals are scored in the second half than in the first half. In 27% of matches, more goals are scored in the first half than in the second. In 28% of matches, the same number of goals is scored in both halves.

The following tables contain the number of times per game teams perform certain actions based on their level.

ACTIONS PER MATCH ACCORDING TO TEAM LEVEL				
POINTS PER MATCH	OFFSIDES	CLEARANCES	SUCCESS. DRIBBLES	UNSUCCESS. DRIBBLES
LESS THAN 1.07	2.19	26.3	8.1	7.3
BETWEEN 1.08 Y 1.26	2.29	26.7	7.9	7.7
BETWEEN 1.27 Y 1.60	2.33	24.1	8.8	7.8
MORE THAN 1.61	2.47	21.9	10.3	8.1

ACTIONS PER MATCH ACCORDING TO TEAM LEVEL				
POINTS PER MATCH	AERIAL DUELS WON	AERIAL DUELS LOST	BLOCKED CROSSES	BLOCKED PASSES
LESS THAN 1.07	16.8	17.8	2.5	5.4
BETWEEN 1.08 Y 1.26	16.0	16.4	2.6	4.4
BETWEEN 1.27 Y 1.60	16.3	16.1	2.4	5.1
MORE THAN 1.61	14.5	13.4	2.2	5.0

ACTIONS PER MATCH ACCORDING TO TEAM LEVEL				
POINTS PER MATCH	INTERCEPTIONS	BLOCKED SHOTS	UNSUCCESS. TOUCHES	DISPOSSESSED
LESS THAN 1.07	15.5	3.3	11.4	11.2
BETWEEN 1.08 Y 1.26	17.2	3.2	11.3	11.5
BETWEEN 1.27 Y 1.60	15.8	2.9	11.8	11.4
MORE THAN 1.61	15.0	2.6	11.0	11.8

The analysis of the remaining variables mentioned in the chapter entitled "How do the best teams play?" is included below. The figures in these tables indicate the percentage of times that a superior team according to the column variable ranked better than a superior team on the row variable the following season.

IT FORECASTS BETTER	SHOTS ON GOAL DIFFERENCE	POINTS PER GAME	TOTAL SHOT DIFFERENCE
TRANSFERMARK VALUATION	49%	47%	45%
GOAL DIFFERENCE	48%	41%	44%
POINTS PER GAME	53%	NA	48%
SHOTS ON GOAL DIFFERENCE	NA	47%	42%
TOTAL SHOT DIFFERENCE	58%	52%	NA
WHO SCORED RATING	52%	50%	47%
POSSESSION	55%	53%	51%
PASS ACCURACY	55%	53%	51%

IT FORECASTS BETTER	WHO SCORED RATING	POSSESSION	PASS ACCURACY
TRANSFERMARK VALUATION	47%	43%	42%
GOAL DIFFERENCE	44%	44%	43%
POINTS PER GAME	50%	47%	47%
SHOTS ON GOAL DIFFERENCE	48%	45%	45%
TOTAL SHOT DIFFERENCE	53%	49%	49%
WHO SCORED RATING	NA	46%	46%
POSSESSION	54%	NA	48%
PASS ACCURACY	54%	52%	NA

For example, let's imagine two teams. The only thing we know about them is that in the previous season team A had more possession but less passing accuracy than team B. This table indicates that team A has a 52% chance of ranking better the following season given that possession is a more predictive variable than passing accuracy.

Finally, we include the tables from the chapter "First and Second Halves" with the probabilities that a match will end in a home win, draw or away win depending on the level of the teams when the home team is winning or losing at halftime by two goals.

LOCAL TEAM LOSES BY 2 GOALS AT HALFTIME	RESULT AT THE END OF THE MATCH		
GROUP	HOME WIN	TIE	AWAY WIN
1. VERY SUPERIOR LOCAL	12%	21%	67%
2. SUPERIOR LOCAL	7%	18%	75%
3. LOCAL SOMEWHAT SUPERIOR	7%	13%	80%
4. LOCAL SLIGHTLYSUPERIOR	5%	11%	83%
5. VISITOR SLIGHTLY SUPERIOR	4%	10%	86%
6. VISITOR SOMEWHAT SUPERIOR	2%	9%	89%
7. SUPERIOR VISITOR	2%	8%	90%
8. VERY SUPERIOR VISITOR	1%	5%	94%

LOCAL TEAM WINS BY 2 GOALS AT HALFTIME	RESULT AT THE END OF THE MATCH		
GROUP	HOME WIN	TIE	AWAY WIN
1. VERY SUPERIOR LOCAL	97%	2%	0%
2. SUPERIOR LOCAL	96%	4%	0%
3. LOCAL SOMEWHAT SUPERIOR	94%	5%	1%
4. LOCAL SLIGHTLYSUPERIOR	93%	6%	2%
5. VISITOR SLIGHTLY SUPERIOR	92%	6%	2%
6. VISITOR SOMEWHAT SUPERIOR	91%	7%	2%
7. SUPERIOR VISITOR	85%	9%	6%[101]
8. VERY SUPERIOR VISITOR	85%	10%	5%

---

[101] It could be expected that the probability of away victory in group 7 would take an intermediate value between that of group 6 and that of group 8. However this is not the case in the available sample.

ANNEX 3: DOUBLE CHANCE BETS

Unlike the fulltime result market, the double chance market has the peculiarity that out of its three options (1X, X2 and 12) two of them will be winners and one will be a loser at the end of the match. The three options of a double chance bet are not disjoint but overlap. This affects how the overround, margin, and implied probability should be calculated.

The overround is calculated as follows:

$$Overround = (1/Odds_{ab}+1/Odds_{bc}+1/Odds_{ac}) / 2$$

The margin is calculated as follows:

$$Margin = 1-(1/Overround)$$

The implied probability of each of the outcomes is calculated as follows:

$$Pimp_{ab} = (1/Odds_{ab})/Overround$$

Since the three options of the double chance market overlap, the sum of the implicit probabilities adds up to 200% instead of 100%.

$$Pimp_{ab}+Pimp_{bc}+Pimp_{ac} = 200\%$$

From the implicit probabilities of each of the three outcomes (1X, X2 and 12), the implicit probability of 1, X and 2 can be calculated as follows:

$$Pimp_{a} = (Pimp_{ab}+Pimp_{ac}-Pimp_{bc})/2$$

Even when working with a single bookmaker, we will observe slight differences in the implicit probabilities of 1, X, 2 in the fulltime result market and in the double chance market.

ANNEX 4: BOOKIE MARGIN IN EUROPEAN LEAGUES

These are the margins charged by bookmakers on the German Bundesliga matches over the last few years:

SEASON	B365	BW	IW	LB	WH	BV	PS	BEST 5	BEST 7
2005-06	8.3%	9.2%	10.8%	11.0%	11.1%	10.9%		4.8%	4.8%
2006-07	7.4%	9.0%	10.2%	11.0%	11.1%	11.0%		4.6%	4.6%
2007-08	6.3%	9.0%	10.2%	11.0%	10.9%	9.8%		4.4%	4.3%
2008-09	6.1%	9.0%	9.1%	10.6%	10.0%	9.1%		3.4%	3.3%
2009-10	6.1%	7.4%	7.7%	10.8%	9.4%	8.0%		3.5%	3.4%
2010-11	6.1%	7.2%	9.3%	6.3%	6.2%	3.8%		2.6%	2.0%
2011-12	6.0%	6.0%	9.2%	6.1%	6.2%	3.2%		2.4%	1.6%
2012-13	6.0%	6.0%	7.8%	6.4%	6.0%	3.0%	2.0%	2.5%	0.9%
2013-14	6.0%	6.2%	7.4%	6.2%	6.0%	3.2%	2.0%	2.5%	1.0%
2014-15	5.2%	6.3%	7.4%	5.6%	5.9%	3.2%	2.0%	2.4%	0.9%
2015-16	4.9%	5.9%	7.5%	6.0%	5.8%	3.6%	2.0%	2.4%	0.9%
2016-17	4.8%	5.0%	5.4%	6.1%	4.7%	3.8%	2.0%	1.8%	0.8%
2017-18	5.0%	4.9%	5.3%	5.9%	5.8%	3.7%	2.2%	2.1%	0.9%
2018-19	5.0%	4.9%	5.1%		5.3%	3.8%	2.8%	2.5%	1.4%
2019-20	5.2%	5.0%	5.1%		4.8%	4.7%	3.2%	2.6%	1.9%

This information is graphically represented below:

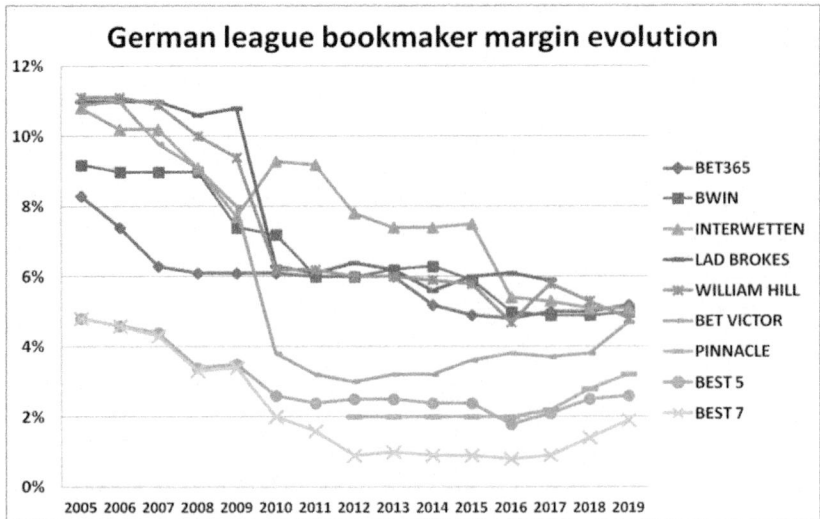

German league bookmaker margin evolution

234

The following table contains the margins charged by bookmakers in the Italian Serie A over the last few years:

SEASON	B365	BW	IW	LB	WH	BV	PS	BEST 5	BEST 7
2005-06	8.3%	9.0%	10.9%	11.0%	11.1%	10.0%		5.2%	5.1%
2006-07	7.6%	9.2%	10.3%	11.1%	11.1%	11.0%		4.9%	4.8%
2007-08	6.3%	9.3%	10.2%	11.0%	11.0%	9.8%		4.4%	4.2%
2008-09	6.1%	9.2%	9.3%	10.8%	10.4%	9.1%		3.9%	3.8%
2009-10	6.1%	7.7%	7.8%	10.8%	9.1%	8.1%		3.7%	3.6%
2010-11	6.3%	7.5%	9.3%	7.7%	6.3%	4.5%		3.3%	2.5%
2011-12	6.1%	6.2%	9.2%	6.9%	6.1%	3.3%		3.4%	2.2%
2012-13	6.1%	6.1%	8.0%	7.1%	6.0%	3.1%	2.1%	2.9%	1.1%
2013-14	6.1%	6.2%	7.5%	6.1%	6.0%	2.9%	2.0%	3.0%	1.0%
2014-15	5.2%	6.0%	7.5%	5.4%	5.9%	2.8%	2.0%	2.7%	0.7%
2015-16	4.9%	5.6%	7.4%	6.2%	5.7%	3.6%	2.0%	2.7%	0.8%
2016-17	4.8%	5.1%	7.4%	6.0%	4.7%	4.0%	2.0%	2.3%	1.0%
2017-18	5.0%	4.9%	5.5%	5.9%	5.8%	3.9%	2.3%	2.2%	0.9%
2018-19	5.0%	5.0%	5.0%		5.1%	3.9%	2.7%	2.9%	1.5%
2019-20	5.2%	5.0%	5.0%		5.5%	5.4%	3.1%	3.3%	2.1%

This information is graphically represented below:

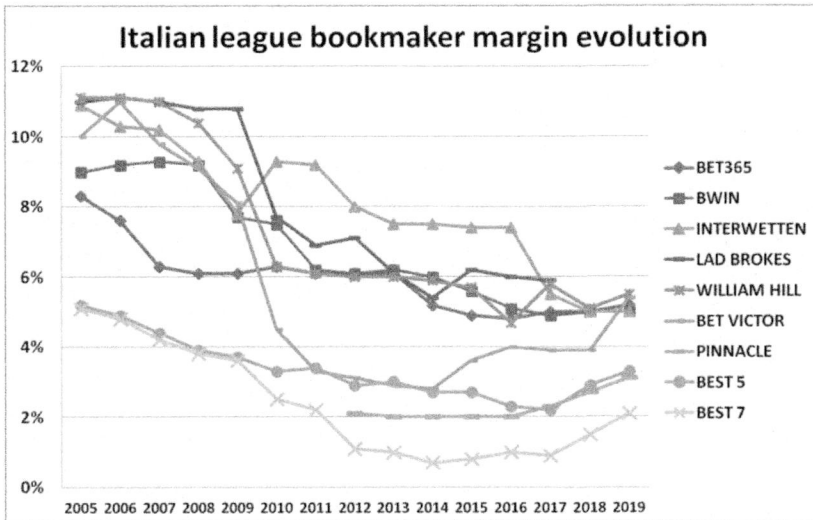

Italian league bookmaker margin evolution

235

The following table contains the margins charged by bookmakers in the French Ligue 1 over the last few years:

SEASON	B365	BW	IW	LB	WH	BV	PS	BEST 5	BEST 7
2005-06	10.1%	9.3%	10.9%	11.0%	11.1%	10.9%		5.2%	5.0%
2006-07	9.3%	9.3%	10.1%	11.0%	11.1%	11.0%		5.2%	5.1%
2007-08	6.7%	9.3%	10.1%	11.1%	11.1%	10.0%		4.7%	4.5%
2008-09	6.2%	9.3%	9.3%	11.1%	10.2%	9.7%		3.3%	3.3%
2009-10	6.1%	7.7%	7.8%	11.0%	9.2%	8.1%		3.0%	2.9%
2010-11	6.1%	7.4%	9.3%	11.0%	6.3%	4.3%		3.6%	2.7%
2011-12	6.0%	6.3%	9.2%	10.2%	6.0%	3.4%		3.3%	2.2%
2012-13	6.0%	6.2%	7.9%	6.7%	6.0%	3.1%	2.5%	2.8%	1.2%
2013-14	6.1%	6.2%	7.5%	6.1%	6.0%	3.1%	2.4%	2.7%	1.1%
2014-15	5.3%	5.8%	7.4%	6.0%	5.8%	2.8%	2.4%	2.6%	1.0%
2015-16	4.9%	5.9%	7.4%	6.5%	5.7%	3.2%	2.4%	2.6%	1.1%
2016-17	4.9%	5.1%	7.4%	6.2%	5.7%	3.9%	2.4%	2.4%	1.1%
2017-18	4.9%	4.9%	7.4%	6.1%	5.8%	3.9%	2.4%	2.4%	1.2%
2018-19	4.9%	4.8%	5.1%		5.7%	3.9%	2.7%	2.9%	1.6%
2019-20	5.0%	4.9%	5.0%		5.7%	5.5%	3.1%	3.1%	2.0%

This information is graphically represented below:

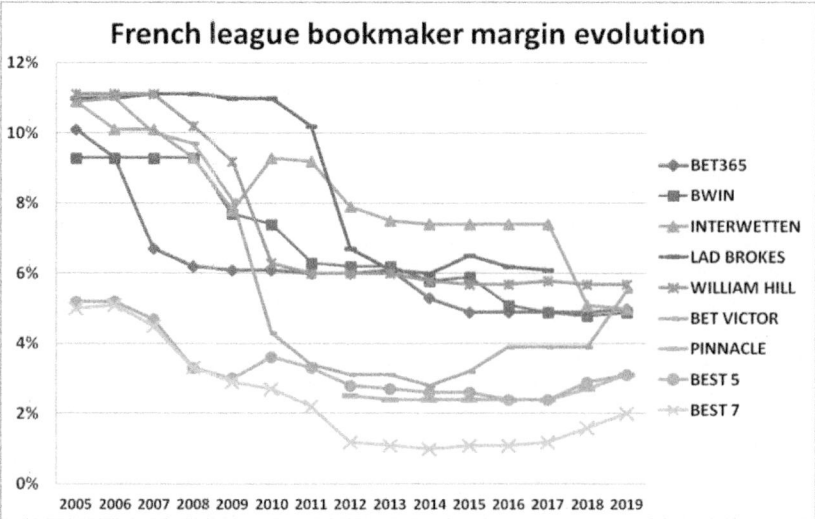

French league bookmaker margin evolution

The following table contains the margins charged by bookmakers in the Dutch Eredivisie over the last few years:

SEASON	B365	BW	IW	LB	WH	BV	PS	BEST 5	BEST 7
2005-06	10.4%	10.1%	11.9%	11.1%	11.1%	11.0%		6.2%	5.9%
2006-07	9.8%	10.1%	11.9%	11.1%	11.2%	11.0%		5.3%	5.2%
2007-08	8.4%	10.0%	12.0%	11.1%	11.1%	10.0%		5.0%	4.6%
2008-09	7.9%	9.4%	12.0%	11.0%	11.1%	9.9%		4.5%	4.4%
2009-10	6.7%	9.3%	11.8%	11.0%	9.2%	9.3%		4.3%	4.1%
2010-11	6.4%	9.1%	11.6%	11.1%	8.8%	6.5%		3.8%	3.4%
2011-12	6.1%	7.3%	11.2%	11.1%	8.8%	5.1%		3.5%	2.9%
2012-13	6.2%	8.9%	10.3%	10.2%	8.7%	4.0%	2.9%	4.4%	2.1%
2013-14	6.1%	9.1%	10.2%	8.9%	8.6%	4.1%	2.9%	4.3%	2.0%
2014-15	6.1%	8.7%	10.2%	6.3%	7.5%	4.1%	2.9%	3.7%	1.8%
2015-16	6.1%	7.4%	9.3%	6.2%	8.2%	4.6%	2.5%	3.9%	1.8%
2016-17	6.1%	7.0%	8.6%	6.1%	8.2%	4.8%	2.5%	3.4%	1.7%
2017-18	6.2%	5.0%	7.5%	7.8%	7.6%	4.8%	2.7%	3.2%	1.6%
2018-19	6.2%	4.8%	7.5%		6.7%	4.7%	3.9%	3.6%	2.5%
2019-20	6.2%	5.0%	7.4%		6.5%	5.9%	3.8%	3.8%	2.7%

This information is graphically represented below:

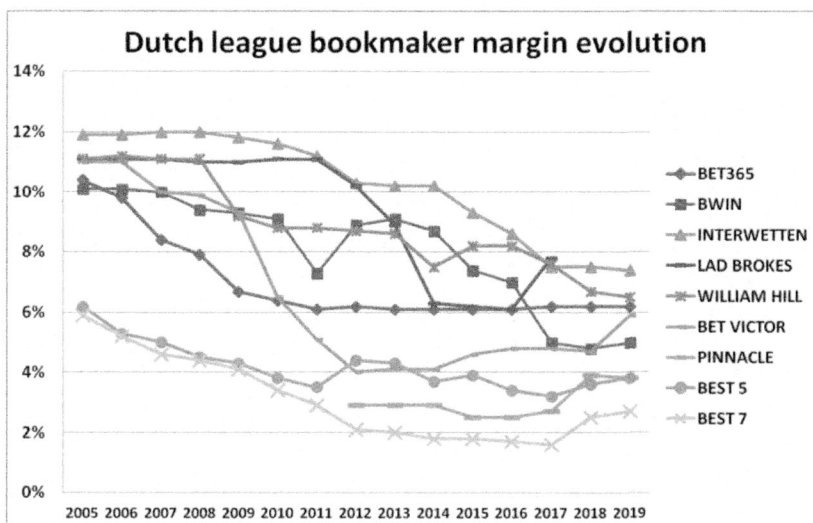

Dutch league bookmaker margin evolution

237

The following table contains the margins charged by bookmakers in the Portuguese Primeira Liga over the last few years:

SEASON	B365	BW	IW	LB	WH	BV	PS	BEST 5	BEST 7
2005-06	10.5%	10.1%	11.8%	11.2%	11.1%	11.0%		6.1%	5.9%
2006-07	10.0%	10.1%	11.9%	11.2%	11.1%	11.1%		6.1%	5.9%
2007-08	8.1%	9.7%	11.9%	11.1%	11.0%	10.1%		4.7%	4.6%
2008-09	8.0%	9.3%	11.9%	11.1%	10.9%	10.0%		4.7%	4.6%
2009-10	6.9%	9.3%	10.1%	11.0%	8.8%	9.3%		4.2%	4.1%
2010-11	6.4%	9.1%	10.1%	11.0%	8.7%	6.2%		3.8%	3.4%
2011-12	6.1%	7.4%	10.2%	10.8%	8.7%	4.6%		4.2%	3.1%
2012-13	6.1%	7.4%	10.1%	9.9%	8.3%	4.0%	2.9%	4.1%	2.1%
2013-14	6.1%	7.4%	10.1%	8.8%	8.3%	4.2%	2.9%	4.4%	2.0%
2014-15	6.2%	7.4%	10.1%	8.5%	8.3%	4.4%	2.9%	4.0%	1.9%
2015-16	6.0%	7.3%	9.1%	6.3%	8.2%	4.5%	2.5%	3.7%	1.6%
2016-17	6.1%	6.9%	8.0%	6.1%	7.4%	4.8%	2.5%	3.3%	1.5%
2017-18	6.2%	6.5%	7.4%	7.7%	8.1%	4.8%	2.5%	3.6%	1.7%
2018-19	6.2%	6.6%	7.4%		5.8%	4.8%	3.1%	3.8%	2.2%
2019-20	6.2%	6.4%	6.2%		5.7%	6.3%	3.8%	3.9%	2.7%

This information is graphically represented below:

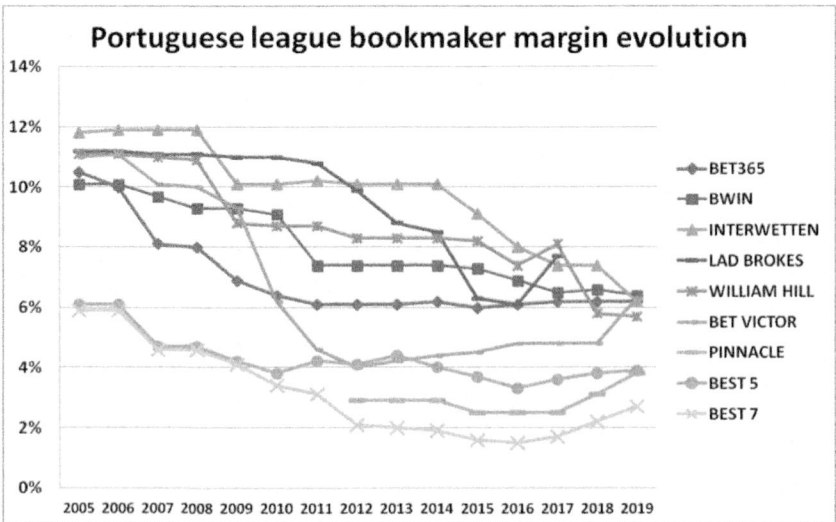

Portuguese league bookmaker margin evolution

ANNEX 5: PREDICTIVE CAPACITY IN EUROPEAN LEAGUES

This is the evolution of the predictive capacity of each bookie for the Spanish Second Division over the last few years:

SEASON	B365	BW	IW	LB	WH	BV	PS	BEST 5	BEST 7
2005-06	36.2%	36.3%	35.8%	36.1%	36.0%	36.4%		36.3%	36.3%
2006-07	36.7%	36.5%	36.5%	36.7%	36.6%	36.6%		36.8%	36.8%
2007-08	36.0%	36.0%	35.7%	35.9%	36.1%	35.9%		36.0%	36.0%
2008-09	37.9%	37.9%	37.4%	37.5%	37.7%	37.7%		38.0%	38.0%
2009-10	36.7%	36.5%	36.2%	36.4%	36.5%	36.7%		36.7%	36.7%
2010-11	37.6%	37.4%	36.9%	37.3%	37.4%	37.6%		37.6%	37.6%
2011-12	39.2%	39.0%	38.5%	38.7%	38.7%	39.0%		39.1%	39.2%
2012-13	38.0%	37.8%	37.4%	37.6%	37.7%	38.2%	38.3%	37.9%	38.2%
2013-14	35.5%	35.4%	35.2%	35.3%	35.4%	35.4%	35.6%	35.4%	35.5%
2014-15	37.6%	37.1%	37.0%	37.3%	37.2%	37.7%	37.5%	37.6%	37.7%
2015-16	36.8%	36.7%	36.4%	36.8%	36.6%	36.9%	37.0%	36.8%	37.0%
2016-17	36.7%	36.7%	36.1%	36.6%	36.4%	36.6%	36.8%	36.7%	36.8%
2017-18	38.2%	38.1%	37.7%	37.8%	37.7%	38.1%	38.3%	38.2%	38.3%
2018-19	37.8%	37.6%	37.6%		37.6%	37.6%	37.8%	37.8%	37.8%
2019-20	35.6%	35.5%	35.4%		35.4%	35.4%	35.5%	35.5%	35.5%

This information is graphically represented below:

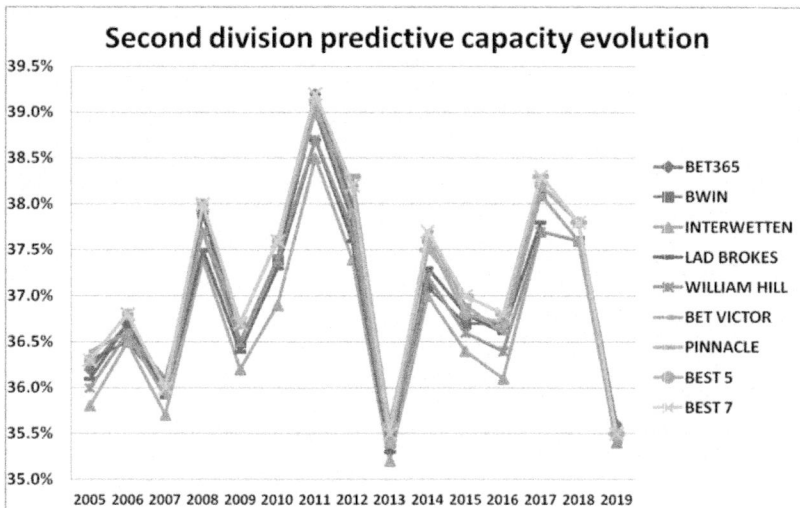

Second division predictive capacity evolution

The following table shows the predictive capacity of each bookmaker for the German Bundesliga over the last few years:

SEASON	B365	BW	IW	LB	WH	BV	PS	BEST 5	BEST 7
2005-06	39.6%	39.6%	39.0%	39.3%	39.2%	39.3%		39.8%	39.8%
2006-07	38.3%	38.0%	37.8%	38.0%	37.9%	37.9%		38.3%	38.3%
2007-08	39.8%	39.6%	39.2%	39.5%	39.1%	39.8%		39.8%	39.8%
2008-09	40.4%	40.2%	39.8%	40.0%	39.9%	40.3%		40.4%	40.4%
2009-10	39.4%	39.3%	39.2%	39.1%	39.2%	39.5%		39.5%	39.5%
2010-11	38.3%	38.3%	37.9%	38.4%	38.3%	38.5%		38.4%	38.5%
2011-12	40.3%	40.1%	39.6%	40.3%	40.0%	40.6%		40.3%	40.5%
2012-13	40.9%	40.8%	40.3%	40.9%	40.6%	41.0%	41.1%	40.9%	41.1%
2013-14	43.1%	43.0%	42.6%	43.0%	42.7%	43.2%	43.6%	43.2%	43.5%
2014-15	40.7%	40.2%	40.0%	40.6%	40.4%	40.7%	40.9%	40.6%	40.8%
2015-16	42.0%	41.6%	40.9%	41.9%	41.5%	42.1%	42.2%	41.9%	42.1%
2016-17	40.8%	40.8%	40.2%	40.8%	40.6%	40.9%	41.0%	40.8%	40.9%
2017-18	40.5%	40.5%	40.0%	40.4%	40.2%	40.5%	40.7%	40.4%	40.6%
2018-19	42.7%	42.5%	42.1%		42.5%	42.6%	42.5%	42.6%	42.7%
2019-20	42.7%	42.6%	42.2%		42.7%	42.6%	42.7%	42.7%	42.8%

This information is graphically represented below:

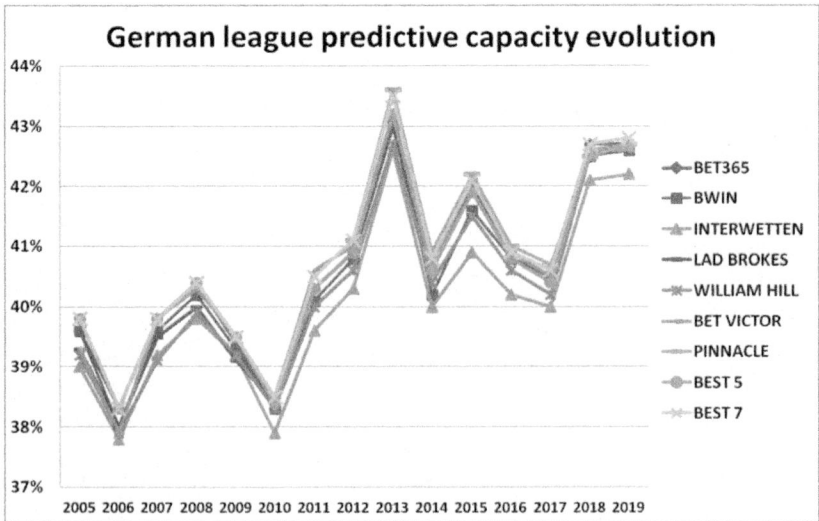

German league predictive capacity evolution

The following table shows the predictive capacity of each bookmaker for the Italian Serie A over the last few years:

SEASON	B365	BW	IW	LB	WH	BV	PS	BEST 5	BEST 7
2005-06	42.9%	42.9%	42.2%	42.9%	42.7%	43.0%		43.2%	43.2%
2006-07	41.5%	41.4%	40.9%	41.1%	41.3%	41.1%		41.7%	41.7%
2007-08	40.8%	40.6%	40.1%	40.2%	40.4%	40.2%		40.8%	40.8%
2008-09	41.0%	40.8%	40.3%	40.5%	40.6%	40.7%		41.0%	41.0%
2009-10	40.9%	40.6%	40.6%	40.4%	40.7%	40.8%		40.9%	40.9%
2010-11	40.3%	40.1%	39.9%	40.3%	40.3%	40.3%		40.5%	40.6%
2011-12	39.8%	39.8%	39.3%	39.5%	39.6%	40.1%		39.8%	40.0%
2012-13	41.5%	41.5%	40.8%	41.1%	41.1%	41.7%	41.9%	41.5%	41.8%
2013-14	42.5%	42.6%	42.1%	42.3%	42.1%	42.7%	42.8%	42.5%	42.9%
2014-15	39.0%	38.7%	38.6%	39.0%	38.7%	39.4%	39.4%	39.0%	39.4%
2015-16	42.0%	41.6%	41.2%	41.8%	41.5%	42.1%	42.2%	41.9%	42.2%
2016-17	45.2%	45.2%	44.4%	45.0%	44.9%	45.4%	45.4%	45.2%	45.5%
2017-18	46.0%	46.0%	45.6%	45.8%	45.7%	46.4%	46.3%	46.1%	46.5%
2018-19	43.3%	43.2%	43.0%		43.3%	43.6%	43.5%	43.4%	43.6%
2019-20	42.6%	42.5%	42.3%		42.6%	42.7%	42.7%	42.7%	42.8%

This information is graphically represented below:

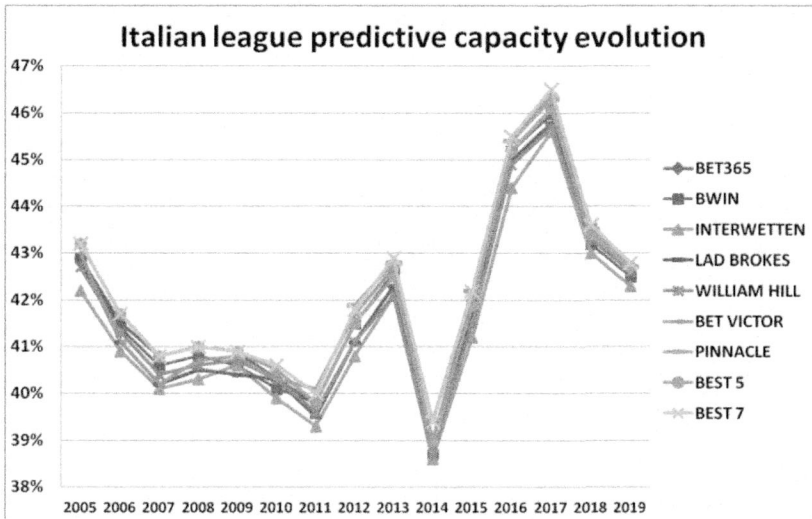

The following table shows the predictive capacity of each bookmaker for the French Ligue 1 over the last few years:

SEASON	B365	BW	IW	LB	WH	BV	PS	BEST 5	BEST 7
2005-06	37.8%	38.1%	37.6%	38.0%	37.8%	37.9%		38.1%	38.1%
2006-07	37.4%	37.4%	37.0%	37.3%	37.3%	37.4%		37.7%	37.7%
2007-08	37.2%	37.0%	36.9%	36.9%	37.3%	37.1%		37.2%	37.2%
2008-09	38.7%	38.4%	38.2%	38.3%	38.2%	38.3%		38.7%	38.7%
2009-10	39.6%	39.4%	39.2%	39.1%	39.3%	39.5%		39.7%	39.7%
2010-11	37.8%	37.5%	37.2%	37.3%	37.6%	37.8%		37.7%	37.8%
2011-12	39.1%	39.0%	38.5%	38.7%	39.0%	39.4%		39.1%	39.3%
2012-13	39.0%	39.1%	38.7%	38.8%	38.8%	39.2%	39.3%	39.1%	39.2%
2013-14	40.9%	40.7%	40.3%	40.6%	40.5%	41.0%	41.2%	40.8%	41.1%
2014-15	40.3%	39.8%	39.9%	40.2%	40.0%	40.5%	40.5%	40.2%	40.5%
2015-16	39.1%	38.9%	38.6%	38.9%	38.7%	39.3%	39.2%	39.0%	39.2%
2016-17	41.3%	41.2%	40.6%	41.1%	40.9%	41.3%	41.5%	41.3%	41.4%
2017-18	42.8%	42.8%	42.0%	42.6%	42.5%	43.0%	42.9%	42.8%	43.0%
2018-19	40.0%	40.0%	39.7%		39.9%	40.1%	40.1%	40.0%	40.1%
2019-20	40.3%	40.2%	40.1%		40.3%	40.3%	40.4%	40.4%	40.4%

This information is graphically represented below:

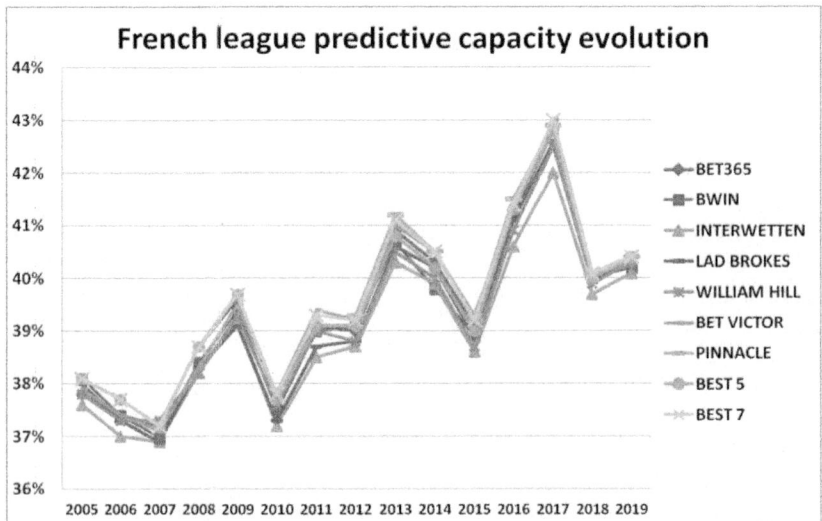

French league predictive capacity evolution

The following table shows the predictive capacity of each bookmaker for the Dutch Eredivisie over the last few years:

SEASON	B365	BW	IW	LB	WH	BV	PS	BEST 5	BEST 7
2005-06	42.6%	42.4%	42.1%	42.8%	42.8%	43.0%		42.8%	42.9%
2006-07	43.8%	43.2%	42.8%	43.3%	43.1%	43.7%		43.7%	43.8%
2007-08	41.7%	41.1%	40.7%	41.2%	40.6%	41.7%		41.6%	41.7%
2008-09	42.5%	42.0%	41.3%	41.7%	42.0%	41.8%		42.4%	42.4%
2009-10	46.7%	46.1%	45.2%	45.8%	46.6%	46.6%		46.9%	46.9%
2010-11	44.6%	44.1%	43.4%	44.0%	44.5%	44.8%		44.7%	44.8%
2011-12	45.6%	45.1%	44.4%	44.3%	45.3%	45.8%		45.7%	45.8%
2012-13	42.0%	41.7%	41.6%	41.6%	41.9%	42.2%	40.9%	42.0%	42.2%
2013-14	41.1%	40.8%	40.6%	41.1%	40.9%	41.3%	41.1%	41.2%	41.5%
2014-15	42.6%	42.2%	41.9%	42.4%	42.1%	42.7%	42.6%	42.6%	42.9%
2015-16	42.5%	42.2%	42.2%	42.3%	42.0%	42.6%	42.5%	42.5%	42.7%
2016-17	43.7%	43.6%	43.1%	43.7%	43.3%	44.0%	43.7%	43.8%	44.1%
2017-18	43.6%	43.7%	43.1%	43.3%	43.1%	43.7%	43.1%	43.7%	43.9%
2018-19	46.2%	46.2%	45.7%		46.1%	46.4%	46.2%	46.4%	46.5%
2019-20	45.2%	45.2%	44.7%		45.2%	45.3%	45.3%	45.4%	45.5%

This information is graphically represented below:

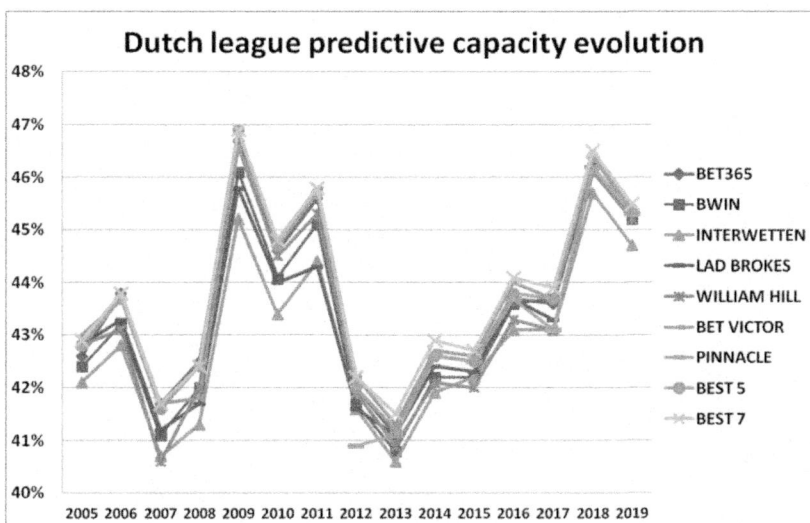

Dutch league predictive capacity evolution

243

The following table shows the predictive capacity of each bookmaker for the Portuguese Primeira Liga over the last few years:

SEASON	B365	BW	IW	LB	WH	BV	PS	BEST 5	BEST 7
2005-06	39.9%	40.4%	39.5%	39.9%	40.0%	40.0%		40.3%	40.3%
2006-07	41.5%	41.6%	41.0%	41.3%	41.0%	41.8%		41.7%	41.8%
2007-08	40.4%	40.5%	40.0%	40.2%	39.6%	40.3%		40.5%	40.6%
2008-09	41.0%	41.1%	40.1%	40.6%	40.6%	40.7%		41.1%	41.1%
2009-10	42.6%	42.4%	41.7%	42.0%	42.3%	42.4%		42.6%	42.6%
2010-11	41.4%	41.3%	40.8%	40.6%	40.9%	41.6%		41.5%	41.6%
2011-12	44.5%	44.3%	44.1%	43.7%	44.1%	44.7%		44.5%	44.7%
2012-13	43.4%	43.3%	42.7%	42.6%	42.8%	43.6%	43.0%	43.4%	43.7%
2013-14	42.5%	42.2%	41.9%	42.2%	42.0%	42.5%	42.4%	42.5%	42.7%
2014-15	44.4%	44.2%	43.2%	43.9%	43.8%	44.7%	44.2%	44.5%	44.8%
2015-16	44.3%	43.9%	43.4%	44.2%	43.7%	44.5%	44.5%	44.3%	44.7%
2016-17	43.0%	42.8%	42.3%	42.8%	42.5%	43.1%	43.1%	43.0%	43.3%
2017-18	46.3%	46.2%	45.3%	45.9%	45.6%	46.3%	46.3%	46.3%	46.7%
2018-19	45.0%	44.9%	44.5%		45.2%	45.3%	45.2%	45.3%	45.4%
2019-20	42.2%	42.2%	42.0%		42.1%	42.2%	42.4%	42.4%	42.5%

This information is graphically represented below:

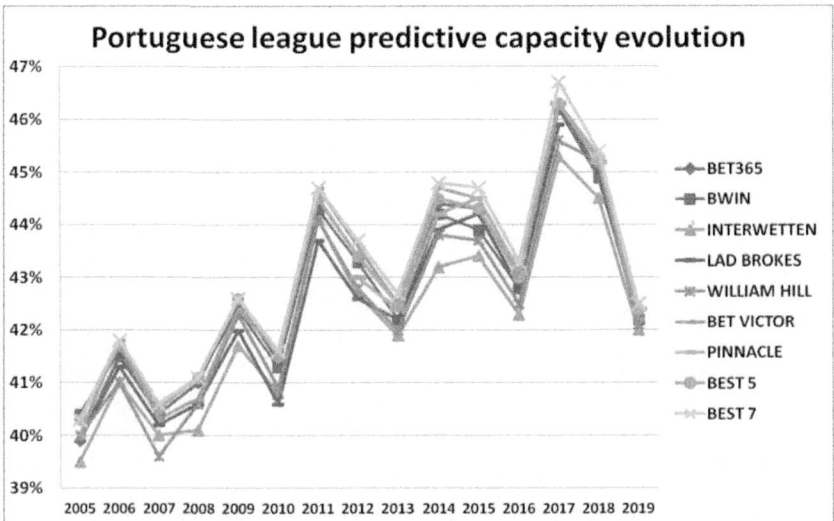

Portuguese league predictive capacity evolution

BIBLIOGRAPHY

Buchdahl, Joseph (2009): *Fixed Odds Sports Betting*, London, High Stakes.

Buchdahl, Joseph (2013): *How to Find a Black Cat in a Coal Cellar*, Harpenden, High Stakes.

Buchdahl, Joseph (2016): *Squares & Sharps, Suckers & Sharks, The Science, Psychology & Philosophy of Gambling*, Harpenden, High Stakes.

Kuper, Simon & **Szymanski**, Stefan (2014): *Soccernomics,* London, Harper Sport.

Anderson, Chris & **Sally**, David (2014): *The Numbers Game*, London, Penguin Books.

Pullein, Kevin (2016): *The Definitive Guide to Betting on Football*, Newbury, Raceform Ltd.

Hagerty, Pat (2016), *Good Teams Win Great Teams Cover*, Hank and Oliver LLC.

Sumpter, David (2017): *Soccermatics: Mathematical Adventures in the Beautiful Game*, London, Bloomsbury.

Holgado, Samuel (2019): *Leer Antes de Apostar*, Independently Published.

Miller, Ed & **Davidow**, Matthew (2019): *The Logic of Sports Betting*, Independently Published.

Palacios-Huerta, Ignacio (2014): *Beautiful Game Theory,* Princeton, Princeton University Press.

Levitt, Steven D. (2004): *Why are gambling markets organised so differently from financial markets?*, London, Royal Economic Society.

Hassanniakalager, Arman & **Newall**, Philip W.S. (2019): *A machine learning perspective on responsible gambling,* Cambridge, Cambridge University Press.

WEBSITES AND INTERNET ARTICLES

Historical football results and odds information available for download in Excel: www.football-data.co.uk/downloadm.php

Odds converter: https://es.surebet.com/converter

Arbitrage opportunity searchers: www.betburger.com, www.rebelbetting.com

Bookmakers and Odds Comparators: www.marcadoresonline.com, www.wincomparator.com, www.oddsportal.com

Historical record of bets and forecasts: www.pyckio.com

Bookmakers licensed in Spain: www.ordenacionjuego.es

Transfermark website in English: www.transfermarkt.com/

Who Scored website in English: https://www.whoscored.com/

Understat Expected Goals Website: https://understat.com/

German TV video in English about home field advantage: https://www.youtube.com/watch?v=YNBBuNAA9oU

Article on the effect of the absence of public on home field advantage during the coronavirus pandemic (Covid-19) in 2020: https://football-observatory.com/IMG/sites/b5wp/2020/wp304/en/

Article by Kiko Llaneras on research on penalty kicks and shootouts (in Spanish): https://elpais.com/politica/2021/07/09/actualidad/1625840281_767960.html

TED talk I gave on the use of statistics and modelling techniques that can be used to predict soccer results (subtitled in English): https://www.youtube.com/watch?v=ir5AGfXGkwI

Talk I gave to the students of the UCAM's Master on Big Data applied to sports (in Spanish): https://youtu.be/p1HXDKm1KFQ

Interview on Radio Marca Barcelona with journalist Carles Escolán (in Spanish): https://youtu.be/_GOIhVVKS0U

Printed in Great Britain
by Amazon